Volume I

From 1000 to The Reformation

WOMEN &
CHRISTIANITY

Volume II:
From 1000 to The Reformation

WOMEN &
CHRISTIANITY

MARY T. MALONE

NOVALIS

ORBIS BOOKS

Maryknoll, New York 10545

Founded in 1970, Orbis Books endeavors to publish works that enlighten the mind, nourish the spirit, and challenge the conscience. The publishing arm of Maryknoll Fathers and Brothers, Orbis seeks to explore the global dimensions of the Christian faith and mission, to invite dialogue with diverse cultures and religious traditions, and to serve the cause of reconciliation and peace. The books published reflect the views of the authors and do not represent the official position of the Maryknoll Society. To obtain more information about Maryknoll and Orbis Books, please visit our website at www.maryknoll.org.

Published in 2002 in the United States by Orbis Books, P.O. Box 308, Maryknoll, New York 10545

Published in 2002 in Canada by Novalis, Saint Paul University, 223 Main Street, Ottawa, Ontario K1S 1C4

First published in 2001 in Ireland by The Columba Press, 55 A Spruce Avenue, Stillorgan Industrial Park, Blackrock, Co Dublin

Manufactured in the United States of America.

Cataloging-in-Publication Data is available from the Library of Congress

ORBIS/ISBN 1-57075-394-6 (hardcover)
              1-57075-393-8 (paperback)

A catalogue record of this book is available from the National Library of Canada

NOVALIS/ISBN 2-89507-253-1 (paperback)

Contents

Dedication

I gladly dedicate this book on the lives of far-distant women to the men of my immediate family: my brothers, John, Des, and Jim; and my nephews, Mark, Niall, Seamus, Francis, Martin, Fergal, Simon, Miguel, Jimmy, John and David. If they manage to make their way through it, perhaps they will experience new amazement at the lives of their friends, mothers, sisters and daughters.

Dateline

An event cannot be isolated by giving it a date, but it serves to anchor the attention and situate the persons involved in an appropriate context.

1000	Most areas of Europe converted to Christianity
1030s	Two decades of confusion between popes and anti-popes in Rome
1042	Reign of Edward the Confessor, builder of Canterbury Cathedral. Died 1066.
1046	Birth of Matilda of Canossa, friend and supporter of Pope Gregory VII
	Synod of Sutri: deposition of anti-popes Sylvester III, Gregory VI, Benedict IX
	Pope Clement II appointed by Emperor Henry III to initiate reform in the church
1049	Pope Leo IX initiates the war against clerical marriage; appoints advisors Hugh of Cluny, Cardinal Humbert, Peter Damian, and the priest Hildebrand.
1050	Mary Magdalen declared the chief patron of the Abbey of Vezelay
	At mid-century, many women's monasteries closed including Wimbourne, Whitby and Ely.
1054	Split between East and West with the mutual excommunications pronounced by Cardinal Humbert and Patriarch Michael Cerularius.
1055	Agnes becomes Empress Regent for her six-year old son, Henry IV. Forced to retire to a monastery.
1058	Pope Nicholas II decress that only Cardinals may elect the pope.
1059	End of Eucharist debate with Berengarius of Tours.
	Council of Rome declares monastic women to be among the laity.
1066	William the Conqueror: Battle of Hastings
1073	Hildebrand becomes Pope Gregory VII
1074	Matilda of Canossa begins her active military support of the papacy.
	Gregory VII suspends all married priests. Initiates lay boycott of married clergy. Reduces priests' wives and children to the status of slaves for compliant bishops.

1075	Decree of Gregory VII against lay investiture. Publication of *Dictatus Papae*.
1076	Decree of excommunication against Henry IV.
1077	Confrontation between Pope and Emperor at Matilda's Castle at Canossa.
1085	Death of Pope Gregory VII as a prisoner of the Normans.
1090	Birth of Bernard of Clairvaux.
1093	Anselm becomes Archbishop of Canterbury.
1094	Initiation of Crusading movement by Pope Urban II at Clermont.
1095	Birth of Christina of Markyate, future recluse and abbess.
1098	Birth of Hildegard of Bingen.
1100	Foundation of double monastery at Fontevrault by Robert of Arbrissel.
1106	Death of Emperor Henry IV.
1113	Bernard enters the Cistercian monastery of Citeaux and founds Clairvaux in 1115.
1115	Death of Matilda of Canossa at the Abbey of Polirone.
1116	Peter Abelard sets up his school in Paris and becomes tutor to Héloïse.
1122	Birth of Eleanor of Aquitaine. Concordat of Worms: End of Investiture dispute.
1120s	Correspondence between Héloïse and Abelard on the nature of women.
1129	Birth of Elizabeth of Schönau.
1132	Abelard's school in Paris becomes known as the University of Paris.
1135	'Waves' of heresy beginning to sweep the church.
1136	Death of Jutta of Sponheim: Hildegard becomes Abbess of the Monastery of Mount St Disibode.
1137	Marriage of Eleanor of Aquitaine to Louis VII of France.
1139	Second Lateran Council: first universal law of celibacy.
1140	Council of Sens: Bernard engineers the condemnation of Abelard. He is forbidden to teach. Publication of Gratian's *Concordia Discordantium Canonum*. Beginning of the mature visionary life of Hildegard of Bingen.
1142	Death of Abelard
1144	Consecration of the Royal Abbey of St Denis. Bernard of Clairvaux preaches and meets Eleanor of Aquitaine, now Queen of France.
1145	Second Crusade called by Pope Eugenius III, and preached

by Bernard and Hildegard. Eleanor of Aquitaine, dressed as the Amazon, Penthesilea, joins her husband, Louis VII at Vezelay to receive the Crusaders' Cross.

1147	Hildegard and Bernard correspond about her writings. They are approved both by Bernard and Pope Eugenius III. Eleanor and Louis return to France planning to divorce.
1150	Hildegard moves her nuns to Rupertsberg, and soon after founds the monastery at Bingen.
1151	Hildegard completes *Scivias*.
1152	Eleanor of Aquitaine marries Henry II of England.
1153	Death of Bernard of Clairvaux.
1154	Arnold of Brescia is executed as a heretic.
1158	Hildegard completes *The Book of Life's Merits*, and begins her preaching journeys
1160	Hildegard preaches in the Cathedral of Trier for Pentecost. Death of Christina of Markyate.
1162	Thomas Beckett becomes Archbishop of Canterbury.
1163	Hildegard begins the third section of her theological trilogy with *The Book of Divine Works*. It is completed in 1173.
1164	Death of Héloïse. She is buried near Abelard at the Paraclete. Council of Clarendon: Henry II clarifies his position against Thomas Beckett. Death of Elizabeth of Schönau.
1167	Hildegard begins her fourth and last preaching journey. Death of Aelred, Abbot of Rievaulx, the 'English St Bernard': Author of a work on the life of a recluse for his sister.
1168	Eleanor retires to her own territory of Aquitaine for six years, having been estranged from Henry.
1170	Murder of Thomas Beckett at Canterbury, December 29. Birth of Dominic Guzman, founder of the Dominicans.
1174	Eleanor imprisoned at Salisbury until the death of Henry II in 1189.
1177	Birth of Mary of Oignies, considered to be the first Beguine,
1178	Hildegard of Bingen (aged 80) and her convent excommunicated.
1179	Excommunication lifted. Hildegard dies on September 17. Third Lateran Council.
1181	Birth of Francis of Assisi, founder of the Franciscans.
1184	Initiation of the Inquisition by Pope Lucius III.
1189	Eleanor becomes Regent of England on the death of her husband Henry II. Richard the Lionhearted is captured while returning from the Third Crusade. Eleanor ransoms him in 1193.

1194   Birth of Clare of Assisi.
1198   Innocent III becomes Pope.
1202   Beginning of Fourth and probably most disastrous Crusade.
1203   Death of Eleanor of Aquitaine, probably at Fontevrault,
        where she is buried.
1206   Dominic preaches against the Albigensians.
1207   Birth of Mechtild of Magdeburg.
1208   Crusade against the Albigensians led by Simon of Montfort.
        Massacre at Béziers.
1209   Approval of first Franciscan rule by Innocent III.
1212   Clare joins Francis at San Damiano, and becomes its Abbess
        in 1216.
1213   Death of Mary of Oignies.
1215   Fourth Lateran Council: Decreed, among many other items,
        that there can be no new Religious Orders.
1216   Death of Innocent III. Death of King John of England. Magna
        Carta.
        Recognition of the Dominican Order by Pope Honorius III.
1221   Death of Dominic.
        Beginning of the twenty-year long mystical life of Hadewijch.
1225   Birth of Thomas Aquinas.
1226   Death of Francis of Assisi.
1228   Publication of *Ancrene Wisse*, written on the life of a recluse
        for three sisters at Hereford.
1229   Mechtild of Magdeburg becomes a Beguine.
1232   Birth of Gertrude of Hackeborn, later Abbess of Helfta.
1239   Clare of Assisi's communities are enclosed by Pope Gregory
        IX, against her wishes.
1241   Birth of Mechtild of Hackeborn.
1244   Massacre of the Albigensians and their final defeat at
        Montségur.
1253   Death of Clare of Assisi.
1256   Birth of Gertrude of Helfta, called the 'Great'.
1258   Death of Juliana of Mont Cornillon, credited with the
        institution of the feast of Corpus Christi.
1260   Birth of Meister Eckhart.
1264   Foundation of Paris Beguinage by King Louis IX.
1265   Discovery of body of Mary Magdalen at Vezelay.
1270   Mechtild of Magdeburg arrives at Helfta.
1274   Council of Lyons: Beginning of decrees against the Beguines.
        Death of Thomas Aquinas and Bonaventure.
1275   Angela, one of the first women burnt as a witch, in Toulouse.

1277	Foundation of the Order of Mary Magdalen for prostitutes by Pope Gregory IX.
1279	Discovery of 'real' body of Mary Magdalen in Provence. End of the dominance of Vezelay as centre of pilgrimage.
1282	Death of Guglielma of Milan. Her disciple, Mayfreda, is named Pope. Beginning of mystical life of Gertrude the Great
1290	Birth of Na Prous Boneta.
1291	End of Crusader presence in the Holy Land. Death of Gertrude, Abbess of Helfta.
1296	Publication of Marguerite Porete's *The Mirror of Simple Souls*. Decree *Clericos Laicos* of Benedict VIII asserting the pope's sole right to collect clerical taxes.
1297	Death of Mechtild of Hackeborn.
1300	Jubilee celebrations attended by thousands in Rome.
1302	Inquisition examines the followers of Guglielma of Milan. Several executed.
1303	Capture and imprisonment of Pope Boniface VIII by French forces at Anagni. He died a month later in October.
1307	Seizure of the French property of the Templars.
1309	Clement V moves the papal court to Avignon.
1310	Execution of 54 Templars by being burnt at the stake in a field outside Paris. On June 1, Marguerite Porete is burnt at the stake in the Place de Grève, Paris.
1312	Final condemnation of the Beguines at the Council of Vienne.
1313	Meister Eckhart moves from Paris to Cologne.
1317	Birth of Bridget of Sweden Four Beguines burnt at the stake in Narbonne.
1318	Four spiritual Franciscans burnt at the stake in Marseille.
1321	Mass burnings of lepers in France.
1325	Na Prous Boneta, a woman mystic and spiritual Franciscan, burnt at the stake in Montpelier.
1326	Canonisation of Thomas Aquinas.
1327	Death of Meister Eckhart. Beginning of fifty year reign of Edward III in England
1328	Posthumous condemnation by John XXII of 17 of Eckhart's propositions.
1337	Beginning of 100 years' war between England and France.
1343	Destruction of the Abbey of Helfta. Birth of Julian of Norwich.
1347	Beginning of plague called the 'Black Death'. About 30 million perished.

1347   Birth of Catherine of Siena on March 25.

1349   Massacre of the whole community of Jews in Basle as
        punishment for supposedly starting the plague.

1370   Ongoing battles between the Gwelfs and Ghibellines for the
        papal states.
        Bridget of Sweden allowed to open two convents in Rome in
        response to her visions.

1373   Death of Bridget of Sweden.
        Julian of Norwich receives her revelations on May 8.
        Birth of Margery Kempe at Lynn.

1374   Catherine of Siena summoned to the Dominican General
        Chapter. Raymond of Capua appointed as her director.

1376   Catherine of Siena sent to Avignon by the Florentines as their
        ambassador to the pope.

1377   Massacre of the whole town of Cesena by Cardinal Robert of
        Geneva, later anti-pope Clement VII.

1378   Catherine of Siena finishes her *Dialogue*.
        Papacy returns from Avignon to Rome. Catherine moves to
        Rome.
        Beginning of Great Western Schism, with first two then three
        popes for several years.

1380   Death of Catherine of Siena on April 29.

1381   Peasant revolt in England led by Wat Tyler.

1382   Denunciation of John Wyclif and the Lollards at Oxford.

1393   Completion of the Long Text of the *Revelations of Julian of
        Norwich*.

1409   Council of Pisa ends the Great Schism.

1412   Visit of Margery Kempe to Julian of Norwich.

1413   Margery Kempe begins her four-year pilgrimage through
        Europe and the Holy Land.

1414   Council of Constance: Condemnation and execution of John
        Hus.
        Battle of Agincourt. Victory for Henry V over the French.

1417   Margery Kempe accused of Lollardy, but successfully
        defends herself.

1431   Joan of Arc burnt at the stake in Rouen on May 31.

1439   Death of Margery Kempe.

1453   Fall of Constantinople.

1456   Decree issued clearing the name of Joan of Arc and read
        publicly both in Paris and Rouen.

1469   Birth of Erasmus of Rotterdam

1478   Birth of Thomas More.

1483   Birth of Martin Luther
1484   Pope Innocent VIII issues decree *Summis Desiderantis*
         officially inaugurating the witch-hunts.
1487   Publication of *Malleus Maleficarum* by Kramer and Sprenger
         as a handbook for witch-hunters.
1492   Christopher Columbus in the New World.
         Pope Alexander VI Borgia begins his reign.
1498   Savonarola, Prior of San Marco in Florence, prophetic preacher
         of reform, burnt at the stake.

Introduction

One of the common observations in the writing of medieval women was that they were living in decadent times, and that such times cried out to God for desperate remedies. Among the remedies that God seemed to enjoy using were the prophetic voices of women. 'Because in these times,' says Elizabeth of Schönau, 'the Lord deigns to show His mercy most graciously in the weak sex, such men (i.e. the clerics) are offended and led into sin.' And she continues, '... while the men were given over to sluggishness, holy women were filled with the Spirit of God, that they might prophesy, govern God's people forcefully, and indeed triumph.' Elizabeth is but one of a whole cohort of such women who took on the task of 'governing God's people forcefully' with courage, wisdom, and astonishing energy. They raged against the perceived corruption of the church, challenged ecclesiastical malfeasance in every area, but most especially called the church to account for its heartlessness, cold rationality, juridical insensibility and glaring infidelity to the teaching of Christ.

This volume explores the origins, contexts and lives of several such women and attempts to present some small sense of their contribution to the medieval church. Unlike the previous one thouand years when the voices of women were relatively rare, the period 1000-1500 CE presents us with abundant testimonies to the intense involvement of many women in the public life of the church. Nevertheless, the writings presented to us under their names must be read and interpreted with great care. Most women had male clerical secretaries, sometimes, indeed, their own brothers, and while the relationship between the holy

women and their clerical assistants was often cordial, it was inevitable that the women's message was sometimes used to serve
an ecclesiastical purpose other than the one intended. Speaking
and writing, as the quotation from Elizabeth of Schönau indicates, was dangerous for a woman, and though it was a common
occurrence, it was always seen as exceptional 'in these times of
stress'.

I have found one temptation to be unavoidable, and that is
the desire to imagine what today's church might be like had the
teaching of Hildegard, Elizabeth, Mechtild, Clare, Marguerite,
Julian, Catherine and so many others been integrated into the
ongoing self-understanding of Christianity. It is Christianity's
great loss that this did not happen, and one is forced to conclude
that the resultant Christian story and the resultant body of
teaching is therefore partial, distorted and unfaithful to the
totality of the message left by Jesus. In line with the common observation that women prophets were raised up to supply for a
deficiency in the contemporary church, it is important to ask
what the women found absent and in need of amendment.
Almost without exception, the medieval women would answer
in chorus, compassion. The great gift of medieval women mystics to the church was precisely in their mystical prayer and its
necessary accompaniment, a life of compassion. Their prayer
originated in the brilliant new experiences of bodily intimacy
and, yes, identification, with Christ especially in the mystery of
the eucharist, and hence the continuance of his life of compassionate care for all was accepted as the central tenet of the life of
mystical prayer. Besides, and again, almost without exception,
these women mystics presented such a life of prayer as the common Christian inheritance of all. Their lives of prayer were always intended to be shared with others, and none of the women
sees herself as uniquely gifted.

It is precisely this opening out of the mystical life as an
invitation to everyone that set the church's teeth on edge. In its
response we meet, for the first time, the appalling acts of ecclesiastical violence against women. The extent of this violence

against all perceived internal enemies of the faith, is unendurable to contemplate today. The actual experience of being burnt at the stake is unimaginable for us. Yet the story of the bravery, dignity and integrity of Joan of Arc, executed on 31 May 1431 and Marguerite Porete, executed on 1 June 1310, among so many others, demonstrates the profound faith and overwhelming courage of these women.

One sure lesson to be learned from the lives and writing of so many medieval women is that there is no truth whatever to the proffered ecclesiastical image of womanhood. Such women were not tied to the biological make-up which was central to the church's official teaching on women then and now. Indeed, what is also remarkable is that the unending preoccupations of clerics about women's sexuality have no answering echo in the women's own sense of identity. For them, their bodies are not the problem; it is ecclesiastical insensitivity to their divinely felt vocation that presents them with the greatest anguish.

For me it has been an undiluted joy to have had the opportunity to delve into the lives and writings of such women. The greater part of the task of interpretation, critical analysis, and even translation of these texts still remains to be done, and awaits someone with much more expertise than I have at my disposal. Nevertheless, I have learned enough, and hope to have communicated enough, to show the shattering relevance of these women and their words to the whole Christian tradition. Extraordinary challenges to conventional Christian understandings occur on every page of their writings. Among the most dramatic of these challenges is the need to penetrate to the very heart of the Christian mystery to try to understand what these medieval women have to tell us about the mystery of God and the mystery of humanity. It is a challenge we dare not ignore.

CHAPTER ONE

Entering the Second Millennium:
Issues and Ideas

The second millennium dawned on a Christianity that was torn apart by the most profound conflicts. For over a hundred years, the papacy had been treated as the private inheritance of several feuding Italian families. It had been bought and sold and passed along as private property to children both legitimate and illegitimate. In fact, many historians seem to ignore the two hundred years from around 850, and start the Christian history of the second millennium with the year 1050, when papal influence begins its ascent to become the great universal power of medieval times. Since the rise of the Ottonian dynasty in Germany, successive emperors had marched into Italy in an attempt to put an end to the chaos, but this had usually resulted in a dual, and sometimes triple papacy of German and Italian popes. The story is a complex one and the arrival of the German Pope Leo IX in 1049 is greeted by both his contemporaries and modern historians with great relief. With Leo and his cohort of German clerical assistants, the papacy begins to bring to realisation some of its most radical claims.

On the one hand, it may seem obvious to begin the history of the second millennium with the position of the papacy. On the other, it may not seem at all appropriate to begin the history of Christian women in the second millennium with this story. Women, however, are integral to the story of the papacy and the papacy is integral to the story of women. As the papacy begins to reform itself, the familiar pattern is repeated. Reform in all cases means clerical reform, and clerical reform, particularly at this period, is rooted in the absolute separation of clergy and women. As clerical reform progresses, particularly through the

first two centuries of the millennium, the accompanying negative theorising about women's lives attains at times the level of
demonisation. For women Christians, the story of these centuries
lies in their astonishing survival skills in the face of this almost
universally negative propaganda. The medieval period introduces
us to some of the most brilliant women to have graced the
Christian story, women like Hildegard of Bingen, Hadewijch of
Brabant, Marguerite Porete and Joan of Arc. Christian women
who sought spiritual sustenance lived their lives as nuns, mystics, pilgrims, recluses, beguines, queens and even prostitutes
and their stories will form the bulk of this volume. What adds an
even more astonishing dimension to the story is that many of
these women wrote as teachers for the women of their time, and
their writings have survived, sometimes against impossible
odds, to our day. These writings will provide the spiritual backdrop to our story, and will reveal the forgotten, but profound influence of these medieval women on the whole of Christianity.
Their writings and stories will delight, frustrate, illuminate and
be deeply moving as we come to know them as sister Christians,
so utterly different and yet so familiar in their shared spiritual
dreams.

As we gain familiarity with the apparently endless procession
of medieval women who have become known to us in recent
times, it is important to remember that these women represent
an infinitesimally small fraction of medieval women. The same
may be said for the much more familiar array of great medieval
men, from Abelard and Bernard to Popes Innocent and Boniface.
Despite the increasingly rich literary resources from these times,
we can come to know only the very tip of medieval life. The fact
remains that ninety percent of the medieval population were
serfs, probably illiterate, and with no possibility whatever of
leaving to us any literary trace of their passing. The face of
Europe, with its landscape of fields, hedgerows, and towering
churches testifies to their work and faith, but as individuals,
they remain forever unknowable. Those we meet, whether female
or male, belong almost exclusively to the aristocratic class. That

is why the story of the 'great' women and men needs to be constantly put into context. Some historians compare the middle ages to a vast concentration camp where most lived in abject poverty and utter dependance, with little or no choice in the disposition of their lives. While this may be slightly exaggerated, it does give us pause for thought. We have become so familiar with the aristocratic and ecclesiastical high points, that we tend to forget the backdrop against which the medieval brilliance was achieved.

Another reason why it is necessary to begin the story of the second millennium from the position of the papacy is that, in this age, the great and critical attack took place on lay control of the churches. This is the period when a succession of ecclesiastical reformers took decisive and often brutal action against the then traditional powers of the laity in order to make of the church an exclusively sacerdotal and hierarchical power. As the medieval centuries progressed, the church became a truly clerical power. The church was equated with the clergy and the clergy were seen to constitute the church. From the mid-point of the eleventh century, the reform of the clergy was one of the central planks in every papal reform. Since the millennium opened with the universally accepted notion and practice of a married clergy, a notion extending, in practice, to bishops and even the papacy, and since marriage was seen to be the most effective instrument for intermingling of clergy and laity, it was here precisely that the reformers aimed their most powerful weapons. The war against clerical marriage began with Leo IX in the middle of the opening century of the millennium, it intensified to fever pitch under Gregory VII at the turn of the century and reached its canonical climax at the second Lateran Council in 1139. This debate, though primarily about the clergy from an ecclesiastical perspective, was also integrally about the role and position of women within Christianity, and the debate extended to an exploration of the very nature of women.

Subsequent church history painted these monumental struggles as a mere wrinkle in the continuous history of clerical celibacy, but we now know that something much more profound was taking place. This was a cataclysmic struggle for ecclesiastical control, and in the process, the nature and self-identity of the church took a radically new turn. As the millennium opened, the church was still primarily lay-owned, with lay lords exercising roles and functions within the church that had been taken for granted for centuries, and were now considered 'traditional'. Some of these lay persons were monks and nuns who had inherited and endowed local churches from their family possessions. In many places the bishops had lost all administrative control, and in others there existed an exquisitely complex set of traditional obligations of vassalage and feudal loyalty between the local aristocrat and the church. The distinctive feature of ecclesiastical reforms in the first two centuries of the millennium was the total disruption of these arrangements, and the restoration of what was considered to be the traditional powers of the clergy. To this end, the gospels, patristic writings and, above all, canon law were brought to bear in an effort to place the reforms on a profoundly spiritual and traditional footing. The resulting features of the church have become so familiar to us that we have come to take them for granted as the only possible set of arrangements. The four great reforming councils, from the first to the fourth Lateran, have painted the church in colours still familiar to us. We have come to believe that this was the necessary path to take, in fact the only possible path. When we look more closely at these developments, however, and see the struggles and conflicts of the time, the choices made and the choices ignored, we will see that other paths might easily have been chosen in equal fidelity to the gospels. When we look, in particular, at the position of women in these struggles, it will be clear that these centuries mark the highpoint of exclusion, because the reforms then enacted were re-inforced by canon law and conciliar decree. It is not an accidental result that this medieval era closes with the pernicious witch-craze, which erased whole populations of women in many localities.

For one of the key elements of these reforms was that women

were seen to be in competition with God for the souls of men, especially the souls of the clergy. In the struggles over clerical celibacy, women were the ones who anchored priests to the local community, thereby taking their total attention from the church. The reforms, then, saw little role for women within Christianity. Women were the negative factor. What is astonishing is that, at the same time, the new breed of scholar, the theologians, were formulating with Aristotle's rediscovered help, the equality of souls and spiritual destinies that women and men shared. The Middle Ages, however, was one period when ecclesiastical theory and ecclesiastical practice did not often coincide. We shall have occasion to look at a great deal of theory and, with more difficulty, at some practice. One of the major problems facing the medieval historian of women is that almost all the literature comes from the pens of clerics. It is the 'clerical gaze' that conveys the notions of women that seem to have been prevalent.[1] Women are presented to us through the eyes of clerics, or more correctly, the 'woman' is presented, she who now assumes the definitive portrayal applied to all women for centuries. Fortunately, we can come into contact with a sufficient number of medieval women to illustrate the failure of the model 'woman' to account for the variety and colour of women's real lives through this period. Before spelling out some features of this universal 'woman', it is necessary to continue to paint a more general picture of the ecclesiastical context at the millennium's dawn.

By the year 1000, most of Europe had been Christianised. The attention now could move from the rather intimate and personal tasks of evangelisation to the much more complex task of creating what was to become Christendom. This involved the conscious elaboration of a centralised programme which would bring the whole world (Europe was beginning to see itself this way) under the law of Christ. This programme was so successful that, as we have said, it has appeared to be inevitable, partly because only the successes were included as history. When the whole story is appropriated, however, other paths seem not only possible, but equally necessary. This is especially the case for the story of women and the laity, as will become clear in the following chapters. Besides, though many features of this structure of Christendom have survived to our day, the cohesion of the whole has been vastly exaggerated by historians, especially by Roman Catholic eccclesiastical historians. According to Peter Levi, the whole was 'something of a ginger-bread palace for some time, and now the gilt is off the ginger-bread. Christendom was a provincial, western and insular parody of the great civilised Roman empire which still haunted the imagination.'[2] For many believers through the ages, this is the highest point the Christian story has attained. For many others, as contemporary historians suggest, the whole was an exercise in the misuse of power.

By the year 1000, society had inherited an array of self-understandings, many stemming from previous reform movements. Among these was the notion of the division of society into three diverse groups, those who prayed, those who fought, and those who worked, in other words, monks, soldiers and serfs. The whole appeared much more harmonious in writing than it was in practice and the following centuries introduced even more wrinkles into this portrait. But there was a new kind of harmony apparent in society from the turn of the millennium. From 1000, the population was beginning to grow again. The invasions of hostile tribes were practically completed by then and Europe began to assume the geographical features known to us today. As we have seen, the majority of the population belonged to the peasant class but even for them, the new century offered some change in a somewhat longer lifespan, a more varied and plentiful diet, and the increasing availability of urban centres with their attendant attractions and distractions. Infant mortality, however, still hovered at around fifty percent, and maternal mortality rates were not significantly different.

Women had no official place in the overall scheme. While all peasants were treated as existing somewhere between the human and the animal, woman was defined by her body and its usefulness. She was bound by innumerable constraints and was rarely seen as an individual in the legal, moral or economic sense. Women's voices are seldom heard, and the few that rise above the silence are usually members of the aristocracy. Within the feudal aristocracy, women were of fundamental importance in forging marriage alliances to the benefit of both families. The endless and intricate story of Queen Eleanor of Aquitaine and her ubiquitous relatives amply illustrates this, as we shall see in Chapter Three. The fall-out from the struggles for clerical celibacy entailed a new elaboration of the nature of marriage. One of the earliest planks in the church's new marriage teaching was the insistence on mutual consent as the core of the arrangement. This was conspicuously ignored in most mariage arrangements known to us through documentary evidence. When one considers that many marriage arrangements took place when the bride was as young as four years of age, one can see that the bride's consent had little to do with the deal. Often, the same could be said for the groom, but in most cases there was a decade or two of difference in the ages of bride and groom. The woman was seen as an available and hopefully fertile womb. Most women would have spent half their lives pregnant until the age of forty.[3]

Several fundamental values prevailed in this early medieval period, values that were constantly to be challenged during the succeeding centuries. Among these were hierarchy, authority and liberty. Hierarchy referred not only to the sacred order of the clergy, but even more so to the divine ordering of society as a whole. Each man (sic) had been placed in his own assigned spot. Trying to rise above this was sinful pride; falling below was shameful. Besides, trying to tamper with the divine and sacred order of society was nothing short of sacrilege. Earth was modelled on heaven and was intended to reproduce heaven on earth. This central understanding of the ordering of society was an extremely effective method of social and ecclesiastical control, but though it remained central for centuries, it was constantly under siege on many fronts. The authority of superiors, at every level, was unquestioned and obedience was the hallmark of the good subject. Obedience and respect were owed especially to God's special representatives, the clergy, the rulers and the husband and father in the family. Authority and womanhood were seen as two antithetical concepts, a real imbalance in nature and a total disruption of the divine will. Religious rebellion was regarded as the greatest possible abomination, and with the growth of the universities and the new learned class, intellectual rebellion added a further horror to the catalogue of acts of disobedience. Nevertheless, so-called heretical movements and some particularly well-thought out intellectual challenges to the traditional faith came to dominate the landscape of the period. As we can imagine, women heretics were seen to be particularly loathesome. In its utter frustration with these endless dissenting movements, the papacy finally instituted the infamous Inquisition.

The much lauded value of freedom had to do primarily with the freedom of the churches from lay control. From the middle of the eleventh century, freedom came to be the password for reform. For most others, freedom was but a dream, and utterly impossible to achieve. Nevertheless, as we shall see, the eleventh and twelfth centuries are seen to be the centuries that discovered the notion of the individual and individual freedoms. It is one of the great ironies of the trials of the inquisition that the freedom of the individual to choose or reject the faith was presumed, when no such freedom was at all possible in most cases. The growth of towns and eventually of the universities during this period did enlarge human consciousness, however, in astonishing ways. Trade and trade routes were constantly being expanded, bringing not only stories from strange and newly discovered lands, but also new tastes, colours, materials and goods of all kinds.[4]

The Ottonian dynasty, successors to the Holy Roman Empire, were the rulers who presided over the new millennium. Otto III reigned from 983-1002. He dreamed of moving his imperial seat to Rome and ruling as co-emperor with the Popes. As a step towards this end, he had appointed his cousin, Bruno, who took the name Gregory V, as the first German pope. After the death of Otto, the throne moved from the Saxons to the Bavarians, and the fairly illustrious series of emperors bearing the name of Henry. Henry III (1039-1056) was a religious man and a close friend of Abbot Hugh of the Abbey of Cluny, the acknowledged centre of church reform. Henry's wife, Agnes, was also a devout woman, seriously committed to the reform of the church in the Cluniac model. Meanwhile, in Rome, the situation was scandalous, with three popes vying for position, the last one, Gregory VI having bought the papacy from his predecessor, Benedict IX ,for 2000 silver pounds. Henry, on the urging of Abbot Hugh and Empress Agnes, decided to intervene. He summoned the popes and bishops to the Synod of Sutri in 1046 and Silvester, the third claimant, and Gregory were deposed. A few days later, Benedict met the same fate. With the way now cleared, and with an eye to the purity of the early church, Henry appointed the Bishop of Bamberg as Pope with the ancient and revered name of Clement II.

Pope seemed to follow pope annually, and eventually, the German Leo IX, a former monk, became pope in 1049. Leo travelled to Rome as a bare-footed pilgrim, and received formal canonical approval from the clergy and people of Rome. In fact, they had little choice, but it was novel for a pope even to go through the motions of the traditional rites. Leo was the first reform-minded pope since Gregory I had died in 604. He set about implementing his vigorous reform programme and for a few short years had the whole-hearted co-operation and approval of the emperor. This constituted the first centralised action of the papacy for centuries and it was both joyfully welcomed by the reform parties and vigorously opposed by those who till then had held Rome as a private possession. Leo's first task was to surround himself with trusted advisers, which meant in practice a thorough reform of the cardinals. Leo found the cardinals, that is the chief clerics in the neighbourhood of Rome, to be all Roman and little inclined to reform. He imported his own men, four of whom were destined to have an extraordinary influence on the church, with results lasting to our own day. These were Abbot Hugh, who became the pope's spiritual adviser, Cardinal Humbert, his legate, Peter Damian, his theological adviser and the priest, Hildebrand, who was put in charge of the financial and practical affairs of the papacy. These men travelled, denounced abuses, held synods, punished offenders and preached the reform throughout much of Europe.

It is time now to look at the agenda of reform. Leo IX began a process that was to continue for the next few centuries. The immediate agenda was the freedom of the church from lay control, a very delicate operation, since it involved attacking the very rulers who had placed Leo in power in the first instance. Two abuses, in particular, received their undivided attention, namely simony and lay investiture. The details of the reform need not detain us here, but the whole impetus was to wrench the church free, once and for all, from lay influence and the exchange of gifts or favours in the appointment of church officials. Obviously, powerful interests were involved here, and there were several major scuffles over the next few years. Rome and the papacy, however, took on an ever increasing confidence in the rightness of their task and refused to brook any interference. One of the earliest and utterly deplorable tragedies of this stage of the Roman reform was the split with Eastern Christianity in 1054, through the excommunication of the Patriarch of Constantinople, Michael Cerularius, by Cardinal Humbert, the papal legate. The language of the excommunication decree is outrageous and illustrates the utter self-righteousness and ignorance of the Roman church with regard to the traditions of the East. Humbert was absolutely unbending in his attitude and utterly without pity or sensitivity. He accused the Patriarch of practising every heresy ever conceived since the beginning of Christianity, including the practice of 'allowing the hair and beard to grow'. Finally, he thunders: 'That is why, being unable to bear these unprecedented injuries and these outrages directed against the chief apostolic see ... we sign against Michael and his supporters the anathema that our most reverend pope has pronounced against them if they do not return to their senses.'[5]

This tragic event, which waited until 1965 to be reversed by Pope Paul VI , gives some idea of the grim determination of this generation of reformers. Eventually, the priest, Hildebrand, became Pope in 1073, taking the name Gregory VII, and the reform movement reached even higher degrees of intensity. Before decribing the monumental moment of challenge between the imperial will of Henry IV and the implacable reforming fervour of Gregory, it will be well to list some of the other items on the reform agenda. Externally, there remained the threat of Islam, which had already deprived the Christian Church of its ancient territories in North Africa, Southern Spain and Italy, and much of the Near East. During these centuries, the tide began to turn in Europe's favour, as Spain and Italy began to reclaim their own territories. Eventually, the ill-fated Crusades, initiated by Pope Urban II in 1095 would carry the opposition deep into the heart of Islam in order to reclaim the Holy Places for Christianity. Again, we are well aware that the decisions made then still haunt Christianity and have stained its relationship with another great world religion for centuries. We will have occasion to look more deeply at the crusading movement later.

One of the major internal challenges for the reform movement in Christianity was the life of the clergy. Chapter Two will explore this struggle in some detail, but here it is important to gain some insight into the spirit and goals of this item on the reform agenda. There is no basis for mandatory celibacy in the scriptures, but there are several scriptural elements which together form the basis to which all pro-celibacy advocates have appealed. These include the apparent preference of both Jesus and Paul for celibacy, some of Paul's admonitions, some of the Levitical regulations for the Jewish priesthood about cultic purity, and the traditional practice of virginity. We know that the debate intensified with the advent of the ascetic movement in the fourth and fifth centuries, and especially the example of the lives and writings of many Church Fathers. The advocacy of pre-eucharistic sexual abstinence was common in these writings, but the presumption that most clergy were married remained intact. It is clear, of course, that such sexual abstinence is impossible to legislate or monitor. The intervening centuries of turbulence had done nothing to make the position clearer; if anything, the practice of clerics with regard to marital chastity seemed even murkier, to judge by the records. An eighth century document, for example, forbids clerics to have more than one wife. Early in the new millennium, however, there is nothing less than an outright attack on clerical marriage. This onslaught was one of the key planks in the reform movements that originated in the eleventh century and carried on with increasing intensity into the pontificate of Gregory VII. Even though the language is often as intense as the fevered tones of Jerome – indeed he was one of the favoured authorities of the time – the eleventh century debate is much more pragmatic than the fourth century version. The eleventh century reformers are seeking freedom from lay control and, consequently, total control over the clergy. The radical reform of the clergy, and their separation from all lay influence is part of the papal struggle for power. It is primarily a power struggle, not a spiritual one at this stage.

For our purposes here, it is sufficient to have given an idea of the general tone of the struggle, but it is also necessary to highlight the devastating consequences for the ecclesiastical attitude toward marriage. It is, of course, clerical marriage that is under attack here, but the language and attitudes transfer easily to all marriage and to the general contempt in which marriage, and especially women's role therein was held at this time. The following quote gives some idea of the tone of the debate. Peter Damian was one of the main crusaders in the celibacy debate. He was absolutely insensed at the horror of clerical marriage and seems to direct most of his hatred at the wives. He urges total chastity on priests in a sermon preached in 1059 and insists that 'the hands that touch the body and blood of Christ must not have touched the genitals of a whore'. He is not speaking of prostitution here, but of marriage.[7] In the end, however, the church was forced to deal with marriage, as its sacramentality came under serious debate. Marriage was, of course, included as a sacrament, but churchmen seem to have felt that it was included in the sacramental listing almost on sufferance.

The medieval debate on the sacrality of the priesthood co-incided with changing attitudes towards the eucharist itself. The Western church had no uniform eucharistic doctrine. One tradition, under the influence of Ambrose, stressed the changing of bread and wine into the Lord's body and blood, without being specific about how this change took place. Another group, broadly Augustinian, stressed the dynamic symbolic unifying power of the sacrament, incorporating all who received it into the mystical body. A debate between theologians had arisen during the Carolingian period, which led to a renewed emphasis on the reality of the change and this ultimately caused genuine confusion between the historical body of Jesus and the eucharistic body of Christ. Berengarius of Tours sought to restore some balance by reminding all of the symbolic dimension of the Augustinian teaching. Berengarius, equipped as he was with some of the new language and concepts of early scholasticism, raised the discussion to a whole new level, and attempted a somewhat metaphysical explanation of the eucharistic change. He was ultimately condemned and forced, in 1059, to sign a statement of faith that included a quite crudely physical statement about the Body of the Lord being torn apart by the teeth of believers. Eventually, following the lines of the scholastic debate, actually initiated by Berengarius, the Aristotelian and non-biblical concept of transubstantiation came to be the accepted explanation for the nature of the eucharistic change.

Though this whole eucharistic debate demands a much more nunanced discussion, enough has been said here to indicate the new emphasis on the actual physical/sacramental body of Christ in the eucharist. This realisation added to the awe in which the eucharist was held and to an increased awe at the radical and awesome power of the priest in bringing about this great mystery. The concurrent debate on clerical celibacy gained great impetus from this new eucharistic understanding, and the task of the reformers was made that much easier. Nevertheless, the battle was a hard fought one, and finally needed the participation of the whole Christian community to carry it to a successful conclusion.

Henry III died in 1056. He had personally presided at the initiation of the reform movement and, together with his wife, Agnes, had brought a new thirst for reform to the church in his realms. He was succeeded by his son, Henry IV, then aged only 6, so that Agnes automatically became the Queen Regent. The church reformers were immediately aware of the ideal opportunity presented to them of pushing their programme of liberating the church from lay control. What possible obstacle could a six-year-old emperor present? There was never an attempt here to destroy the emperor, or wrest total control for the church, but a final push to separate the two powers into their respective spheres. The ensuing battle has always been termed the 'investiture' struggle. Lay investiture was considered to be the symbolic induction of the clergy into their office by the emperor and the bestowing by him of the symbols of office, namely, the ring and the crozier. From the emperor's perspective, this was a clear, though symbolic demonstration of the source of the new bishop's temporal power. Emperors willingly conceded the spiritual power to the pope. The emperor saw himself standing surely on the traditional ground of feudal obligation and loyalty, and with less certainty, by this time, on the ancient divine right of kings. But this latter was also an ancient claim. The emperor was no ordinary layman. He was the anointed of God, uniting in his person symbolically the divine and human natures of Christ the King. Besides, this ancient and traditional role had been proven over and over again in actual deeds. Who, in fact, had saved the church, most recently in the person of Leo IX?

Against this, the reformers held up the priestly ideal of sacerdotal power, based on election by the clergy and people, though by now this claim was quite fuzzy, as the people had little say in the matter. The ideal, however, survived and formed an essential element in the reformers' goals. With a six-year-old emperor and an apparently friendly Queen Regent, the time seemed ideal to push the church's claims to the limit. Agnes of Poitou, the second wife of Henry III, had been crowned Holy Roman Empress in 1046. She was a well known supporter of the Cluniac monks in their reform efforts, and was also a patron of arts and letters. Simply by becoming Queen Regent, she gained enemies on all sides. The German barons, no less than the papacy, were awaiting just such an eventuality. As the German barons began to grab land, and as the papal demands began to be articulated, it seemed that anarchy would prevail in Germany. Henry IV was finally removed from her care and Agnes abdicated the regency. In the traditional manner, Agnes retired as a penitent and spent the rest of her life as a pilgrim in Italy, lending whatever support she could to the pope. Her contemporaries pointed to these events as yet another example of how women did not have the competency to govern.[8]

Pope Gregory VII and his associates prepared well for their move against the Emperor. They had studied the forged Donation of Constantine, a document which supposedly outlined the powers and properties bestowed on the papacy by the Emperor Constantine in the fourth century. Though previous popes had based many claims on this document, in Gregory's view it gave too much credit to the emperor. From his perspective, all papal powers came directly from God – no emperor had anything to offer a pope, except obedience. In the case of the election, appointment and ordination of bishops, the pope alone held authority. All the emperor could claim was to be notified as a courtesy. Henry IV, on the other hand, desperately needed the traditional feudal powers of episcopal investiture in order to keep his empire together. A monumental conflict was in the making, and when it happened, it shook the world, and changed the concept of the papacy forever. In February 1075, Pope Gregory published his decree against lay investiture: 'We decree that no one of the clergy shall receive an investiture with a bishopric or abbey or church from the hand of an emperor or king or of any lay person, male or female. But if he shall presume to do so he shall clearly know that such investiture is bereft of apostolic authority, and that he himself shall lie under excommunication until fitting satisfaction shall have been rendered'.

Shortly afterwards, in the same year, Gregory laid down his

own claims to authority in a document which has garnered him both extravagant praise and vicious blame, the famous *Dictatus Papae*. This is an extraordinary document, laying out in what appear to be chapter headings, the papal claims. There are twenty-seven in all, but a few of them will give an idea of the whole:

1. That the Roman Church was founded by God alone.
2. That the Roman Pontiff alone is rightly to be called universal.
8. That he alone may use the imperial insignia.
9. That the pope is the only one whose feet are to be kissed by all princes.
10. That his name alone is to be recited in the churches.
11. That he may depose emperors.
19. That he himself may be judged by no one.
22. That the Roman Church has never erred, nor ever ... shall err to all eternity
23. That the Roman Pontiff, if canonically ordained, is undoubtedly sanctified by the merits of St Peter.
26. That he should not be considered as Catholic who is not in conformity with the Roman Church.
27. That the pope may absolve the subjects of unjust men from their fealty.[9]

As historians point out, this document, and indeed many more similar ones, express the basic ideas which remain central to all subsequent medieval papal claims: the pope has the fullness of power in both church and world, and has personally become holy in assuming the papacy.

It would indeed be a strange emperor who would not react to these claims. Henry, the Bavarian, was engaged in constant warfare with the Saxons. When the war was going well, he felt free to defy the pope; when it turned against him, and he needed the support of the pope and all the German bishops, he was able to write in pious submission to the pope asking for his prayers. Milan proved to be the test case that inflamed the final conflict. Henry appointed his own candidate against the pope's wishes and in a general assembly coerced the German bishops into denouncing Gregory VII as a papal usurper, guilty of all kinds of immorality and abuse of authority. Inevitably, the decree of excommunication against the emperor followed in February 1076. The emperor's initial response opened with the words: 'Henry, King not by usurpation, but by the pious ordination of God to Hildebrand, now not pope, but false monk.' It was definitely not a letter of submission, but the ensuing months showed that Henry had overplayed his hand. The moral power of the pope's actions astonished the world. The German nobles and bishops were glad of an opportunity to defy their emperor, now excommunicate and deprived of royal authority. Henry found himself alone and was obliged to begin negotiating his surrender and pardon.

The subsequent events are well known. The pope was to travel to Augsburg to judge the emperor on his own ground in February 1077. In January, the pope paused in his travels at the castle of Canossa to enjoy for a time the hospitality of his friend, Countess Matilda. To the astonishment of all, Henry, not wanting the pope on German soil, slipped away to Canossa, and presented himself as a barefoot penitent at the gates of Matilda's castle. This scene took place in the depths of an Alpine winter and intentionally placed the pope in an impossible situation. As a politician, he should have sent Henry back to Augsburg to await the planned judgement. As pastor, he was faced with a penitent sinner seeking absolution. After three days, the pastor won out, the excommunication was revoked, and Henry was absolved of wrongdoing. This was probably the best moment of Pope Gregory's spiritual career, but politically, it was disastrous. Some German nobles had elected another king, and when Henry returned, a vicious civil war raged in Germany for three years. Eventually, Henry was excommunicated again, but this time, the whole of Germany turned against the pope, who had remained deaf to all pleas for help, thus allowing the civil war to continue for three years without intervention.

Henry called together his bishops and nobles and, going with the popular feeling, denounced Pope Gregory again as a false pope and elected Clement III as the real pope. Eventually,

in 1084, the anti-pope was installed in Rome by Henry and
Gregory was forced to flee. The Normans in the south of Italy,
supposedly papal allies, arrived too late to help the pope and instead looted the city, putting almost half of it to the flames.
When they returned south bringing the pope with them, the
people of Rome had turned against Gregory, blaming him for all
their suffering. He died, a lonely and apparently bitter man as a
prisoner of the Normans. The life of Pope Gregory VII has presented historians with a dilemma. We shall return to him in
Chapter Two, but offer here the two main strands of judgement
in subsequent assessments of his life. One group sees him as a
greedy and ambitious ruler, as culpable as those he condemned,
his main flaw being his utter inability to bend. It is said that his
assistant, Peter Damian, called him 'My holy Satan'. The other
group sees him as a selfless servant of the church, with astonishing energy, but little penchant for self-analysis. However one
judges him, Pope Gregory VII set the agenda for much of the rest
of the Middle Ages. No one was untouched by his influence. His
career as pope brought him from the heights of influence and
love to the depths of hatred and rejection. Much of the remainder of this volume will examine the effects of these papal claims
and actions on the life of women.

First of all, we return briefly to the Countess Matilda,
Gregory's supporter and host at the time of his greatest test. In
1074, late in the year, the pope had addressed her as 'my most
beloved and loving daughter' and added that 'you can hardly
imagine how greatly I may count on your zeal and discretion'.
Matilda was then in her late thirties and had inherited vast
Italian estates from her father while she was still a child. To assert her independence in this fairly unusual position, she had
amassed a huge army and put her self at the service of the papacy
in the person of St Peter. It is said that her soldiers shouted 'For
St Peter and Matilda' as they charged into battle.[10] She signed
herself 'Matilda, by the grace of God'. In her lifetime, she was
treated as a saint, as befitted the anointed protector of the pope,
but her enemies suggested that there was more than friendship

between Pope Gregory and herself. Matilda, however, seems to have been an extremely religious and high-minded woman, backed by enormous wealth, and fond of quoting St Paul to the effect that nothing, 'neither principalities nor powers', would separate her from the love of Peter. No wonder people wondered about their personal relationship.

Matilda had been born around 1046 in the castle at Canossa, centre of her family's huge land holdings. Her father, the Margrave Boniface II, as well as all her brothers, died before she was six, and an extremely turbulent childhood followed. Her inheritance remained precarious – Emperor Henry III was casting the envious eye of a feudal overlord in her direction – and it was inevitable that she turn to military activities in order to preserve her inheritance. In theory, her possessions were secure, but it was the actual practice that counted. Claims to inheritance had to be enforced, usually in a case like Matilda's by male relatives. Where Matilda differs, is that she took such obligations on herself. Matilda's tutors are said to have had great difficulty teaching her embroidery, as all she wished to learn was the practice of martial arts. She learned to ride with spear and lance and to fight with pike, battleaxe and sword, all the while wearing the required heavy armour.

Matilda did, however, excel in the arts considered suitable to a female. She even learned embroidery and sent gifts of her work to William the Conqueror. She was fluent in four languages and was able to write and sign her letters, unaided by a clerk. Matilda married twice, but the truth of these arrangements is hard to discern in the welter of legends about chastity that always surrounded her memory. It is clear that neither marriage was what one might call a success, since Matilda seems to have disliked intensely the carnal requirements of married life. With the very well-timed death of her first husband in 1076, she was free and available for the papal agenda in the struggle with the Emperor Henry IV.

Matilda's first public appearance seems to have been at the Council of Sutri in 1059, together with her mother and step-father.

This council was occasioned by the death of Pope Stephen IX and the ensuing play of pope and anti-pope. Matilda's family was connected either by marriage or loyalty to one line of popes in the following two years of confusion. Her first battlefield experience seems to have been in the defence of Pope Alexander II in 1061 at the age of fifteen. Here her reputation as the new leader of the Amazons was made and it had much opportunity to develop over the next few years. Her exploits became the stuff of legend, so it is difficult to extract fact from fiction, but there seems no doubt that her military efforts were always on behalf of the Italian-backed papacy. Pope Alexander II was ably supported by the monk, Hildebrand, and the first meeting of Matilda and the future Pope Gregory VII must have taken place during these battles. A any rate, as soon as Gregory became pope in 1073, Matilda declared herself to be his faithful handmaid, as devoted to him, as she said herself, as Paul had been to Christ. Their friendship seems to have been as intense as the mission they shared, but the suggestion of carnal relations between them, which appeared regularly in later accounts, seems unsubstantiated. It was, however, an intense, continuous and deeply satisfying relationship for both of them, with Matilda acting the part of devoted daughter, and the pope, fittingly, acting the part of holy and loving Father.

Matilda's mother, Beatrice, as well as her first husband, the hunch-back Godfrey, died in 1076, so she was free and independent. We have already mentioned that Gregory had stopped off at Matilda's castle at Canossa, en route to the excommunicated emperor's trial in Augsburg. From Canossa, delegations raced back and forth, working out the terms of a possible reconciliation. Matilda's troops had provided the pope's armed escort from Rome to Canossa. She seems to have ridden out to join the pope at Florence in order to be his personal escort to her home. Canossa was a huge impregnable fortress, well chosen for the pope's protection. Matilda's chaplain was so excited by the whole proceedings that he wrote a song, put into the mouth of the castle itself: 'Lo, I possess at once the Pope, the King [Henry],

Matilda, princes of Italy, of France and of those beyond the mountains'.[11] We know that among the guests were Bishop Hugh of Cluny and his assistant Odo, the future Pope Urban II, who summoned the world to the First Crusade in 1095.

As the news of Henry's precipitate journey to Canossa became known, Matilda was sent to meet him as a kind of go-between papal ambassador. Matilda seemed the best one to plead with the determined pope. She was, in fact, a second cousin of the emperor and he begged her: 'Go therefore to him, O most valiant cousin and make him bless me once again.' We are told that she pleaded the emperor's case so eloquently that the pope became irritated with her. Eventually, on the fourth freezing day, the emperor was admitted and pardoned. As later events were to reveal, the pope had to be content with this one glorious moment of imperial submission. Nothing in Henry's further conduct showed any kind of remorse for his actions and the great Pope Gregory was to die in captivity in Salerno, while the emperor's anti-pope sat on the papal throne. No wonder, he died a bitter man.

Matilda's star did not rise much further either. The emperor, far from being grateful for her intercession, accused her of treason in not extending her feudal loyalty to him and placed her under the imperial ban. This meant that all her goods were forfeit. The papal side then assured her of the eternal riches awaiting her in heaven, but were powerless to help her further. Matilda did not lose heart and definitely did not stop fighting. Her loyalty to the papacy continued unabated. We are told of some victories by Matilda and her troops as she fought back against the emperor's harrassment – even that she stood tall in the stirrups as she massacred the enemy. She adamantly refused, over the next fifteen years, to make peace with the emperor until he abandoned his succession of anti-popes. The succession of Odo, her former friend and ally as Pope Urban II was one bright spot in her very turbulent life, and offered her a second loving papal relationship. For Pope Urban's sake, in 1089, she was married off to the seventeen-year-old Welf of Bavaria, thus bringing

Bavaria into the papal alliance. Welf soon tired of his powerful wife and separated from her six years later.

By now, Matilda was universally known as the 'daughter of Peter', surely one of the strangest titles any woman has ever borne. The emperor now unceasingly tried to make peace with her, but as long as there was an anti-pope in his retinue, Matilda would not hear of it. In the end, Matilda out-lived pope (Urban died in 1099), anti-pope (Clement died in 1100) and even the emperor himself, who died in 1106. She continued fighting on behalf of the papacy, however, seeming more at home on the battle-field than anywhere else. The new emperor, Henry V, opted for courtesy and co-operation in his dealings with his father's old enemy and swore that 'in the whole earth there could not be found a Princess her equal'. As Matilda aged, she spent most of her time in the nearby Benedictine monastery of Polirone. The illuminated 'Matildine Gospels' which she presented to the monastery illustrate her final achievement of some kind of spiritual peace.[12]

Matilda died at Polirone on 15 July 1115, without direct heir. Her feudal possessions were left to the emperor and all her other possessions to the See of Peter, thus causing endless difficulties for the next several years, as claim followed counter-claim. Matilda was buried in the monastery, but her body was transported to St Peter's in the seventeenth century. Matilda was so unique that her contemporaries sought for models with which to compare her. Penthesilea, the Amazon queen, was one of the few models available, as well as the Queen of Sheba. All her admirers – to this day – hasten to assure us of the femininity and compassion of this woman warrior. Her devotion to the See of Peter cannot be doubted and, for most of her Italian admirers, this serves to excuse the embattled state within which she lived her life. In any case, Matilda is almost unique in the annals of women's Christian history. Chapter Three will explore the life and times of Queen Eleanor of Aquitaine, another extraordinary woman, whose bravery was no less doubted, but whose devotion to the papacy was much more questionable.

It remains to comment briefly on general attitudes towards women during this profoundly formative first century of the second Christian millennium. Things had not been going well for women during the eleventh century. Even the great abbey of Gandersheim, from where Hroswitha had challenged negative images of women, fell prey to the new almost universally hostile attitudes towards women. Emperor Henry II had gladly availed himself of the support of the two great abbesses of Gandershem and Quedlinberg to secure his imperial election, but then he began systematically to destroy the power and influence of such powerful women. He peremptorily placed the abbeys under the authority of the bishop and his successor, Henry III, combined both Gandersheim and Quedlinberg into one huge estate for his daughter. It was an age of intentional institutional reform and, following the example of the church reformers, the lay leaders could find no place for women in their new schemes. As women in monasteries were subjected to unwanted episcopal power, they lost touch with the old monastic networks. This was only exacerbated as the reformers forced abbots to be ordained as bishops and forced most monks to be ordained as priests. Much of the dispossession of women's convents was motivated by greed, as emperors and bishops sought rich rewards for those who supported them. As the century wore on, however, and the goal of clerical celibacy came to be more and more the driving force of reform, old forms of misogyny were everywhere apparent.

The Synod of Rome in 1059 had taken the first step in making the church a woman-free zone. Women were designated as irreparably lay, lost in some grey world between the celibate cleric and the disempowered laity. Wealthy women patrons soon saw which way the wind was blowing, and instead of endowing convents as they would have in a previous age, they began to endow male monastic institutions. Besides, what had the nuns to offer that competed with the Mass for the Dead and the celebration of the eucharist? Women had become a very insecure investment indeed.[13] Dozens of convents were emptied of nuns and turned over to monks. These included the old and famous convents of Ely, Whitby, Repton and Wimbourne in England. New shades of propaganda proposed that women were too weak to follow the Benedictine rule without very strict supervision. 'Mary became a consolidated stereotype of feminine virtue comfortably ensconced in heaven and exquisitely malleable to monkish visions and fantasies, which filled the yawning gaps in the sources'.[14] And if Mary had become the model of obedient and submissive feminine virtue for nuns, who was the new model for married women? Mary Magdalen, reformed and penitent prostitute. Gregory the Great, who had died in 604, is said to be the one who combined all the Marys of the scriptures into the one model of penitence. These two Marys now became the sole models for women: the one a virgin-mother, and the other a penitent whore. As the propaganda used to back the imposition of celibacy became more outrageous, all women were demonised and seen as the enemies of the clergy. In such a case, only penitence and exclusion from society were required from women, both for their own good and especially for the good of men's souls. All through the eleventh century, claims were made by various churches and abbeys to possession of the relics of Mary Magdalen. The great abbey of Vezelay in Burgundy, the greatest surviving Romanesque church in France, however, claimed to have miraculously discovered her whole body, thereby dislodging all other claims. In 1050, Pope Leo IX had established her as the chief patron of the abbey, placing her even head of the Virgin Mary. From that time on the abbey flourished as a centre of devotion and pilgrimage in honour of this outstanding example of womanly repentance.[15] In Chapter Ten we will pick up again the threads of devotion to these two womanly symbols of holiness. The point here is to demonstrate the paucity of spiritual images and examples for married women during the opening years of the millennium.

Having celebrated the opening months of the third Christian millennium, it seems appropriate to enquire about the conditions of Christians at the beginning of the second. The mood was certainly not one of celebration. Most Christians were probably not aware of the moment and the papacy was certainly otherwise engaged in the final decades of its corrupt decline. But, as Norman Cohn has illustrated in his classic writing, there were stirrings abroad which were to have enormous influence on the church, even to our own day.[16] These stirrings have been collectively termed 'millenarianism'. The term refers to a particular quality of religious dissent at significant moments in the history of the church, and the early centuries of the second millennium certainly constituted one of these moments. As the church imposed the eleventh century version of reform, it displayed yet again its constant flaw. As a religious community it failed to satisfy the religious aspirations which it had evoked. It seems that the official church is usually astonished at the fervour of lay spiritual aspirations and when it fails to satisfy them, it is judged by the very standards it has set for itself. The evocation of the purity and fervour of the New Testament community touched a chord in the lay population. As the centuries progressed, as we shall see, these aspirations were nourished by a succession of leaders such as Joachim of Fiore, and eventually produced the great mendicant orders of the Franciscans and Dominicans, but also, from the church's perspective, spawned many heresies along the way.

The problem was that for many of the laity, the enemy of reform was the church itself, with its wealth, clericalism and increasing lack of attention to lay spiritual sustenance. The very reforms of Gregory VII had created a longing for holiness, while at the same time illustrating that this newly reformed clerical church had little need for either women or laity. From the eleventh century on, the religious dissent of the poor and revolutionary movements of the poor became increasingly frequent. There was serious over-population, rapid economic and social change, greater divergence between the rich and the poor, and a growing and unbridgeable gap between the clericalised church and the ordinary person. Such millenarian fervour always needs a named enemy. In the eleventh and twelfth centuries, this enemy was variously seen as the Jews, the papacy, the whole clericalised church, and eventually women. In some ways, the Crusades, as we shall see, channelled some of this fervour away from the European continent, but when they failed, disillusionment was even greater. Eventually, in true millennarian style, the poor believed that only they could set things to rights, since the great, the wealthy and clergy had so significantly failed. These currents underly much of the next few hundred years. No group is untouched by them. The greatest fear and also the greatest hope was that the lowly would rise up against the great. It was Joachim of Fiore who named the period the 'Age of the Holy Spirit', the third age. This latter notion became the common stock of European social mythology, and is not unknown in our day. One of the keys to the understanding of these movements is the desire for personal religious experience, and this will be one of the major themes in the lives of women as the second one thousand years begin.

Women in the Gregorian Reform: Marriage and Celibacy

The Gregorian reform, so-called after Pope Gregory VII, was neither initiated nor brought to completion by him. The reform had picked up momentum some thirty years earlier in the papacy of Leo IX, gained legal trappings during the four Lateran councils, and achieved some kind of completion in the fourth Lateran Council of 1215, called by Pope Innocent III. The stated goal of this reform was the 'freedom of the church', not to be understood as our modern notion of individual personal freedom, but rather the freeing of the church from lay control. This entailed the disentanglement of the church from the ownership and control, both actual and symbolic, of the lay lords, and what is of more immediate interest here, the disentanglement of the clergy from all worldly concerns. The primary ingredient of this endeavour, however, was the imposition of celibacy on all clergy, achieved finally at the second Lateran Council in 1139. Thus marriage became a diriment (i.e. absolute) impediment to priestly ordination and, in fact, to the whole gamut of clerical life. It was a sweeping reform, closing the door on a way of life that had been part of ecclesiastical understanding for almost 1000 years. It was socially disruptive and took centuries to implement. Nevertheless, in the papacy of Gregory VII, a mindset was created that would alter the face of Christianity forever. No ecclesiastical reform is kind to women – inevitably they have been seen as God's competitors for the souls of men – but this particular reform was directed against women in particular. Women were demonised and vilified in order to attempt to make marriage less attractive to the clergy. In the process, a new misogyny was born, and a new understanding of marriage and priesthood was articulated. The fact that similar debates still rage in the churches show how significant the work of Gregory VII was, and also the effectiveness of what today we might call his propaganda machine. This effectiveness is also demonstrated by the complete historical amnesia over centuries about the very vocal opposition to mandatory celibacy, and by the fact that, though clerical marriage became legally impossible, the goal of clerical chastity was not attained, as concubinage continued to flourish, again invisibly to most historians.

As we have seen, there was no basis for mandatory celibacy in the New Testament, but several scriptural themes lent themselves readily to pro-celibacy advocates. These included the apparent unmarried state of Jesus and Paul, Paul's encouragement of singleness 'in these times of stress', (1 Cor 7:26), the ascetical practices of some 'heretical' sects, and the proffered option of a life of dedicated virginity for both sexes. The married household, however, continued to be the normative model of ecclesial life in the New Testament, and far beyond. Many of the great conciliar bishops known to us were married. The fourth century blossoming of desert and urban ascetic monasticism led to a quasi-epidemic of voluntary virginity for both women and men. A kind of ascetic competitiveness led to new demands on ordained clerics to practise pre-eucharistic abstinence from sex for reasons of cultic purity. These fourth- and fifth-century debates took place in an atmosphere of high emotional and spiritual intensity, as the new conciliar teachings about the divinity of Christ altered the conception and practice of priesthood. As daily celebration of the eucharist became the norm, the demands for clerical sexual abstinence reached a crescendo.

In this context, sex and impurity were seen as practically synonymous. To engage in sex was to lead an impure life, and such a life was seen as diametrically opposed to the cultic purity required of the clergy. There was strong opposition to these cultic requirements and one, at least, of the opposing reasons was silenced forever. This had to do with the presentation of Mary, the mother of Jesus, as model for all as virgin, wife, mother, widow.

On the contrary, Mary's perpetual virginity, it was said, presented her as the model of virgins and celibate clerics for all time. All opposing views were declared heretical and have disappeared almost entirely from subsequent history. The total turmoil throughout the western world from the fifth to the ninth centuries meant that survival, not clerical celibacy, was the main issue. The vast majority of clerics known to us were married, and marriage was seen to be essential to survival. Besides, in the developing feudal world, such choices were not always left to individual clerics, as ownership of land decided who the decision-makers were.

From the time of the accession of Pope Leo IX, there was an onslaught on clerical marriage. A succession of local synods forbade priests to marry. The popes themselves and their advisers travelled the length and breadth of Europe preaching against clerical marriage and seeking out those who continued to disobey. Finally, at the second Lateran Council in 1139, the first universal law of celibacy was articulated and promulgated. In other words, marriage was now forbidden to priests, their children were declared illegitimate, and their wives were reduced to the status of concubine. Priests were forced to divorce their wives and both the wives and children often became serfs, or slaves of the church. In most instances, such women and children were sent as slaves to compliant bishops, lay lords and abbots. Huge social disruption followed, both in terms of the lives of the married clergy, their wives and children, but also in the re-distribution of land. Here again, those who were compliant benefitted enormously, and contrariwise, priests' sons were forever prevented from inheriting church land. It is no wonder that this Gregorian reform is seen as one of the four great revolutionary moments in the western world. The implications for women are not usually to the forefront of the mind of the traditional historian, but such will be our main concern here.[1]

When Leo IX had become pope in 1049, clerical marriage was widespread and considered normal, despite six hundred years of decrees about clerical abstinence and increasingly harsh penalties.

It is to these decrees and especially the fourth century patristic writings on virginity that Gregory VII appealed in his imposition of clerical celibacy as the 'traditional' teaching of the church. Gregory thought of himself as a traditionalist, not realising that traditional forms in a wholly new setting are revolutionary in their implications. He brought about a completely new order in western Christianity. Gregory's language was often as heated as that of Jerome in the fourth and fifth centuries – indeed Jerome became again one of the favoured authors of this period. Gregory wrote of the 'foul plague of carnal contagion' affecting the church through priestly marriage. He accused non-compliant bishops of 'loosening the reins of lust' upon the world and summoned them to Rome for exemplary punishment. Since 1059, there had been an effort, initiated by the inflexible Cardinal Humbert, to ban the laity from taking part in services conducted by married priests. It was Humbert also who threatened excommunication on married priests who did not divorce their wives. As all this indicates, the reformers were thus content to cause total social disruption in the furtherance of their aims.

One of the aims of this programme was to achieve total power over the church and the world. We have already seen the outlining of this power in the *Dictatus Papae*.[2] It was based almost totally on the pseudo-Isidorian decretals, that is the earlier forgeries used to justify the pope's temporal power. Pope Gregory's method was to give orders and to compel obedience. He instituted a kind of mysticism of obedience as a way of achieving the *plenitudo potestatis*, the fullness of power, that he thought appropriate to the office of the papacy. In 1074, Pope Gregory, in his first Lenten synod, suspended all married priests and mobilised the laity to reject all ministry from such priests and bishops. This remarkable decree occasioned a boycott of the clergy by the laity, organised by the Pope. Eventually, almost forty years after Gregory's death, the marriage of priests became a legal impossibility at the Lateran Council of 1139.

What were the consequences? Despite the tendency of ecclesiastical historians to view legislation as effective as soon as it is enacted, priestly chastity was not immediately achieved. What was achieved, however, was the legalising of celibacy, and perhaps, even more important, the placing of the priesthood in an entirely new context. To all intents and purposes, the clergy now constituted the church. They were always and everywhere superior to the laity. The old 'divine right of kings' was loosened and henceforth was largely symbolic. Priests were removed from the people and an unbridgeable gap was created between clergy and laity. Perhaps the greatest consequence was that the clergy were forever hedged off from women. A new language of misogyny was created during this debate from which the church is only slowly recovering. It will not go amiss to report again the astonishing language of Peter Damian in his campaign against clerical marriage. For him, the women are clearly the enemy:

> I speak to you , O charmers of the clergy, appetising flesh of the devil, that castaway from paradise, poison of the minds, death of souls, companions of the very stuff of sin, the cause of your ruin. You, I say, I exhort you women of the ancient enemy, you bitches, sows, screech-owls, night-owls, bloodsuckers, she-wolves ... come now, hear me, harlots, prostitutes, with your lascivious kisses, you wallowing places for fat pigs, couches for unclean spirits...[3]

Wives, mothers, children and families were pawns in this epic struggle. The violence and, one would have to say, unChristian nature of the language gives some idea of the intensity and tone of the struggle. This was a battle for power that the papacy was going to win and there was no tradition of ecclesial compassion for married women on which to draw. Instead, the reformers could re-ignite centuries of hatred for women in literature, theology and real life and, in fact, this constituted much of the substance of their reforming stance. There was also a great deal of concern about the loss of church property and income and the growth in some places of a kind of hereditary priestly office. The reform aimed to put an end to such practices once and for all.

The attack on women was forecast in the words of Pope Leo IX about the *damnabiles feminae*, or 'those damned women'. The wife of a priest was not *uxor*, the ancient and honourable Roman term for wife, but a harlot. All such wives should be seized and become slaves of the church. Their children, equally damned, should be sold into slavery. The pastoral care that later characterised Pope Gregory's dealings with Emperor Henry IV were in no way visible in his dealings with the wives and families of priests, nor with the priests themselves. One way by which such pastoral care could reasonably be by-passed was by naming the offending priestly families as heretical. They were called Nicolaitans with constant reference to Revelations 2:6-14: 'You hate the works of the Nicolaitans which I also hate.' The word 'wife' was forbidden to be used in connection with priests, and even the story of Patriarch Paphnutius who was said to have counselled against the imposition of celibacy at the council of Nicea in 325, was banned from public discussion. The argumentation grew quite bizarre. One sermon argued that since all female laity were the spiritual daughters of priests, it would constitute incest to sleep with such a close relative.

All priests were commanded to move to a common residence, dormitory and refectory, in order to support one another, and to report on one another's obedience. The reformers appear to have been quite alarmed at the resistance of the clergy to their aims. Priests are said to have replied that they would prefer to desert the priesthood rather than marriage, and that it was impossible to require priests to live like angels. We hear of whole parishes attacking and chasing reformers out of town – Peter Damian himself was chased out of the city of Mantua by the irate townspeople. Between 1075 and 1082 we know that Gregory had to depose 15 bishops and 4 archbishops for non-compliance. Gregory invited the German princes and the laity to judge the clergy for themselves. We hear of laity stamping on consecrated hosts as a sign of contempt for the clergy. When the clergy objected to such behaviour, Gregory let them know that celibacy was the absolute pre-requirement for any further discussion. He was totally unbending in this and this inflexibility set the scene for the achievement of his aims. When Gregory died in 1095 he had not yet reached the goal of clerical celibacy, but he had succeeded in totally disrupting the ministry of married priests and in changing public opinion. Even the anti-popes were coming around to Gregory's point of view, and eventually, the laity themselves insisted on celibate ministers. The boycott had worked.

The one voice that is nowhere heard here is the voice of the wives and children. We hear that many wives committed suicide in preference to serfdom. Others, it is reported, banded together to attack their local bishops. It was to be in vain. As the pope's power over the bishops increased, the bishops, in their turn, gained more control over the lower clergy. The priests, again, gained more control over the laity, especially as the theology and practice of the sacraments changed dramatically. The power of the priest in eucharist and penance gave him entrée into the inner lives of the laity, thus controlling the most intimate decisions of families. This was especially the case for nuns. Where before, the intimate life of the convent was built on a relationship between abbess and nuns, especially with regard to confession of sins and spiritual direction, now there was the intrusive presence of the priest. Ordination was now deemed to take precedence over every other vow, and the sacrament of priestly orders appears almost to invalidate the sacrament of matrimony. Part of the propaganda for the imposition of celibacy was to name all sexual activity, whether extra- or intra-marital as unclean. Even the papacy and curia were changed forever as a result of this celibate war, as they were to be consumed for centuries with mountains of legislation concerning priestly concubinage.

Anne Llewellyn Barstow marshalls the evidence to illustrate the opposition to this ecclesiastical onslaught.[4] As we have seen, a huge defence against the imposition of the practices of ascetical virginity had taken place in the fourth and fifth centuries. The issues then dealt with the example of Mary as model for wife, mother and widow, as well as for the virgin, and with the importance of baptism in determining the nature of ecclesial life, rather than sexual activity. The influence of Ambrose, Jerome and Augustine ensured that the ascetic agenda prevailed, though even Augustine suggested that clerical marriage was preferable to concubinage and secret vice. Henceforth, Mary appears primarily as Virgin, even when addressed as Virgin-Mother, and the Christian life was inevitably divided into a first-class group of Christians, who practised strict sexual asceticism, and a much lower second-class group who 'fell into marriage', as Jerome had said.

For the next five hundred years, i.e. from approximately 500-1000 CE, there was no active debate, despite volumes of reminders about clerical abstinence and cultic purity. There was no strong centralised papacy and, in any case, much of the decision-making was in the hands of the feudal land-owners. By the eleventh century, however, there is a strong new and more detailed defence of clerical marriage, because the new legislation was more specific and all-embracing in its enactments. The lack of scriptural evidence for imposed celibacy was widely quoted; in fact, the scriptures implied the opposite, it was pointed out, as most of the male apostles were married. Paphnutius and his advocacy of the essential element of choice in the matter of celibacy at the council of Nicea was so widely quoted that it was finally condemned. A one thousand year custom of priestly marriage was invoked against the innovatory behaviour of the reformers, who falsely claimed tradition on their side. Several anti-celibacy authors comment on the violence of the proceedings, where new legislation is imposed against the will of all, against biblical precedent and against ancient custom.

Furthermore, the opposition insisted, the lives of married priests offer, in most cases, a wonderful example of married chastity. Why are such lives vilified? When there is such inhuman legislation, priests will inevitably practise a 'false continence' or they will turn to homsexuality. The writing of Ulric makes this point over and over again: enforced celibacy leads to homosexuality, and such homosexual priests are now presented as being more obedient to the pope. The point is, these defenders of clerical marriage allege, that women have been set up as the major problem.

But this is not true. The major fault here lies with the imposition of a law which requires that people act contrary to their nature. Celibacy is a gift of grace and all the legislation in the world will not make a man celibate. What about those who cannot be celibate? Is this legislation driving priests into fornication, incest, sodomy and no end of new scandals? And are not the natures of clergy and laity the same? This legislation is not geared to moral reform but to papal control; it is more about power than service. Besides, the imposition of celibacy will produce a different kind of priest, one obsessed with power and obedience rather than one who leads by love and example. Priests who practise imposed celibacy will learn a new contempt for marriage and this injures the whole church. The pope forgets that all baptised persons are holy, including priests' wives and children. Here, the pope is in direct conflict with the Holy Spirit. This legislation causes utter chaos in the churches. What is gained by having the laity boycott their clergy, burn their tithes, trample the eucharistic hosts underfoot and confirm their own children with the wax from their ears? Is the pope ready for the revolution that will ensue, since he has taught the people to despise their local authorities? Even the authority of the father of the family has been destroyed.

All these writers support the ideal of celibacy, but are utterly against its imposition, seeing this as a legal impossibility. Nevertheless, the papal party was in a position to pass such a law and to make it effectual. Barstow mentions some of the reasons why it eventually worked to create a completely new sense of the Christian reality. Eventually, most monks were ordained to the priesthood, thus destroying forever the old equality of a lay monasticism that included women and men on a fairly equal footing. Such women were now deemed to be the enemies of the clergy and even the enemies of monks. Before too many years had passed, monks were condemning women as the greatest danger to their lives. They refused to work with women and resented bitterly any time they had to spend in ministry to women:

We and our whole community of canons, recognising that
the wickedness of women is greater than all the other
wickedness of the world, and that there is no danger like that
of women, and that the poison of asps and dragons is more
curable and less dangerous to men than the familiarity of
women, have unanimously decreed for the safety of our
souls, no less than for that of our bodies and goods, that we
will on no account receive any more sisters to the increase of
our perdition, but will avoid them like poisonous animals.[5]

Women were equated with insatiable sexuality and irrationally
demonic temptation. There was a systematic defilement of
women needed in order to attract men to celibacy. Such demonised women were less desirable. Sexual union was projected into
a mystical realm of erotic spirituality, and endless commentaries
on the Song of Songs – the favourite biblical text of the period –
invited men to direct their longings to the one safe woman,
Mary, the perpetual virgin.

Other contemporary developments fed into the eventual vic-
tory of the reformers. The development of university education,
available only to clerics, created another level of division and elevated the clergy even more above the common or 'lay' person,
now also unlettered in Latin, the sacred and priestly language of
the church. The dramatic change in the celebration of what was
then seen as the eucharistic miracle in the liturgy added yet another dimension. The priest seemed to occupy a quite different
realm from the people, a new powerful realm of godly gifts
brought about by his cultic purity. Besides, the sacrament of
penance gave the priest a very localised power over the people
of his immediate parish. The peoples' lives were now known to
him and he decided how God's gifts would be distributed.
Inevitably, a new ecclesiology, a new understanding of church
arose from this which practically identified the clergy and the
church. Nothing was required of the laity but obedience and
compliance and the observance of fairly minimalistic church
laws. As Barstow points out, even the use of the word 'laity' is a
misnomer. There was no lay identity, except that they were not

ordained, no lay spirituality, and no lay education. Nevertheless, the laity have a way, historically, of rediscovering the
biblical heart of Christianity, and before very long, lay movements, as we shall see, make of the church a very turbulent place.
The priesthood now becomes a state, a race apart, with its
own power and authority attached to celibacy and the new theology of priestly ordination, and completely divorced from the
ancient and traditional roots of community. At the time, clerical
celibacy was the powerful symbol for clerical freedom from all
taint of secular life, lay power and most especially women. The
symbol of celibacy is the refusal to acknowledge the importance
and maturity of the laity. In the end, the symbol and practice of
celibacy was the church's message to women that their gifts
were superfluous to the life of the church. Nevertheless, in the
succeeding years, there is an explosion of womanly involvement
in the life of the church, a power that no pope or legislation
could stop. Though misogyny was intrinsic to the establishment
of the culture of clerical celibacy, women do not seem to have
noticed that their presence was not required. Despite the demonisation of women that was the flip-side of celibacy, a treasury of
womanly spirituality was produced by generations of women,
both lay and religious, who quite simply saw themselves as responding to the voice of God. Before turning to these women, it
is important to try to discern what women were, in fact, doing
behind all the negative stereotypes. Here again the researcher is
limited almost entirely to the pens of male authors. From them
we can get a clear idea of what male writers said their society expected of women and we can draw some conclusions. From the
women, however, there is still no voice. It is no wonder that one
of the classic histories of women at this period is called the
'Silences of the Middle Ages'.[6]

   Women became a major pre-occupation for church reformers.
Having created a culture and literature of misogyny, or rather
re-awakened it, the church now was faced with the task of controlling women and solving the problem of marriage. In the
course of the celibacy debates, marriage had been denigrated

almost, one would think, beyond repair. Despite such feverish debates, however, marriage was still the lot of the vast majority of people. In the preceding centuries, there had been a great deal of ad hoc theorising on marriage, occasioned by the utterly capricious lives of most of the aristocracy. Children were given in marriages at their parents' whim and just as easily taken back and bestowed elsewhere. We hear of one girl, called Grace, who had been married three times before the age of eleven. The whole of England seemed to have been involved in the negotiations around her welfare. Theoretically, marriage was by now given meaning only by the exchange of mutual consent. With the connivance of the King of England, the Archbishop of Canterbury and the great Bishop Hugh of Lincoln, Grace was first married off at four years of age. Two more husbands followed in quick succession, each more vicious than the previous one. We do not know the end of the unfortunate Grace, supposed daughter of Agnes and Thomas, but as an aristocratic child, she was seen as fair game from the moment of birth. Whatever most suited the family's land-holdings was what influenced marriage decisions, and church and aristocracy found little way around this. So, even though the theory of freedom of consent within marriage was on the books, the actual implementation of such a theory was not possible for centuries. Such stories are legion.[7]

Nevertheless, from the eleventh century on, the church gave marriage its modern form. Till then, the church had had very little influence on the practice of marriage, and its subsequent influence was sporadic for centuries, but once marriage attained – with great difficulty – the status of a sacrament, the power of the church over its celebration increased. Just as the clergy had resisted interference with their marriage rights in the eleventh century, so too did the aristocracy in the twelfth. The whole story is full of paradoxes. As the church tried to sacramentalise marriage, it had to delineate its real nature. Till then, Germanic marriage practice which focused on the act of intercourse, Celtic marriage practice which focused on the handing over of the bride, and Roman marriage practice which focused on the free exchange of consent, had been the dominant forms and these had been acknowledged or ignored to suit the ecomomic goals of the aristocracy. Now the church canonists adopted elements of all three but chose to focus on the free exchange of consent. This, paradoxically, in theory, freed marriage from the power of the clergy. This choice, consciously or unconsciously, was a strategic manouevre. The clergy and the aristocracy would be merrily engaged for centuries in sorting out the most extraordinary variey of marriage conundrums. Brides, and often grooms too, were simply pawns in the exercise. During the twelfth century, the age of the groom at marriage rose until there were usually ten years or more between him and his bride. There are cases where it is clear that the church tried to protect women in such cases, but it took centuries before free consent had any reality whatever in the bride's marriage arrangements.

There was a huge disparity, then, between theory and practice. For one thing, the caste system meant that no nobleman was allowed to marry a serf, no matter who desired this relationship. In this, as in so many medieval cases, caste outweighed any influence of the gospel, and to an even greater degree, sex outweighed any evangelical notion of equality. Having engaged in decades of vicious misogynystic writing, late eleventh and twelfth century authors, both lay and clerical, began to pour forth volumes of words about the social and ecclesial roles of women. Most of these words were designed to show the reasons why women were utterly incapable of choosing anything for themselves, certainly not anything as significant as a husband. Eventually, a consensus was arrived at – that is, in writing – about the nature of *the woman*. Most of the writers were reduced to speaking about this mythical figure, since, for both clerical and lay writers, women were largely unknown to them in actuality. The church was becoming a women-free zone, and other pursuits, mostly military, occupied aristocratic males. As these writers scoured through ancient texts, including the scriptures, to reach a definitive delineation of *the woman*, they found themselves immensely reassured by the similar discussions in the newly discovered writings of the greatest philosopher of all, Aristotle.

Females came to be described according to a hierarchy of value, set up by the males themselves. The eleventh and twelfth century writers had centuries of previous writing to support their opinions. 'Women were the theoretical and practical testing ground on which the whole of society created and experienced a particular concept of sexuality'.[8] Women were first and foremost bodies to be committed either to the church or to the family. Their lives were seen as static, products of nature, designed by nature and God for one particular purpose. A woman's choice had little to do with the outcome. Virgins, widows and wives were seen as three rungs on a ladder of virtue. On the moral scale, virgins were seen to be the equivalent of queens on the social scale. The main criterion was chastity and this over-rode all other social and religious categories.

The first requirement for women was to be kept out of the public gaze. Just to be seen was a sin for a woman. The very sight of a woman would arouse men's lust, cause discord, violence, adultery and revenge. Even the journey to church was mired in possible difficulties. Such women, even when obeying church law by attending the Sunday service were seen as 'arsonists of sacred places'.[9] Much worse was the devastation associated with women who went out socially to dances and parties. Here, flushed cheeks and lowered glances vastly increased the sin. A woman sinned even by looking out the window, obviously longing for the world of men. The writers warned men especially about women who sat by their windows sewing. It is said that these women can get so excited by the passing male scene that they sew their fingers by mistake. The usual advocacy of sewing as a suitable activity for women was designed to impose immobility, keeping both hand and eyes occupied, and therefore free from harm.

Contemporary women might be relieved to know that one of the greatest faults of women was deemed to be a restless curiosity.

They were always seeking for something new and better. At that time, however, this was seen as unnatural, and a sign of woman's inconstancy and unreliability. They surmised that women's souls must be equally irrational, inconstant, limp and unreliable, and were delighted to have this suspicion scientifically confirmed in the writings of Aristotle. Woman is a *mas occasionatus*, a faulty and incomplete male, irrational and easily led astray. The only solution was to keep women in custody. This came to be one of the key words in all pastoral, pedagogical and spiritual literature. For religious women, it was soon translated into the world of the cloister. The intention of cloister and custody was to protect and care for woman like a 'jewel of inestimable value', but also to repress, imprison and supervise her for her own good. Modesty was said to be a noble custodian for some women, and occasionally modest women could act as their own custodians. This was rare, however, even in convents. Eve's sinful heritage remained powerful in women's lives and this sin had been aggravated by the history of so many evil women. Therefore it is clear that personal modesty is never enough; it always needs the re-inforcement of male custody.

A remedy for such inconstancy was total submission to men, whether father, brother, husband, bishop, priest or spiritual director. With such a history behind them, one would think that most women would have become accustomed to submission. But women are slow learners. Even after centuries, some still resist such submission. Men learn more quickly. They are destined for command, leadership and decision-making and they have learned their lessons well. Men have become confident in their own superiority. It is this confidence of superiority, of course, that the celibacy debates were all about. Paul's graded headships in 1 Cor 11:3 is usually quoted here. It is clear, then, that women, according to philosophy, scripture, theology, custom and church teaching are always inferior to men.

Another of the medieval paradoxes emerges here as the medieval theologians re-discovered the patristic teaching about the equality of souls in women and men. How could it be that God had endowed women with souls equal in dignity to those of men? The problem was solved by relegating this teaching to the level of pure spirituality. Any sane observer could say that women and men were not equal in practice. The natural superiority of the male remained unquestioned, as did the natural inferiority of the female, designed at creation and even more aggravated by the sin of Eve. God's curse on Eve was re-echoed in the life of every single woman – another excellent reason for custody. It was deemed to be clear, then, that freedom for women was a sin against nature and the order of creation.

The ancient strictures of Tertullian against women's dress, cosmetics and ornamentation are repeated with even more urgency in the Middle Ages as the range of such commodities expanded with the opening of new trade routes. Dressing for show is equivalent to idolatry. Instead women should wear the necklace of doctrine, the earrings of obedience, the ring of faith, the linen of chastity and the sash of discipline. Wives, of course, should be an adornment for their husbands, but they should be aware that they no longer owned their bodies. The only reason for such ornamentation was for his honour. Apart from ornamentation, the woman's body should always be as immobile as possible. When she walked, 'she should take little steps of equal size', and keep her eyes so low that 'nothing but where you put your feet matters to you'. They were not to treat Sunday worship like the market, discovering there 'all their neighbours, friends, and relations in God's church'. Today's reader might take heart from these rare glimpses of how life really was for women. Going to church must have presented women with one of the few opportunities to meet and greet others. Even the contents of the woman's diet was discussed by these men – no wine or spices and always a more meagre diet than that of men.

Idleness was another anxiety for these male writers. With most women having annual pregnancies and either running a home or trying to survive, women must have had very little opportunity for leisure. Idleness, however, seems to be a particular bugbear of the clerical writers. They saw work as another form of custody for women. It kept them busy, exhausted the body, and provided the suffering for which women were naturally suited. Even more important than endless work was complete silence. Centuries of clichés came into play here. Women were chatterboxes, expert liars, malicious gossips, constant arguers, persistent whiners, all illustrating the model of Eve, who when she spoke wrought only destruction. It was even suggested that Jesus chose Magdalen as witness of the resurrection, because he knew she would gossip about it. The apostles preached the resurrection, the women only gossiped. Most medieval men showed unconcealed scorn for women's words. Speaking in public was absolutely forbidden, so a woman's contribution was specifically excluded from church, university, lawcourt and every public forum. The language of power, government, church, justice, philosophy, theology, salvation and gospel were all masculine. Scripture, exegesis, the teaching of the Fathers, canon law and endless examples all prove that women are unsuitable for preaching and teaching. Their intellects were defective, thus depriving them of any authority.

The strictness of these prohibitions against speaking, teaching and preaching stand out because women were, in fact, engaged in all three pursuits at this time. From Hildegard of Bingen on, hundreds of women questioned these clerical regulations, and won the right of being heard through the sheer brilliance of their discourse. The claims of women to be sent by God to speak caused great heartbreak to the churchmen, placing them in very precarious circumstances. When they claimed the right to judge whether it was God or the devil instructing the women, they were often severely rebuked. Most medieval men were superstitious enough to ponder such activity of God. They might not agree, but God's instructions were often clearly articulated in the exemplary lives of the women.

Women's speech was praiseworthy only when comforting husbands, responding obediently or consoling children. Otherwise all women's speech was irrational, fickle and incoherent. As thousands of stories illustrated, they were utterly incapable of keeping a secret. Noble women and nuns were allowed to study and read what was appropriate, but the material that they were allowed to read constituted only another form of custody. Even confession of sins was not seen to be wholly necessary for women. Their confessors reported that they made fairy tales of their sins.

A whole series of words rang in women's ears for centuries: chastity, obedience, submission, silence, modesty, sobriety, humility, suffering. This feminine model had already been around for centuries, but had never been articulated in such a complete and comprehensive way. This medieval picture was one articulated by clerics and was rooted in their own projections, supported by philosophers, fabulists, law-makers, theologians, scripture and tradition. It is a model with great staying power and has had untold influence on the life of every woman who has grown up in the Western world. On the other hand, the frequency and feverishness of these utterances illustrates the hidden power of women, their ability to terrify men even while living in such prescribed circumstances. The question every historian wishes to explore is the extent to which these prescriptions actually formed the lives of women. Did the medieval women see themselves in these descriptions? Did they change their lives accordingly? Did women actually think of themselves as a blight on the face of the earth, worthless, irrational and closer to the animals than to humans? It is still impossible to answer these questions satisfactorily. The frequency with which such admonitions appear would give one to believe that it was a wasted task for the clerics to keep on reiterating such precepts. The women we will meet in the remaining chapters give the lie totally to such a picture of womanhood. Nevertheless, such prescriptions meant that they had to live their lives in particular ways, surmounting enormous obstacles and taking great personal risks simply to dare to speak publicly. But speak and write and preach they did, and the surviving texts attest to their brilliance.

On the other hand, the enormous social, cultural and ecclesiastical changes following on the battle for the imposition of celibacy, created a setting where the value of women was vastly reduced. Wealthy women no longer donated money to convents when nuns could not render any of the important services that the ordained monks now rendered. Priests could celebrate the eucharist, pray for the dead, give absolution for sins and perform no end of spiritual and secular service to those who were willing to fund their establishments. We know that even the most worthy of male monastic establishments, the Cistercians, eventually suffered grievously from their very success. We have already seen that nuns now occupied a strange misty place in the hierarchical ordering of the church. They did not belong to the clergy and there was never any question whatever of their being ordained in the sense this word came to hold in the eleventh century. In the male clerical stronghold that was now the church, women were a negative value. As a Spanish proverb of the time said, 'The honourable woman is locked in the house with a broken leg.'[10] Just as the wife was confined to the home under her husband's supervision, so were the nuns enclosed in their convents. 'The sacralisation of monks shattered the symmetry of female and male monasticism, making nuns second class monastics'.[11] As we have seen, women had been excluded from the monastic reforms originated in the monastery of Cluny and then castigated for not being reformed. The vilification of women, then, could be extended to apply to these nuns. During the eleventh century, the numbers of convents decreased rapidly. As Jo Ann McNamara points out, the misogyny of the age was reinforced by greed. Powerful wealthy women and powerful articulate nuns were, in the spirit of the times, seen as a sign of degeneracy.[12] Nuns also generally lost the right to elect their own leaders, and as we have already said, the new clerical situation meant that the intimacy of an all-female community was disrupted by the intrusive presence of male confessors and celebrants. Many convents tried to reform themselves, but their efforts were constantly thwarted by clerics. It was now impossible for most convents to be immune from the authority of the local bishop, and local clerical politics often determined the affairs of the convent to an extent not otherwise experienced. As male monasteries began to flourish under the influence of the reform, and then the advent of university education and the study of theology, women's convents floundered as such benefits were denied to them. Miraculously, within another few decades, the tide would turn as women forced themselves and their spiritual gifts on the church once more.

Having ruled out the possibility of clerical marriage, and having vilified the very notion of marriage itself in the process, it remained to the generation after Gregory VII to try to rehabilitate that institution in the eyes of the church. Marriage advice was directed almost completely to wives since they were the ones seen to constitute the problem. Sarah was a particularly loved model, especially for her obedience, chastity and devotion. Eventually a complete educational system for wives was built around her biblical image.[13] Even though wives were still seen to be at the bottom of the scale of perfection, after virgins and widows and just above prostitutes, they still deserved some attention, since they constituted the vast majority of church female membership. As the church moved toward defining marriage as a sacrament, it was incumbent on the theologians and canonists to praise it as a source of grace, but this did not come easy. The writers are much more comfortable with Jerome's fourth century fulmination against the miseries of marriage. Eventually a new doctrine was built up based on the creation story, the wedding feast of Cana and the virginal motherhood of Mary. This was all interpreted through the injunctions of Paul about the headship of the male and the silence and subjection of the wife. The wife was key in this new notion of marriage, especially in her role as constant peacemaker. For aristocratic wives, this meant being an ambassador between their family of origin and their husband's family, since most aristocratic marriages were politically motivated. It was especially accomplished, however, through the constant submission of wife to husband. She was instructed to expect an imbalance of love – she was to love totally, but not to expect a similar devotion in return. She must believe that 'no one is wiser, stronger or handsomer than her husband'. Everything he does is to be seen as right and just. She is to be blind to his faults through her love. The husband cannot afford such love; his must always be measured, because too much love will make the man lose his essential rationality. Adam was the exemplar here – he allowed himself to be ruled by sentiment, not reason. He was utterly led astray by loving his wife more than God.[14]

Eventually Aristotle's definition of marriage as the relationship of two unequal partners dominated the writing. Thomas Aquinas was to add his own contribution about the different levels of virtue in husband and wife and the necessary justice involved in evaluating them differently. A husband was to receive more love because he was essentially more just, more reasonable, and thus capable of greater virtue. A wife, being naturally inferior, receives a lesser kind of love. Wives continued to be central to such writings for several hundred years as the sacramentality of marriage was worked out with such tortuous reasoning. Women were caught in an impossible bind in such talk – their call to selfless love was the very mark of their inferiority. Even today, such talk of wifely love pervades papal documents. Women, especially wives, are described as experts at giving all for a very limited return. Women had the added responsibility of making themselves constantly lovable so that husbands would not stray, while on the other hand, too much attention to their appearance and their own interests was a mark of sinfulness. What all the authors really imply is constant submission. The harmony and unanimity in marriage that was the goal was never the result of a commonality of desires and aims, but was always seen as the wife's responsibility in making sure that the husband's decisions were reinforced by constant submission. The 'love patriarchy' of the deutero-Pauline literature had returned once again to the forefront of the church's teaching. Love and obedience were identical for a woman and the burden of maintaining the marriage was laid squarely on the shoulders of the weaker and inferior partner.

The accompanying debate on the nature of sexual rights within marriage need not detain us here – it will be necessary to tackle this equally tortuous subject again. The one point to be made here is the absolute necessity of wifely fidelity. Husbands were theoretically bound by a similar law but, as the previous instructions to the wife point out, many doors were left open to him. Most of the aristocratic marriages known to us in the sources bear not the slightest sign of such fidelity, but the teaching was useful in bringing about the end of an unwanted relationship. Aristotle's insistence that the wife's fidelity was more necessary in order to ensure the purity of the family blood-line became a standard part of the teaching, to such an extent that fidelity became a uniquely female virtue. In this way, the inequality of the marriage relationship was sealed. The wife's main task was to 'generate children continually until her death'. Thus, she atoned for the sin of Eve, gained her own salvation by acting out God's plan for her, and fulfilled her natural and supernatural destiny by being a help to man.[15]

Such were the contradictions of a woman's life in consequence of the division of the church into a woman-free clerical zone and a vast lay zone which seemed to depend totally on the submission and the blameworthy natural love of a wife for her husband, and of the mother for her children. There are few if any similar instructions for husbands and fathers. He was the rationally endowed member of the relationship, and as such did not need further instruction. It was the irrational wife who was in constant need of correction, advice, and admonition. There is little opportunity to discover the extent to which this teaching was followed in its detail. We certainly have no wifely testimony to the living out of such admonitions. It is clear, however, that this constant teaching did penetrate and form the characters of women in a general way over the next several hundred years. The creation of a male-dominated church did nothing to improve the lot of women. In fact, the contrary is clearly the case. There was no real place for women because there did not seem to be any need for them within the confines of this male church.

Here they were a liability rather than a help. In the eleventh century, misogyny found a life of its own and the effects continue to our own day. It is remarkable then, that the array of extraordinary women presented to us as the history of the middle ages unfolds lived their lives with such vigour and high purpose against such a backdrop. Most of the women known to us have survived in the record because of the holiness of their lives. The woman who will next claim our attention has not been remembered for her holiness, but she nevertheless led a most remarkable life as the wife and queen of four kings. This is Eleanor of Aquitaine.

CHAPTER THREE

The World of Queen Eleanor of Aquitaine

The lives of two women cover the whole span of the twelfth century: Abbess Hildegard of Bingen and Queen Eleanor of Aquitaine. There seems to be no evidence that their paths ever crossed, even though the lives of both were intermingled with the great names of the age. Both knew Bernard of Clairvaux, for example, and each was subjected to his critical gaze for very different reasons. Both lived through the saga of Thomas Beckett and the quite different saga of Abelard and Héloïse. Both lived through the early crusading years, the founding of the universities, the appalling and endless warfare between the French and English kings, not to mention the quarrels of both with the Holy Roman Emperor. Both lived through ten anti-popes and some seventeen genuine popes throughout the twelfth century, and the lives of each crossed both happily and quite unhappily, the lives and plans of these popes. Each lived under papal interdict – again for very different reasons – and both found it necessary to defy the popes when their own purposes were being stalled. Hildegard, visionary, mystic, theologian, author, pharmacist, musician, artist, preacher and abbess will occupy us in the next chapter. Eleanor, who was variously Queen of France and Queen of England, crusader, mother and grandmother of kings, queens and even saints, will be the focus of our attention in this one.[1]

The twelfth century presents us with an inexhaustible, and annually increasing store of sources and studies of its amazing vitality. The discovery of the notion of the 'individual' in that century has occupied historians as well as theologians and philosophers. The burgeoning of new forms of community, both secular and religious, has occupied others. The multitudinous religious revivals, the search for new forms of spirituality, in fact the very notion of search and quest, are central to the histories of the period. As a religious grouping, the Cistercians dominate the age and the crusading movement, initiated in 1095 by Pope Urban II, forms a continuous backdrop to all twelfth century affairs. The rise of the universities and of theology, the 'queen of the sciences', presents the western world and more especially the western Christian church with a new figure of power – the theologian of the scholastic variety. New forms of thought emerged with the rediscovery of some of Aristotle's writings, and new trade routes were opened up with the interminable crusading projects of the age. All of this brings an expansion of thought and action which is visible in the lives of the main figures of the age, but the old feudal relationships continue to dominate their main decisions. The end of the old order is brought about through the trickery and misrule of Eleanor's last son, John Lackland, who succeeded in alienating all his allies, both religious and secular. By the time of the *magna carta*, Eleanor had been dead for a decade, but she had outlived both her husbands and most of her children and contemporaries in a life that had lasted three times the average twelfth century span.

In all of this, women form a negligible part according to conventional historians. Even such extraordinary women as Eleanor and Hildegard are rarely mentioned, except as backdrop to more important stories. This, of course, is somewhat true for their contemporaries also, even more so as the ideas of Aristotle about women begin to infiltrate the theology and philosophy of the period. Aristotle provided the concepts and reasoning for the justification of the hierarchy of the sexes, the need for the custody of women for their own and society's good, the exclusion of women from all public activities, the essential superiority of the male in decision-making, especially as husband, the limitation of women's access to spirituality and spiritual resources as a waste of the valuable time of clergy, and the limitation of the mother's role in the education of her children.[2] Nevertheless, as the life of Eleanor shows clearly, such strictures did not always

work. They did work, however, for the vast majority of people
in a general way, but were never as tightly structured as many
histories would indicate.

To be born a woman or a man in the twelfth, as in other centuries, was more than a biological fact. There were social implications. Church, society and custom assigned roles to women in
particular that had nothing to do with innate characteristics, but
were the result of a whole ideological system. This was the system that found new support in the writings of Aristotle. This
was the system that led kings such as Louis VII of France to
speak of his 'frightening superfluity of daughters' and to pray
for an heir of the 'better sex'. This was the system that saw Alais,
surely one of the most tragic figures of the age, daughter of the
same king, kept virtually under lock and key for twenty-five
years, until Henry or one of the Plantagenets would finally agree
to marry her. This marriage never happened, but Alais was too
great a piece of booty to be allowed out of her prison. Eleanor,
herself, of course was partly responsible for this state of affairs,
but she also experienced her own share of imprisonment at various times in her life. The mystery of Eleanor's life, as of the lives
of Hildegard and the other women known to us by name from
this period, is that somehow she managed to outwit the system
and evade its consequences on so many occasions. The life of
Eleanor will not tell us much about the lives of the majority of
twelfth century women, but it will illustrate the extent to which
some few women were able to penetrate the all-embracing nega-
tivity about women's lives. Women, those quintessential creatures
of nature, according to the twelfth century scholars, were occasionally powerful enough to affect the culture of an age in remarkable ways.

In the third decade of the twelfth century, William, Count of
Poitou and Duke of Aquitaine died at Compostela. The pilgrimage to the shrine of St James beckoned many a hoary old sinner
at the end of his days, and this William had much to repent of.
His death left his fifteen-year old elder daughter, Eleanor, as one
of the wealthiest women in western Europe. She was also a vassal

of Louis VI, King of the Franks, otherwise known as Louis the Fat, who could now, in her father's absence, bestow her as bride wherever he wished. As it happened Louis also lay dying and the thought of adding Eleanor's lands to his Capetian heritage seemed to be the ideal solution to his battle with the ever-encroaching Angevins from England and Normandy. The acquisition of Eleanor's patrimony in Aquitaine and Poitou would double Louis' possessions and vastly increase the numbers of vassal soldiers. Louis' dynastic problems were known to all. His eldest son and heir had died and his second son, Louis, sent early to the monks to be trained as an archbishop, had been 'brought blinking from the cloister' at the age of ten to be crowned at Rheims as the Capet heir. Now in 1137 young Louis was sixteen, still hankering, by all accounts, for the cloister, but destined by his father's decision to change the history of a good part of Europe. He was dispatched to Bordeaux to woo Eleanor and his success would gain him possession of most of modern France from the Loire to the Pyrenees.

Eleanor had been born in 1122 to a family of soldiers who were also poets and troubadours. It was one of the proudest families of the West, claiming descent from Charlemagne, and intricately involved in the great movements of the age. That they seemed to prefer the association with anti-popes rather than genuine popes seemed only to reinforce their reputation for independence of spirit. Eleanor was reputed to be beautiful and gifted with all the matured arts of her heritage. Neither Eleanor nor Louis had much choice about their union and the nuptials were celebrated in the church of St Andrew by the Archbishop of Bordeaux. As they wended their way back towards Paris, Louis the Fat died, so that in the late summer of 1137 they arrived as King and Queen of the Franks. Not long afterwards, the new king returned to the cloister to continue his education with his beloved monks. He was always regarded as being more a monk than a king, though he was to be the instigator of many future unmonk-like actions. Indeed, within a few years, the king and his whole household were excommunicated over the matter of the appointment of the Archbishop of Bourges. Eleanor seems to have gained some education in Paris at this time, though there are no details about this. Indeed, education would have been almost impossible to avoid as Paris was becoming the educational centre of the world with students flocking there to hear the teachings of the great Peter Abelard.

Several educational traditions had come together towards the mid-twelfth century to feed into the founding of the universities. At Paris, a number of schools had grown up around the cathedral and the monasteries and, with the arrival of Peter Abelard, the left bank of the city was now home to students from all parts of Europe. Abelard's presence made Paris the intellectual capital of Europe. Though owing something to predecessors such as Anselm of Laon, Abelard placed his own particular mark on the combination of reason, logic and faith that came eventually to be called scholastic theology. While still in his early twenties, Abelard started teaching theology in Paris, and is said to be one of the first teachers to request payment for his efforts. It is more than likely that the young Thomas Beckett and John of Salisbury were among his students. The city was awash with intellectual controversy and dialectical conundrums. There was new questioning in the air and Abelard added considerably to the excitement by listing almost two hundred doctrinal questions on which he had found divergent authoritative opinion among previous church teachers. He assembled all the authoritative texts pro and con and published his book, *Sic et Non*, or *For and Against*. Abelard was attempting to challenge his students into solving the resulting faith dilemmas as logical problems which could be solved by dialectical reasoning, with close attention also to context, grammar and language.

In a word, the whole traditional concept of authoritative knowledge was being challenged. Abelard provided no answers to his problems, but suggested new methods of thought, methods that were quite unsettling to the church authorities, while marvellously exciting to the students, whose average age would have been around fifteen. Besides, all these students would have been clerics and under the protection and patronage of the church. Women were totally excluded from the whole process but, as we know from Abelard's own life, some women were privileged through birth or wealth to participate in this exciting educational process. The best known of these, in Abelard's life, is, of course, Héloïse and their story of star-crossed love provided the troubadours with songs for centuries into the future. Heloise was the niece of Canon Fulbert and was consigned to Peter Abelard as his private student around the year 1116. Abelard was about 37 at the time and had studied at Tours, Paris and Laon. In 1116, Abelard had just returned to Paris to set up his own school, having found his latest teacher, the great Anselm of Laon, to be dispensing 'smoke instead of truth'.

The eventual affair with Héloïse interrupted his career and almost ended it. After Héloïse became pregnant, Abelard secretly married her and rushed her off to his family estates in Brittany. A child, Astrolabe, was born to them and they returned to Paris to face the music. It is said that Abelard was castrated by the horrified Canon Fulbert and the couple was forcefully separated. Héloïse was placed in the convent at Argenteuil to become a nun, while Abelard resumed his teaching on the mystery of the Trinity. Such are the bare bones of the story. Abelard, however, is painted in recent research as a much more sinister figure who planned the seduction of Héloïse as a distraction from his momentary intellectual boredom between his experiences in the schools of Laon and the founding of his own school. Eventually, nine years later, Abelard wrote a kind of autobiography, giving his own version of the whole affair.[3] It is said that Héloïse was outraged when she read this, and initiated a correspondence with him in order to give a more accurate account of what happened. Héloïse had been praised by several great teachers of the age for her wisdom and learning, including Peter the Venerable, who wrote: '...you have surpassed all women in wisdom and have gone further even than almost every man'.[4]

The correspondence which is generally acknowledged to be genuine makes fairly dismal reading. Héloïse challenges Abelard on questions of ethics, his knowledge of the religious life and his theology. Abelard treats her generally with disdain and rebukes her for her undisciplined mind, which he says is a particular weakness of the female sex. Héloïse accepts his criticisms with humility, and this just seems to encourage Abelard into an out-pouring of contempt for women's speech:

> The more subtle [the tongue] is in you (*vobis*), and the more flexible because of the softness of your body, the more mo-bile and prone to words it is, and exhibits itself as the seedbed of all evil. This defect in you is noted by the apostle when he forbids women to speak in church …

He even acknowledges that he assumed that her uncle gave him complete licence to do whatever he wished to Héloïse and that he used 'threats and blows when persuasion did not work'. Abelard's teaching style is full of military terms and in his writings he describes himself as a professional fighter for the truth. Eventually, Héloïse dissociates herself from such forms of philo-sophical logic, and begins to assemble her own arguments which point out the flaws in both the method and content of his reasoning. In fact, it is the growing confidence of the Abbess Héloïse, speaking in her own voice, in direct disagreement with one of the greatest teachers of the age, that has led some modern commentators to dispute the authenticity of her letters.

Héloïse seems to have had as much difficulty in her own day as with her critics today in getting her own point of view across. She was in an extraordinary situation. Her former and disgraced lover ended up as her main advisor and the author of the rule for her convent. Contemporaries admire Abelard for his patience with her and rebuke Héloïse for her audacity, constant com-plaints and criticisms of the master's work. Many contempo-raries continue in this vein, but as the writings of other abesses become more familiar, it is clear that Héloïse is trying to articu-late her own philosophy from her own experience. She accuses Abelard of never having truly loved her because his actions show none of the personal responsibility that should be a mark of true love. Héloïse speaks clearly about sexual passion and says that she no longer needs this from Abelard – impossible, at any rate, since his castration – but that she does require of him that concern, care, and actual presence that should accompany his words of love. It is now clear to her that what had driven Abelard was simply genital craving, not true love. Héloïse says that Abelard married her just to possess her as the object of his craving, but that love was not part of it. She calls upon him now to take up his responsibilities for love. In response, Abelard tells her that she is a good abbess, that he is available if she needs spiritual counsel, but that otherwise, she should leave him alone.[6]

No wonder Abelard and his contemporaries were shocked at the free and forceful language of Héloïse. Here was a new voice, the voice of a woman who was intelligent, learned and struggling to find her own identity. The twelfth century offers us many examples of such women's voices, but each one is faced with the same struggle for a respectful hearing. It should not be thought, however, that this is a modern feminist voice. Even Héloïse, though she demands respect, still accepts that increasingly widespread Aristotelian view of women as weak and utterly different from men. This can be well seen in her arguments with Abelard about the rule which he wrote for her convent. As the genders were becoming more polarised in the twelfth century as a result of Aristotle's influence, nuns and their male counsellors began to have many disagreements about the rule and its effects on women. Héloïse claimed that she could not follow the Benedictine rule because it was insensitive to the particular needs of women. Héloïse wanted a rule that would organise details of dress, food and daily regimen more suited to women. She even claimed that the monastic costume, which was more or less similar for women and men, was simply not suitable for women because of menstruation. She said that woollen garments worn next to the skin were extremely uncomfortable and unhealthy.

Héloïse insisted on having the decisive voice in the community in all regulations for her nuns, particularly since nuns now in their imposed cloister were more dependent on the intrusive presence of priests. Abelard allowed this but added that abbesses who ruled over clergymen were acting against nature, 'leading them on to evil desires in proportion to their dominance'.[7] Abelard referred to Héloïse as a deaconess, because she had demanded more freedom for herself than was permitted in the usual regulations for the abbess. Furthermore, Héloïse was not a virgin, she continued to be involved in the business of the world, and she refused to be entirely cloistered.

It is not clear whether or not Héloïse actually achieved the freedoms and changes she desired. The pressures of the day were against her. We know that she built up a considerable institution, with several daughter houses. It seems to have flourished at least until the end of the century. Abelard, too, had critics other than Héloïse. In 1121, he was summoned to appear before the Council of Soissons, where he was condemned. He eventually set himself up in the abandoned house called the Paraclete, and there his students gathered around him once more. It was there also that Héloïse and her nuns had eventually joined him in 1129. Abelard returned to Paris in 1132 and his school there became the nucleus of the University of Paris. Abelard seemed to attract enemies and one of his severest critics was the great Cistercian, Bernard of Clairvaux. At Bernard's insistence, indeed after an amazing display of the one-up-manship for which Bernard was famous, Abelard was condemned at the Council of Sens in 1140 and forbidden to continue teaching. He set out for Rome to appeal to the pope, stopping en route at the Abbey of Cluny. He was welcomed there and the Abbot, Peter the Venerable, persuaded him to stop struggling and retire. Abelard died there in 1142, and the news was conveyed to Héloïse with great sympathy by the Abbot. He was buried at the Paraclete and Héloïse was buried beside him in the abbey church after her death in 1164. From the thirteenth century on, Héloïse was regarded as the ideal beloved and her tomb was visited by poets and lovers for centuries. Abelard and Héloïse lay more peacefully in their death than either had known in their lifetime.

Bernard of Clairvaux was not unknown to Eleanor of Aquitaine and her family. Eleanor's father, Duke William X, had been excommunicated for his free-wheeling approach to the appointment of bishops. On one Sunday, Bernard, knowing that William was at the door of the church, rushed down the aisle with the consecrated host in a pyx, and confronted the Duke, apparently thus causing him to have a stroke. William lay on the ground foaming at the mouth to the astonishment of all, and in due course all the bishops were properly restored to their rightful sees. Eleanor's family, however, did not easily forgive such public displays of humiliation. It is likely that Eleanor was present with her husband King Louis at Sens for the condemnation of Abelard, and it may have been her dress on that occasion which caused the next outburst from Bernard.

For an abbot who is reputed not to have noticed whether he was riding a donkey or a handsome steed, Bernard shows himself to have been remarkably observant as he describes to his nuns the kinds of dress they should avoid at all cost. In this outburst, it is generally believed he is also addressing and condemning Eleanor:

> The garments of court ladies are fashioned from the finest tissues of wool or silk. A costly fur between two layers of rich stuffs forms the lining and border of their cloaks. Their arms are loaded with bracelets; from their ears hang pendants enshrining precious stones. For head dress they have a kerchief of fine linen which they drape about their neck and shoulders, allowing one corner to fall over the left arm ... Gotten up in this way, they walk with mincing steps, their necks thrust forward; and furnished and adorned as only temples should be, they drag after them a tail of precious stuff that raises a cloud of dust.[8]

Eleanor's sister had also run foul of the church over a question of marriage annullments, so the house of Aquitaine was enduring a double excommunication for a time. Bernard was intimately involved in all these battles. King Louis was wearied of all the church politics, and on one fateful occasion sallied forth with an

impulsiveness which became his trade-mark. He invaded the
territory of Eleanor's stubborn brother-in-law, torching and
burning everything in his path. The townspeople and villagers
took refuge in their church and hundreds were burned to death,
all innocent, and mostly women and children. King Louis was
stricken with remorse, and the stain of this appalling tragedy
clouded the royal couple for some time.

A letter of rebuke from Bernard sent the King into a panic of
remorse, In all these instances, Bernard laid the blame on the
queen, who was loved by Louis with 'a foolish fondness'.
Finally, we know that Bernard and Eleanor came face to face at
the magnificent celebrations for the consecration of the rebuilt
Royal Abbey of St Denis on 11 May, the feast of St Barnabas, in
1144. This was the national shrine of the patron saint of France
and the burial place of its royal house. The royal couple arrived
on the eve and the king joined the monks in vigil and penance
for his war crimes. On the following day it was reported that the
'spirit of penitence shone in his whole aspect'. This pattern of
atrocity and penance was to be repeated many times in Louis
VII's life. Even Bernard was impressed with the king's 'dovelike
humility' and laid aside the rebuke he had intended to deliver in
person. Instead, Bernard is said to have had a talk with the
queen. He encouraged her to use her wifely influence to keep
the king from such dastardly behaviour, but was amazed to find
that Eleanor was not impressed with his counsel. She had assembled arguments to defend her sister's honour in the recent
debacles and Bernard found himself unable to do anything but
leave the room. He then had a sudden illumination that showed
him Eleanor as the evil genius of the king, giving him only
'counsel of the devil'. Bernard berated himself for not noticing
sooner that the devil was up to his old tricks in using the wiles of
a fair woman to deceive. He then rebuked the queen sternly for
her godless influence on the king and warned her to stay away
from the affairs of state. This meeting between Bernard and
Eleanor shows the abbot remarkably at a loss for words, if only
momentarily. We know that Eleanor, despite their mutual hos-

tility, sought the abbot's prayers in the matter of the royal descent. She eventually got pregnant and produced for King Louis the first of his 'frightening superfluity of daughters', Marie.

All the internal problems of Europe were eventually put on hold as St Bernard and Pope Eugenius III called the fighting forces of Europe to the Second Crusade. Even Abbess Hildegard of Bingen joined in the preaching on this occasion. The crusading movement had been initiated on 26 November 1095 by Pope Urban II at Clermont. In the previous March, while engaged at the Council of Piacenza, an appeal from Emperor Alexius I had galvanized the pope into action. He conceived the idea of gathering a huge papal fighting force and sending them far away from the continent of Europe to free the holy places. Urban's rallying speech at Clermont shows clearly that he had many goals in mind as well as freeing the holy places – something that emperor Alexius had not asked for in the first place. Urban wanted to rid Europe of its superabundance of soldiers. He wanted to direct their energies to a worthy cause far beyond the seas. He wanted to re-enact the ancient Truce of God, 'made by our holy ancestors long ago'. He wanted all to act like pilgrims and to leave their possessions in the full knowledge that they would be safe till their return. 'Moreover, the sins of those who set out thither, if they lose their lives on the journey, by land or sea, or in fighting against the heathen, shall be remitted in that hour; this I grant to all who go, through the power of God vested in me'.

It had been a brilliant and moving beginning to what was ultimately a tragic series of events, the results of which are still being played out in east-west suspicion and distrust. Eventually, the Latin Kingdom of Jerusalem had been established in July 1099, after the most appalling scenes of butchery right across the face of Europe and in Jerusalem itself. This western intrusion into the holy places completely ignored the presence of the Eastern emperor and the Eastern church. Nevertheless, a whole panoply of western organisations flourished with Jerusalem as their centre until 1144. These included the Military Orders of monks – the Knights Templar and the Knights Hospitaller of St

John, as well as all the organisation of dioceses, trade and all the feudal arrangements of the home countries.

It was this Latin Kingdom which was now under siege and the call for another crusade went forth. This time, the enthusiasm was not as immediate, but crusading did offer feuding kings the advantage of a breathing space. It was St Bernard who called the world at the end of Lent to the huge church of St Mary Magdalen at Vezelay so that the papal bull could be read. Even the church was too small, so the throngs of knights gathered outside. As kings and princes made their obeisance to Abbot Bernard, all were astonished to see the Queen Eleanor and her ladies doing likewise. King Louis was dissolved in tears as he received the crusader cross, but Eleanor's face was joyful. There were so many soldiers that Bernard ran out of crosses, but there were also many stragglers. All at once, it is said, Queen Eleanor and her ladies appeared on white horses, dressed in gorgeous fighting finery. Dressed as Queen Penthesilea and the Amazons they raced around the crowd encouraging and rounding up the stragglers and they were so successful that even Abbot Bernard's white habit had to be cut up to provide crosses for all.[9]

The force did not finally leave for several months, but from the beginning, the so-called Second Crusade was headed for disaster. The chroniclers later said that despite the preaching of Bernard and the pope, this crusade had never been pleasing to God. We hear tales of horrors all along the way occasioned by treachery, greed and sheer mismanagement. After the betrayals of the earlier crusaders, the Greeks were less than welcoming. We hear that Louis and Eleanor were dazzled by Byzantium, rich and cultured beyond their wildest imaginings. As they neared their destination, the disasters only intensified. The troops got lost, German and French troops deceived each other and led each other into traps. Some tragedies were laid at Eleanor's door as she and her followers and vassals often took their own counsel, without consulting the king. Eventually, the relations between king and queen were stretched to breaking point. There were rumours of an affair between the queen and her uncle,

Raymond, prince of Antioch; whatever the truth of this, there was more cordiality there than Louis could countenance. Eleanor, at twenty-five, felt at home and extraordinarily light-hearted in Antioch. Her role as Queen of France seemed so use-less and boring by comparison. Here, she was at the centre of councils of war and in the midst of a city whose culture and riches delighted her. Eventually, she told the king that she was separat-ing from him on the grounds of consanguinity, as Bernard had pointed out originally when they were first married. She felt that remaining together would put both their souls in jeopardy. This reasoning about consanguinity was used constantly by the arist-ocracy to make and break marriages. The king's council fell into a panic – what were they to do with Eleanor of Aquitaine on the loose? They made the only possible choice. In the middle of the night the queen was seized and the French army departed Antioch before daylight. There were many rumours and eventu-ally folk-songs about this whole affair – Eleanor does not emerge well from any of them, but the mystery surrounding the separ-ation certainly added to her mystique.

Eventually, after more disasters and shipwreck on the home-ward journey, Louis and Eleanor both arrived back in Europe and went to see the pope, himself in exile in Tusculum. Eleanor was again pregnant, but still a year later, she insisted that she wanted a separation from Louis. Pope Eugenius blessed them, announced that there was no consanguinity and sent them on their way. Eleanor was profoundly angry at this turn of events and poured out her resentment at her capture and imprison-ment since Antioch. It is said that the pope prepared a sumptu-ous bed for them and sent them off to sleep together in the hope that the rift would be solved. They were still at loggerheads when they left the pope and arrived back in Paris in November 1149. They had been away for over thirty months and the citi-zens of Paris rejoiced at their return. Despite the rejoicing, the utter failure of the endeavour was obvious to all – even Bernard said that he almost lost faith in God. There was total bewilder-ment because God seemed to have been on the side of the enemies of the Christian faith. To add to the king's misfortunes, Eleanor was delivered of another daughter, Alix.

In 1151, young Henry Plantagenet, aged 18 and Pretender to the English throne, visited Paris in the company of his father. His mother was the Empress Matilda and young Henry was in the market for a suitable wife. He was originally intent on one of the daughters of Louis and Eleanor, but eventually, his eyes turned to Eleanor herself, now aged thirty. The chroniclers do not relate the details of what occurred next, but in the early spring of 1152, Eleanor retired alone to Poitiers. On the following Palm Sunday, Louis and Eleanor were declared to be separated and their two daughters, now declared legitimate, were to remain with the king. In May, Henry came to Poitiers, and he and Eleanor were married on 18 May, just eight weeks after the separation from Louis. Eleanor was now the wife of her former husband's greatest enemy and had added several new titles to her escutcheon. Shortly thereafter Henry left for England and Eleanor, left to her own devices, created the first of many courts of culture, literature, poetry and song at Angers. In 1153, Eleanor gave birth to her first son, and this event was followed a few days later by the death of her old nemesis, Bernard. Twenty-one years later Bernard was named a saint and we shall meet him again in the context of our discussion of the Cistercians. King Louis went off to Compostela on pilgrimage and returned with the King of Spain's daughter as his wife. In 1154, Eleanor was crowned as Queen of England.

Henry and Eleanor set out to unify their vastly scattered domains into one kingdom. They travelled the length and breadth of their territories and, since both preferred to live on the continent, they needed a chancellor of impeccable credentials to run the affairs of England in their absence. The choice fell on the young archdeacon Thomas Beckett. Beckett had the dingy palace of Westminster restored as a suitable residence for Eleanor, and eventually it became the new cultural centre of the world. Eleanor is reported to have turned London into a great European city, with touches of Byzantium. Stories of Tristram and Isolde, as well as the ancient tales of Arthur and his knights add to the almost legendary aura around the new royal couple. Eleanor is said also to have brought manners to the English – men no longer appeared in her presence with their hair like an 'ill-dressed shock of barley'. Men like John of Salisbury, one of Eleanor's guardians and the source of much information about her, worried that the sturdy men of England were being made effeminate. It is reported that Eleanor even influenced the music of the church adding new hymns and harmony to sweeten the service.

During the next few years, Eleanor supplied Henry with an abundance of sons and daughters, even though their first son, William, had died: Henry (1156), Richard Coeur-de-Lion (1157) who was always Eleanor's favourite and designated heir to her own territories, and Geoffrey (1158). These were followed by Eleanor (1161), Joanna (1165) and finally John Lackland (1166). The territory of Henry and Eleanor stretched from Scotland to the Pyrenees in strips always bordering on the territory of King Louis of France. It was inevitable that such an arrangement would lead to endless wars, intrigues, betrayals, professions of friendship and vassalage that were interminably renewed and broken, and tore apart the face of Europe over the next several decades. Both Henry Plantagenet of England and Louis Capet of France dreamed the same dream – that their descendants alone would become the kings of a huge empire of France and England together. At the beginning, however, the fates seemed to smile on Henry and the Plantagenets. Between 1155 and 1165 they had altered the destinies of peoples and changed the map of Europe.

But the destinies of peoples can be altered by more than the ambitions of kings and queens. In 1161, the Archbishop of Canterbury died. Thomas Beckett seemed ideal to be his successor, especially since he and King Henry seemed to be bound in a great mutual friendship. Within three days, Beckett had been ordained, consecrated and installed as Archbishop on 3 June 1162. Within six months, the worldly and worldly-wise Beckett had

become a model archbishop and the friendship between himself
and the king was severed irreparably. What was at issue was the
eternal argument about the power of the king and the power of
the church, or about 'custom' and the 'dignity of the church'.
More specifically, the king invoked custom to allow clerics to be
tried in the king's courts. Beckett resisted absolutely and insisted
that clerics could be tried only by the church. After several false
moves on both sides, the Council of Clarendon in 1164 stated the
king's position clearly and even pushed the case to extremes.
The row between the two former friends was now a huge international incident, and Thomas Beckett fled just in time to the
court of Louis of France, who was finally rejoicing in the birth of
a male heir, Philip. The affair dragged on interminably, drag-
ging the whole of Europe in its wake, including the two royal
houses, their vassals, the Cistercians (Thomas had put on this
habit), and Pope Alexander III, who was in and out of exile and
captivity.

In this utter turmoil, the news came that Queen Eleanor had
returned to her own domains with her favourite son, Richard,
and though she joined Henry for Christmas in 1168, she then returned to her own city of Poitiers. One of the fateful meetings of
the century happened on the Feast of the Epiphany, 6 January
1169 at Montmirail. Henry of England, with his three eldest
sons, and Louis of France with his daughters and son, met together and in the presence of a huge assembly of knights, archbishops and vassals. Thomas Beckett was reconciled momentarily with Henry. Then Henry divided his kingdom among his
sons, and to his second son, Richard, now aged twelve, was betrothed Alais, aged nine, daughter of Louis. The eldest, Henry,
was crowned as the future King of England, known henceforth
as the 'young king'. What was supposed to be a resolution of difficulties merely aggravated the situation beyond control. By the
end of the following year, on 29 December, Beckett had been
murdered – or martyred – and the three sons of Henry II, joined
soon after by the fourth, John Lackland (he had missed the royal
allottment of lands because of his age), were ranged in implac-

able revolt against their father, possibly instigated by Eleanor. Thomas Beckett was canonised four years later in 1174, and Henry Plantagenet never quite recovered his prestige or his old enthusiasm.

Eleanor's departure from the English court aroused much speculation, but it is perhaps Giraldus Cambrensis, one of the chroniclers who never really liked her, who gives us the reason. And the reason was Rosamund Clifford, the king's mistress. Henry had engaged in several dalliances and had many bastard children around England. Rosamund, however, seems to have been installed at court, and the king seems to have been totally besotted by her. The affair continued publicly for eleven years until Rosamund died in 1177. Eleanor's actions were quite inexplicable to her contemporaries, but were quite in line with the Eleanor that had been known to St Bernard. From 1168 until 1174, Eleanor presided over her own court at Poitiers. She resurrected the ancient symbols of St Valerie, patron of Aquitaine, and had her son Richard crowned and installed in the church of St Etienne as the Abbé of St Valerie. Then Eleanor set out to enjoy her independent sovereignty as the ruler of Aquitaine and her other dominions. She presided there over an extraordinary household, where most of the junior aristocracy of Europe lived. They included her own sons at various times, and their assorted fiancées, Marguerite (betrothed to Henry, the young king), the unfortunate Alais who was more or less imprisoned for the next twenty five years, and Louis' other two daughters, Constance and Alix. There were also Eleanor's own daughters, Eleanor and Joanna, as well as dozens of other royal children and about sixty royal ladies. To be the guardian, nursemaid and teacher of all of these Eleanor brought in Marie, her eldest daughter with Louis of France and with Marie came her chaplain, known to history as Andreas Capellanus.

This household then became the centre of royal patronage, and a new kind of literature, culture and what one might today call lifestyle were created. All these assorted heirs were trained in the arts of royalty and love along the lines of the Latin poet

Ovid's *Art of Loving*, as well as the legends of the court of King
Arthur.

Unfortunately, the whole courtly educational experiment
came to an abrupt end as Henry's sons mounted more and more
serious rebellions against their father, and Eleanor, finally captured trying to escape disguised as a man, was brought back in
disgrace to England and imprisoned in Salisbury in 1174. From
that time until the death of Henry in 1189, Eleanor was kept constantly under surveillance. She learned of the great events shak-
ing the world from her virtual prison. Louis, her former husband, died in 1180, and a new crusade was called the same year,
It was rumoured that old king Henry was not treating Alais, his
son's betrothed with the respect she deserved, and then, within
a very short time, both Henry, the young king, aged twenty-
eight, and his brother Geoffrey died in 1183. Eleanor heard the
dreadful news from Jerusalem about yet another terrible defeat
inflicted on the crusaders by Saladin, the new leader of the scattered Turks. Among the crusaders, who somehow managed to
survive were her son, Richard the Lion-Hearted, Philip, now
King of France, and of course, her husband, King Henry, now
aged fifty-five. The news was so fearful that two popes in quick
succession died of shock, Lucius and Urban. Then, alone and
friendless, Henry Plantagenet, King of England, died on 6 July
1189. Even his funeral clothes had to be borrowed, for his burial
at the Abbey of Fontevrault. It seems that neither wife nor any of
his children attended the obsequies.

Queen Eleanor, now aged sixty-eight, was released from captivity after fifteen years. She immediately assumed the regency
of England, gathered her scattered family together and persuaded
them all to swear oaths of allegiance to the new but absent king,
Richard. Eleanor demonstrated again her extraordinary energy
in travelling the length and breadth of the Plantagenet domains
demanding allegiance and marrying off all the surplus princesses
to ensure the alliances – all that is, except for Alais. Eleanor held
courts of justice, attached her own seal to documents, and ruled
as virtual sole monarch, even expelling the papal legates who

had entered England without her permission. Having been a prisoner herself for fifteen years, she knew well that one way of gaining the peoples' loyalty was to open all the prisons. She endowed and repaired monasteries and built up the coffers of a church and country exhausted by the tithes collected for the crusade. Her journeys became legendary – to Rome to ring concessions from the pope; to Messina to visit her daughter Joanna, Queen of Sicily; to Rouen to re-establish broken alliances, all the time signing herself, 'Eleanor, by the grace of God, Queen of England'. Her energy and wisdom amazed all and she became the marvel of the age. From the time of her release, her dominance was never questioned. She had now but two sons and two daughters left and of these, John Lackland, her youngest caused her the most anxiety. She addressed the pope in impeccable Latin and, in her utter frustration at his inactivity, signed herself 'Eleanor, by the wrath of God, Queen of England'. She berated the pope for his lack of concern in the matter of her son, Richard, who had been shipwrecked and kidnapped by the Holy Roman Emperor, on his return journey from the crusade. This, of course contravened every crusader ethic, including the Truce of God. 'If my son were in prosperity, we should have seen them (that is, the legates) running at his call, for they well know the munificence of his recompense ... alas, I know today that the promises of your cardinals are nothing but vain words.'[11]

In January 1193, Eleanor set off on another of her great journeys, carrying the ransom to redeem her son Richard. To collect this she had been forced to cover hundred of miles collecting yet more tithes from her already despoiled vassals and serfs, but she was the only one trusted by all sides to carry such huge riches. She was now seventy-two and when she and Richard arrived back in England in 1194, everyone thought they were seeing ghosts. Some even died of fright. There is a delightful legend about Richard and Eleanor meeting Robin Hood at this time as they made their way through Sherwood Forest to London. Thereafter, Eleanor frequently accompanied Richard on his travels through their scattered domains, and finally persuaded John to cease his treachery and return his allegiance to the Angevin cause. It seemed that her work was now complete, so Eleanor retired to the Abbey of Fontevrault where her husband, Henry was buried. One of the final acts of this last stage of her life was to see Alais finally brought from captivity and married off into comparative obscurity in 1195. There is so much unrecorded drama in the life of Alais. We know nothing of her, except that, as the daughter of Louis and sister of Philip, both kings of France, she was used as a pawn in endless dynastic alliances. Her life readily gives the lie to the then recent definition of marriage as an alliance based on the free consent of the partners.

The drama of Eleanor's life was not yet over. In 1198, she witnessed the accession of the youngest and most powerful pope of the middle ages, Innocent III. The following year brought her perhaps her greatest grief. Her son, Richard, was fatally wounded by a stray arrow in a minor skirmish on 25 March 1199. Eleanor went at once to his side and summoned John. He who had been named Lackland was now the heir of the domains of his father and all his brothers because Richard, at forty-two, had no other legal heir. Eleanor mourned, 'I have lost the staff of my age and the light of my eyes.' Bishop Hugh of Lincoln celebrated the funeral rites for Richard and he too was buried at Fontevrault at his father's feet, as he had humbly requested. Even as the obsequies were being celebrated, and Bishop Hugh was trying to lecture John about the difference between good and evil kings, Philip of France was attacking the Angevin possessions. Eleanor, again to everyone's amazement, took to the road to defend her possessions, travelling as far as the border of Spain to ensure the allegiance of her subjects. She created new towns and communes, discerning with her usual foresight, the future importance of the bourgeoisie and, at the same time, endowing monasteries and convents wherever she went. In the heat of summer, she covered over one thousand miles, and then crossed the length of France again to rejoin John at Rouen. Her extraordinary family had yet more surprises for her. Her daughter Joanna was also in Rouen. She was in the last stages of pregnancy but, to the consternation of all, was demanding to be made a nun of Fontevrault. Joanna would accept neither excuses nor canonical explanations and she was finally admitted to the community by the Abbess of Fontevrault just in time for her own death and the death of her baby in September 1199. Joanna, after a most extraordinary life as queen, crusader and much abused marriage pawn, was only thirty-four. Two more graves were added to the plot at Fontevrault.

Just as everyone thought that Eleanor would now finally retire in peace, she decided that one more task needed her attention. She realised that Philip of France was still without a married heir and she decided to make one last effort to bring peace to both houses by remedying this lack. Her daughter, Eleanor, was Queen of Castille, so the old queen set off across the length of France and across the Pyrenees to visit her and, if possible, bring back one of her grand-daughters to wed Louis, the son of the King of France. En route she was captured and held for ransom, but finally escaped, crossed the Pyreneees in mid-January, and reached Castille. She had not seen her daughter for thirty years. She chose the second daughter, Blanche, and, on their return journey, reached Bordeaux in time for Easter. Eleanor left little Blanche in the care of the Archbishop of Bordeaux and set out herself for Fontevrault. The marriage eventually took place and Blanche is remembered as the mother of Saint Louis IX.

Eleanor's last few years were among the most turbulent of her extraordinary life. She defended her territories yet again, joined in the universal revulsion when her son John murdered his nephew, Arthur of Brittany, a possible rival for the throne of England. The whole of Europe was again in tortuous uproar as John of England and Philip of France tore each other and the whole of the west apart. Eleanor worked tirelessly to heal these ancient rifts, but finally gave in and retired one last time to her old home in Poitiers. She died either there or in Fontevrault in 1204 at the age of eighty-three and was buried in Fontevrault beside her husband, son, and assorted other relatives.

Eleanor had covered in her life all the possibilities open to

women of her class, and, because her life span was three times
the normal span for either women or men, she was able to add
roles undreamed of by others. By 1100, any religious pretensions
of kings and queens had been well and truly quashed, and the
conflict between Thomas Beckett and her husband Henry had
demonstrated very clearly and publicly that the realms of church
and monarchy exercised separate powers. It is also clear that debates on the nature of such powers continued for centuries. The
life of Eleanor, though thoroughly intertwined with the church,
its politics and its main characters, from popes to saints, gives us
remarkably little evidence about her own faith. We know that
she was present at many of the great events of the day, including
the confrontation between Bernard and Abelard at Sens, and the
re-dedication of the royal abbey of St Denis in Paris, among others. She visited and bullied popes, she went on crusade, and she
lived at the Abbey of Fontevrault for several years, yet we have
no inkling about her attitudes towards the Christian faith. When
she needed a model, she seems to have chosen Penthesilea, the
ancient queen of the Amazons rather than any Christian saint.
Eleanor lived at one of the great crossroads of history, and
showed herself to be an extraordinarily competent ruler, a
founder of hospitals, schools, dynasties, and indeed was patron
of a whole new culture and literature. She was also an instigator
of rebellion, a participant in and sometimes director of some of
the most vicious calamities of the age and, at one and the same
time, a lover of direct action and an equally capable manipulator
of events from behind the scenes. Her independence of spirit
and tenacity are astonishing, and leave one marvelling at her extraordinary ingenuity and energy in an age when opportunities
for women were rapidly disappearing. Eleanor's life cannot fail
to impress the historian, while at the same time the tragedy of
another woman's life, that of the imprisoned pawn, Alais, who
started life with an even greater lineage than that of Eleanor,
illustrates that the courses of a person's life are so often quite
fortuitous.[12]

It remains to say a word about the Abbey of Fontevrault,

where the remains of Eleanor, her husband, Henry, and her
favourite son, Richard I and his wife Berengaria lie together in
more peace than they ever knew in life. Robert of Arbrissel, a
priest of Brittany, like many another member of the clergy and
laity in the early twelfth century, felt a call to the genuine life of
the gospel – the *vita apostolica*. This movement of Christians
seeking a form of Christian life more in continuity with the life
of Jesus and his first followers was spreading rapidly through
many parts of Europe. As an apparent backlash to the intense
period of institutionalisation of the clerical and monastic life,
with its deliberate separation of women and men, and especially
its neglect and denigration of women, many new forms of religious living began to make their appearance. They are characterised by a desire for poverty, the imitation of the life of Jesus
and his first followers and the desire to preach the gospel to all.
In 1095, while Pope Urban II was at Piacenza preaching the First
Crusade, it seems that the preaching of this reclusive priest,
Robert, made a deep impression. Robert, with the pope's encouragement, became an itinerant preacher and began to attract
multitudes of both sexes. Eventually, he founded the Abbey of
Fontevrault to house his followers, probably in the year 1100.

Baldric, the biographer of Robert, tells us that these followers
included 'rich and poor, widows and virgins, old and young,
prostitutes and man-haters alike'.[13] Donations began to pour in,
often accompanied by the gift of a daughter or son for the foundation. It was an extraordinary establishment, intentionally differing from the strict monastic patterns of the Benedictines and
the Cistercians. St Bernard, among others, condemned such
attempts to live the evangelical life as ill-considered. One was
either lay or monk – there was no middle ground. Most twelfth
century popes, canonists, monks and jurists would have agreed
completely. Nevertheless, Fontevrault was just one of many
such foundations. Robert of Arbrissel intended his foundation
as a place for the benefit of women, primarily. Contact between
women and men was strictly limited, and tasks were divided
according to sex: 'the more tender and weaker sex to psalm-

singing and contemplation, while he applied the stronger sex to the labours of the active life'.[14] Robert insisted, however, even on his death-bed, that Fontevrault was always to be ruled by a woman. Just before his death, Robert called the brothers to his bedside and gave then the choice of leaving for another monastery or remaining under the rule of an Abbess. Apparently, all the men chose to stay. Robert intended the men to serve the women and provide for them, not only the hardier chores, but also the necessary liturgical and sacramental ministrations. As an added innovation, Robert decreed that the abbess should come from the group of lay sisters, someone who had been married and not one of the virgins who had spent all her life in the cloister. Better also, that she had been poor rather than rich. Petronilla was therefore chosen as Abbess to succeed Robert himself in the direction of the community, and he instructed the local bishops that women were to continue in this position. About Petronilla, he wrote: 'Petronilla ... is to have and maintain the power of ruling the church of Fontevrault and all the places belonging to the church, and they are to obey her. They are to revere her as their spiritual mother, and all the affairs of the church, spiritual as well as secular, are to remain in her hands, or be given to whomever she assigns, just as she decides'.[15]

Fontevrault, under these unique conditions, flourished for the next two centuries. Its innovative constitution gave the nuns more liberty of movement and contact with the larger world, while at the same time, providing them with a constant male staff to conduct such affairs of the abbey as were necessary. It is not surprising that Fontevrault, despite its mixed membership at its inception, soon became quite an aristocratic establishment. The abbey, however, remained under the authority of women, and throughout its existence, the men served the women. 'What was unique about Fontevrault was not that it had some men associated with the community, but that it had a particularly large group of men actually integrated into the community, by the original design of the founder'.[16]

This abbey, then, was chosen by Eleanor, as both her last

home and her burial place. It provided her with an excellent listening post in her closing years, situated as it was on the boundaries of Anjou, Poitou and Touraine on the banks of the Loire. The Nuns' Kitchen, a small archictectural gem, was said to have been built by Eleanor and her daughter, Joanna, and can still be seen. The abbey flourished for several centuries, and provided a fitting resting place for Eleanor and so many members of her once widely scattered family.

CHAPTER FOUR

Three Twelfth-century Visionaries: Christina of Markyate, Hildegard of Bingen, Elizabeth of Schönau

After the profoundly disruptive ecclesiastical reforms of the second half of the eleventh century, the twelfth century inaugurated a period of social restratification. Cities were expanding and, because they immediately provided new opportunities for employment and accommodation, they became a mecca both for a host of society's rejects and also for a new breed of entrepreneur. The bourgeoisie had arrived. The horizon of the West extended eastward through colonisation and trade, all made possible by the crusading movement, which in fact continued right through the century. The disastrous struggles between France and England and between each of them and the German emperor continued unabated, and though national languages and identities were beginning to emerge, it is impossible to designate yet any one nation by its definitive spoken tongue. The boundaries around aristocratic, royal and even imperial possessions and fiefs remained extremely porous, and always in danger of penetration by ambitious or penurious neighbours.

The rise of the universities provides one of the most stabilising and formative elements of the period. Though young clerical students continued to roam from teacher to teacher in search of truth or intellectual titillation, their presence and attention were eventually concentrated in a few central locations, such as Paris for theology, Bologna for law and Salerno for medicine. For decades into the century, teachers like Abelard were the magnets, but by degrees the schools became permanent institutions. While law and medicine attracted thousands of students, it was theology, the queen of the sciences, which seemed to offer the most intellectual excitement for students. The old monastic theology had been oriented toward prayer and contemplation. The new theology set itself to discover the truth of the mysteries of the faith and aimed at a systematic and total view of truth, gained through intense rational reflection and dialectical argument. The dialectical method of argument and counter-argument proved enormously stimulating and the buzz-words of the day were 'faith' and 'reason'. Both the intellectual world of Islam and the newly discovered Aristotelian corpus provided added stimulus to this new movement. Peter Abelard was considered to be the greatest teacher of the West and is thought to have created and perfected not only the dialectical method of reasoning but even the word 'theology' itself.[1]

This was the age of the extreme institutionalisation of the church and the creation of what has come to be called Christendom. Hans Küng attributes five characteristics to Christendom, the ecclesiastical framework which he sees as the dominating force of the twelfth and thirteenth centuries. These he names as: centralisation around the absolute power of the papacy; legalism, rooted in the new science of canon law, especially after the publication of the great lawyer Gratian's work in 1140; politicisation, or the primacy of the issues of ecclesiastical power in the dispensing of justice rooted in law; militarisation, continued in the crusading movement, but also in the continuing dependence of pope and monarch on military solutions to society's problems; and clericalisation, or the almost total identification of clergy and church, and the intense concentration of clerical effort on the control of church and society through the administration of law and sacrament.[2] The whole structure was designed to create an ordered society by applying the principles of gospel and canon law, but despite the claims of absolute and sacred power, the whole continually foundered. Nevertheless, Christendom provided the West with many of the structures which survive to this day, even though the intense debate and the often ruthless oppression of other possible options tend to be forgotten.

It is not surprising that this huge ecclesiastical enterprise, while laying the foundations for many western institutions, also gave rise to a series of movements which vehemently opposed the whole system while using the same spiritual and traditional sources. Since the crusaders first made contact with the Holy Land and came in touch again with the historical and spiritual roots of the Christian tradition, a new form of spiritual quest had swept across Europe. A new longing for the *vita apostolica* made itself felt in every corner of the West, sometimes in the desire to imitate exactly the life of Jesus and his followers, sometimes giving rise to a profound disgust with the increasing power and wealth of the institutional church. The ecclesiastical reform had not lived up to its advance billing, so to speak, and a widespread need to reform the reform was expressed. The clergy were perceived once again as the obstacle to reform and the people turned against them. The conventional memory of the monolith of Christendom has hidden from us the resistance which the hierarchical ideals aroused. It was the end of a long process where the church interposed itself between the ideals of scripture and the actual practices of Christianity. In many ways, the twelfth century revolt of the laity was the last organised opposition to this project, even though the laity, as a whole, did not at this time achieve a separate identity.

Not surprisingly, it was the ideal ground for dissenters of all kinds, some forging their own path, and some organising themselves into vast movements which terrified the hierarchy. For decades, anti-clerical, anti-ecclesiastical, and anti-sacramental ideas had been floating around Europe. These were descended from ancient semi-Manichean ideas which had always survived in the Middle East and had probably accompanied the crusaders on their return to the West. What made these movements so challenging for the hierarchy was that they were often rooted in genuine evangelical ideas and experiences which had vastly influenced the lives of some crusaders when they encountered the Holy Places. A new devotion to the life and person of Jesus was being disseminated and a longing for an ideal gospel life built on the imitation of the life lived by Jesus and his followers. This provided a trenchant critique of the actual highly institution-alised life of the clerical establishment and responded to a wide-spread need for spiritual sustenance.

Such ideas, in the air almost everywhere in a variety of movements, were occasionally systematised and preached by individuals. Such a preacher-founder was Arnold of Brescia, who called for an itinerant church of apostolic poverty, with bishops who would be noted only for their humility. Arnold denounced the ecclesiastical establishment at every opportunity and was eventually executed in 1155 as a heretic. His life demonstrates the church's endemic difficulty with the implementation of evangelical ideals, and whatever Arnold's intention was, his ideals of poverty, itinerant preaching of a vernacular gospel and a non-hierarchical ministry, became ever after tainted with the notion of heresy. From about 1135, such 'heretical' notions were widespread. Historians write about 'waves' of heresy affecting all corners of the church, but what was most alarming for the clerical establishment was the mass movement generally called Cathar which became prominent from around 1140 – ironically the same year as the publication of Gratian's great tome on canon law, *Concordia Discordantium Canonum*. Eventually the Cathars, most notably the Albigensians in the region around Albi in the south of France, were organised as a church within a church. It was this confrontation with an enemy within which most alarmed the hierarchy, and it must be said, the royal rulers of France and England. From around 1184, the combined papal and royal forces instituted the inquisition and initiated an on-slaught of orthodox preaching by the newly founded Dominicans, but the Albigensians only grew in numbers and popularity. Eventually, a new crusade against the Albigensians was promoted and set out to extirpate the enemy within by force of arms. It was the old Augustinian solution and represented in the starkest possible way the scarcity of solutions available to a highly institutionalised church. Thousands perished in this on-slaught and the last years of the Albigensians are marked by horrific massacres in which no distinctions were made between the innocent and the guilty.[3] The viciousness of the ecclesiastical response to these groups only served to create a fearful, resentful and passive laity, and this lay/clerical divide was further aggravated by the eventual redrawing of the lines between the respective powers and roles of laity and clergy. The laity were to be always subordinate and the threat of violence, used so terribly against the Albigensians, was never far from the surface. Lay preaching was utterly forbidden and the access of the laity to the Bible was hedged around with all sorts of legal impositions. The clergy were freed forever from the threat of lay accusation or complaint and their sacramental powers were further hedged around by canon law.

It is in this context that we now turn to examine the possibilities of spiritual sustenance and practice for women. We have seen the activities of Héloïse and Eleanor of Aquitaine, each in very specific contexts. Women played an active part in all of the twelfth century movements. In fact, it was often the leadership roles of women in groups such as the Albigensians, which ultimately aided their destruction. Behind all the turmoil of the period, historians of spirituality pinpoint one of the main operative principles of the movements as the new concern with self-discovery. They discern an increased sensitivity to the spiritual needs of the self and the need to define the boundaries between self and other. The twelfth century is rife with new religious groupings, such as the Fontevrault and Norbertine foundations, and with the revival of old institutions such as that of the hermit. There is an upsurge of interest in charting the inner spiritual landscape of the individual and the main focus of such search concerned the human life of Jesus and his followers.[4] The special place taken by women in this development is now acknowledged by all, but it is a complex story with many strands. One of the best ways of describing women's spiritual traditions at this time is through the lives of the individual women, three of whom will concern us in this section, but some general comments on women's twelfth century spiritual experiences are in order, by way of introduction.[5] One of the major elements in the study of the spirituality of medieval women is the fact that women were specifically excluded from the outstanding development of the age, namely the founding of the universities. This educational disadvantage became a major force in women's history, altering as it did, the relationship of women to their past, present and future. From this time on, women had to prove their intellectual capacity, create their own educational opportunities, and, for the most part, invent their own spiritual traditions. For the vast majority of women no educational opportunities were available, and so we must return to the convents. Even though the educational ban extended also to nuns, religious women had access to the leisure and library resources that made some education possible. The range of women's accomplishment under such strictures is astonishing, but their inability to participate in the major intellectual movements of the day forever marks the history of women and their spirituality.

The fact is that we have access to an enormous amount of women's spiritual writing for this period, and it is not only abundant, but among the best spiritual writing of the whole period. Almost without exception, this writing belongs to the convent, where women wrote for the benefit of their sisters. This is devotional and didactic literature, written both to promote heightened feelings of religious devotion, and also to point women toward proper relationships with the divine and with one another. Among the principal goals of this writing was the need to teach women the art of prayer, especially in its mystical and visionary dimensions. These women spiritual writers seem to have been driven by a profound inner need to communicate what they themselves had learned, but the writing is always couched, initially, in a rhetoric of self-protection. For writing was an extremely dangerous act for a woman, and in an atmosphere highly sensitised to hints of heresy and female insubordination, the women had to learn to wield the authorial voice very carefully. Almost universally the women attribute their boldness in writing to the urgings of God in a specific visionary experience. They are writing because God directed them to write.

Often, the actual act of writing down their visionary experiences comes after a long resistance to such divine encouragement, a resistance usually characterised by illness. As soon as the women put pen to paper, sometimes personally, sometimes through a secretary, the illness disappears.

The specific qualities of this writing will appear as we study the lives of some of the individual women, but a brief overview of qualities may be helpful. This writing , in direct contrast with the contemporary quality of reasoned and objective clerical theological reflection, is rooted in experience and describes and reflects on the women's own mystical and religious experiences. The writing is highly emotional and makes few distinctions between bodily and mental religious experience. Through their religious experience, the women have experienced an inner transformation, a profound self-knowledge and a sense of power and authority that is striking in its self-confidence. Scholastic theology never assimilated this female religious experience and indeed such experience so far outdistanced the contemporary theological concerns that the women were understood by very few of their contemporaries.[6]

The abundance of such mystical and visionary writing is hard to understand at this time unless it can be seen as part of the lay reaction to the extreme institutionalisation of the church. These writings are, in fact, very critical of ecclesiastical corruption, especially as exemplified in wealth, abuse of power and hypocrisy. The mystical spirituality of these women was rooted partly in a reaction to the worldliness of the church. Deprived of the normal access to education and learning, the women were driven to depend on their own internal resources, and there they discovered and encountered their God in a new way. This mystical experience was influenced by the liturgical round of biblical readings, and is forever associated with an intense new devotion to the person of Jesus. Devotion to the eucharist played an all important part in this development as the women experienced their unity with Jesus Christ in the eucharistic bread and wine. Their mystical devotion, then, was intensely participatory, and since they recognised that the most human act of Jesus was his suffering, their own lives were marked, at the initial stages of their mystical lives, by the most horrific experiences of self-inflicted suffering. Such images of fasting, flagellation and the apparent deprivation of all physical comfort can horrify the contemporary reader. The conventional explanation has always been that the women had internalised the official ecclesiastical truth about themselves as the source of sin and the gateway to the devil and were thus engaging in the normal response of penance for such great disservice to the church. Women historians, while acknowledging some truth in the above analysis, discern rather in the women's actions a greater need to participate more directly in the human suffering of Jesus as one step in their journey toward mystical unity.

Such mystical spirituality, in its emotional intensity, its claims to direct access to God and its bestowal of a sense of personal authority, has always placed the ecclesiastical authorities in a dilemma of enormous proportions. They are being asked to sanction a pathway to authority which explicitly by-passes their own claims. Most of the women to be studied here were explicitly committed to the orthodox ecclesiastical agenda but, without exception, they were also profoundly convinced that their experiences came directly from God and that their fidelity to these was a prior commitment. Two responses to ecclesiastical criticism recur in almost every piece of writing. First of all, the women and their supporters point out that the constant biblical tradition shows God choosing the weak to confound the strong and, secondly, each individual voices her conviction that God must be obeyed first, not man. The fact that the church claimed the right to be the only mouthpiece for God only shows how complex the women's lives were. Finally, and again almost without exception, the substance of the women's mystical experiences is concentrated on the life of love and compassion. The women seem to side-step the contemporary dialectical argumentation between faith and reason and choose instead the path of love. Marguerite Porete makes this such an explicit theme in her teaching that it eventaully contributes largely to her execution in 1310.

Christina of Markyate

The story of Christina of Markyate is one of those marvellous accounts of a medieval holy woman which seems to drop like a pebble into the stream of history.[7] Nothing prepares us for such an extraordinary story, including, as it does, all the themes found in the whole tradition of Christian holy women from the beginning. This Anglo-Saxon woman, born to affluent and influential parents in Huntingdon around the year 1096, was given the baptismal name of Theodora. While on a visit to the nearby Benedictine Abbey of St Albans at the age of thirteen, she felt called by God to make a private vow of chastity and sometime later she assumed the new self-given name by which she has always been known to history, Christina, she who belongs to Christ'. Christina's *Vita*, written by an unknown monk of St Albans, provides us only with the details of the early and most turbulent part of her life. It is, indeed, an extraordinary tale.

Without her knowledge, Christina was betrothed to Burthred, a suitable local young man, but when her parents informed her of the engagement, Christina absolutely refused to marry him, claiming that she was betrothed only to Christ. The ensuing family conflict, sometimes horrific in its details, seems to have had repercussions throughout most of England, involving the parents, local influential friends, the bishop of Lincoln, the bishop/husband of her maternal aunt, the Abbot of St Alban's, a host of local hermits and recluses and finally the Archbishop of Canterbury. Christina's initial refusal to marry was greeted with laughter, but her persistent refusal to co-operate turned the whole family against her. The fury and rage of her mother, Beatrix, are among the most memorable features of this story. Christina is put under house arrest, beaten viciously by her mother on a daily basis, and in one unforgettable scene, is displayed at a banquet as an object of ridicule: 'There was one time when on impulse she [Beatrix, the mother] took her out from a banquet and, out of sight of the guests, pulled her hair out and beat her until she was weary of it. Then she brought her back, lacerated as she was, into the presence of the revellers as an object of derision, leaving on her back such weals from the blows as could never be removed as long as she lived.'[8] Beatrix tried every artifice known to her to overcome her daughter's refusal. These included old women with love potions designed to drive Christina out of her mind with impure thoughts and a Jewish woman, noted for her wisdom, who immediately advised Beatrix to cease persecuting her daughter because 'I can see two phantoms ... dressed in white, who accompany her at all times, and protect her from assaults at all points.' Beatrix even planned to have her daughter raped, and to this end exposed her as the wine servant at a banquet. The very nature of this task implied very provocative clothing, tied back to facilitate the pouring of wine and the need for the servant to taste the wine as a guard against poisoning. The mother hoped that a tipsy and provocatively clad girl would force some man to attack her daughter, but without result. In the end, she is reported to have remarked that 'she would not care who deflowered her daughter, provided that some way of deflowering her could be found'. On another occasion, Burthred and his drunken friends were admitted to Christina's room while she slept in order to take her by surprise, but again Christina escaped by hanging from her finger-tips between the wall and the bed-curtains. Foiled again, poor Burthred was ridiculed by his friends and called 'a useless and spineless fellow' who was losing his manliness.

Christina's father, Autti, seems to have taken his frustrations to the powerful civil and religious leaders of the area. Initially, the bishops took Christina's side, but abundant bribery seems to have caused everyone to side with Autti in an effort to defend the family honour. Her father's complaints sound a familiar theme and might even have been spoken by a twentieth-century parent in the midst of an adolescent revolt. 'Why must she depart from tradition? Why should she bring this dishonour on her father? Her life of poverty will bring the whole of the nobility into disrepute. Let her do now what we wish and she can have all that we possess.' On one occasion, after the Bishop of Lincoln – prior to the bribery – had lectured the father on the need for mutual consent in marriage, the father burst out in indignation: 'Well, we have peace today, you are even made mistress over me: the bishop has praised you to the skies and declared that you are freer than ever. So come and go as I do, and have your own life as you please. But don't expect any comfort or help from me.[9] As the bribes turned the bishop against Christina, she and he engaged in a battle of biblical texts, each defending their respective positions.

What of Christina in all of this? Her family's fury seems to have left permanent physical and mental wounds, but she was not without her supporters. We hear of recluses, priests, nuns, in fact a whole network of religious support. The Archbishop of Canterbury, when approached by Christina's childhood friend, the priest Sueno, is reported to have said that he could cheerfully murder her mother. Christina's constant refrain was: 'I am free to love Christ above all.' While the church – in its pre-Gratian days – wondered about who had the ultimate authority in this case, Christina was eventually forced into marriage. It seems to have been the same archbishop who suggested that Christina should run away and, as the burdens of maintaining her virginity became almost intolerable, that is precisely the route that Christina took. It was a cloak and dagger affair including, on a day when her parents were away, secret assignations in a nearby meadow with Loric, the wearing of male dress and riding horseback like a young man, as well as a kind of underground railway of religious friends. Eventually, after a mad thirty mile ride to Flamstead, the resident recluse Alfwen gave her shelter for two years and refused to admit any member of Christina's family.

Christina's next home was with the hermit, Roger. Here she lived in appalling conditions, hidden in a corner of Roger's cell in a hole in the ground. The space was so small that she could not move or even wear winter garments. He allowed her out at night to take care of her bodily needs, but otherwise the conditions were hellish. 'The airless little enclosure became stifling when she was hot. Through long fasting, her bowels became contracted and dried up. There was a time when her burning thirst caused little clots of blood to bubble up from her nostrils.' After four years and a terrifying vision, Burthred, without knowing of the presence of Christina, arrived at Roger's cell in order to release Christina formally from her marriage vows. Fittingly, it was March 27, the day of the resurrection. And so, finally, Christina was released to live out her commitment to Christ for the rest of her life.

We know little of the circumstances of the next several years of Christina's life. In all, she spent sixteen years as a recluse, mostly in Roger's cell which she had inherited after his death, and then some thirty-five years as head of a community of women attached to the Benedictine Abbey of St Alban's. The fame of her holiness had spread far and wide and many young women came to join her. This was an almost inevitabe pattern across the whole history of monasticism: the holy recluse attracts followers, and eventually the solitary becomes the leader of a community. Before exploring the two chief features of Christina's life, apart from her initial struggles, a mention must be made of the St Alban's Psalter, which all agree must have been created for Christina. It is a beautiful work, distinctively illustrated, and containing a calendar detailing the deaths of her parents, two brothers, and her great friends, the hermit Roger and the Abbot Geoffrey. The Psalter is now housed in Hildersheim.

Apart from her extraordinary will to resist her family's plans and follow her own vocation, Christina's life is marked by her male friendships and by her frequent and very convenient visions. Christina's life is unique not in the fact of these male friendships, but in the frank and open way with which these are discussed in her life. During her four year confinement, Roger and Christina had become intimate friends through the freedom attained by their joint commitment to life-long chastity. Though others were 'pierced by the lance of envy', and though they were often unfavourably compared to Paula and Jerome, their friendship persisted. 'Furthermore, through their dwelling together and encouraging each other to strive after higher things their holy affections grew day by day like a large flame springing from two brands joined together ... And so their great progress induced them to dwell together.' It seems to have been a relationship of complete mutuality, which witnessed to an equality in Christ where there was neither male nor female.

After Christina's move to St Alban's, her apparently even closer friendship with the Abbot, Geoffrey, occasioned more malicious gossip. In this relationship, Christina was the dominant partner. She had converted Geoffrey from being a powerful and worldly ecclesiastic so that he became a changed man from what he once was . They came to admire, respect and love each other. 'He had deep respect for the maiden and saw in her something divine and extraordinary. She became his spiritual director and he consulted her about every decision. She was assured that Jesus blessed their friendship because as she dreamed that she and Geoffrey were embracing each other after another round of malicious gossip, she saw Jesus joining with them, adding power to the strength of her embrace.

One student of the life of Christina tells us that there are accounts of over forty-two visions in this one short *Vita*. It is this visionary element, in particular, that distinguishes the medieval context from all others. In many ways, Christina's life is a bridge. She is a member of the old Anglo-Saxon aristocracy in a world and church that is now Norman. The companions and supporters of her religious journey are mostly Ango-Saxon also, but the higher clergy come from a Norman background. Christina's life is also a bridge in its blend of Anglo-Saxon practicality and the new visionary experiences that now characterise religious life. Christina's visions are rooted in her experience of an affective relationship with Christ. This close relationship was gained through her absolute fidelity to her initial vow of virginity. Christ has become her one love. God has assured her that '... the key of your heart is in my safekeeping and I keep guard over your mind and the rest of your body. No one can enter except by my permission.' Her relationship with God and Christ had all the marks of a love affair. At each stage of her life, whenever Christina was in the depths of despair or doubt, a vision would restore her equilibrium. On one occasion, the Christ-child remained with her all day, and Christ as a youth had appeared to console her at the most trying moments of her four year confinement with Roger. One of her earlier visions had presented her in her sleep with a good mother in the person of the Virgin Mary to replace the bad mother of real life. It was at a time when, as Christina says, she could not stop crying. When she awoke and found her pillow wet with tears, she was reassured about the authenticity of her visionary experiences. The frequency of visions of the Virgin Mary in the life of Christina is fairly unusual in the tradition of female visionaries, though the details of Christina's own life provide a good reason for this very significant method of spiritual healing.

As Christina was grappling with the most intimate and personal spiritual struggles, the best minds of Christendom were being exercised by the same dilemmas of marriage and sexual ethics. One of the key new elements in this debate was the role of the intention – a question raised in the work of Peter Abelard. Scholastic theologians brought all the resources of the ancient traditions of Christian theology and Aristotelian philosophy to their task. Christina and the women like her, excluded from this whole development, were left to their own resources. Instead of being moved forward by the workings of faith and reason, they were helped by their visionary experiences. The visions helped to give encouragement, explain conversion, challenge to a change of heart, and allow the visionaries to read the hearts of others. Above all, the women called to a life of virginity, received the added authorisation of divine aid in some very explicit heavenly instructions. Christina, like many of the later women visionaries, speaks of sudden insight and an inundation of knowledge. Women had no training in logic or argumentation, but they knew from their experiences about the sudden illuminations of love, and the ongoing ethical requirements of intimacy. In so many ways, women such as Christina lived on the margins. As an Anglo-Saxon woman, she was among the last generation of her kind. It is likely that she conversed in Old English. The only English words in her *Vita* are spoken to her by Roger when he calls her 'my Sunday daughter', that is the one as superior to all other women as Sunday is to the other days. As a woman, Christina also lived on the margins of church life, and through her heavenly obedience and earthly disobedience had margin-alised herself from her family and all normal human interaction. As a recluse, Christina was also marginalised. The practice of living as a recluse was common in England, though no one is sure of the origins of the practice. Being a recluse could repre-sent either the beginning of a spiritual journey, as it did for Christina, or for a member of a women's religious community, it could represent the very peak of spiritual attainment, to be granted only after a long apprenticeship.[10] The life of a recluse has been called a 'permanent condition of sacred outsiderhood' and it is when she is living as such that we hear of Christina. Once this extraordinary woman who had the 'true gaze of one with spiritual eyes', becomes a more or less regular religious, we hear no more of her. Her death is placed in the year 1160.[11]

Hildegard of Bingen

Born within a year or so of Christina of Markyate in 1098, was Hildegard of Bingen, one of the most accomplished persons, male or female in the whole western Christian tradition. If we have no word from the mouth of Christina herself, except as re-ported by her anonymous biographer, that lack is more than recompensed by the voluminous and multi-faceted writings of Hildegard of Bingen. It is likely that no one today has heard of Christina except for medieval specialists, but Hildegard's name has become well known not alone in the realm of medieval mys-ticism, but also in the worlds of liturgical music, drama, pharmacy, medical science and art. Her writing is at once exhilarating and profoundly frustrating for the modern reader, unaccustomed as we are to the intricacies of the kind of symbolic writing used by her. This fascinating woman, the first from whom we have a systematic body of writing, is also mystifying in her paradoxical attitudes to the role of women. On the one hand, she is utterly orthodox in her support of the reform movement in the church and in its assessment of women as the weaker sex from whom obedience and submission are forever required. On the other, her writings on women are entirely revolutionary and her own ecclesial life is marked, not so much by obedience as by a profound self-confidence in her own prophetic role. On at least two occasions in her life she was insistently disobedient, when the church authorities clashed with her own profound convictions. It would be impossible to do justice to the depth and breadth of Hildegard's corpus here. Instead, after a brief biographical outline, we will concentrate on three areas where her work is unprecedented, the anthropological study of women based on her own observations, the delineating of the feminine divine, and the invention by Hildegard of the category of complementarity in the area of female-male relationships.[12]

Hildegard, born to an aristocratic family in the Rhineland in 1098, was the tenth child in her family, and as such she was sent as a child oblate, a tithe, to the recluse Jutta of Spanheim at the age of eight. Jutta, apparently a family relative, was attached to the Benedictine Abbey called after an Irish monk at Mount St Disibode. At the age of fifteen, Hildegard seems to have made her profession of religious vows and entered seriously on her life as a Benedictine. Hildegard had been aware of visions from the age of five, but around this time she began to be embarrassed by them and decided to lay them aside with other childish things. Throughout the following years, other women were attracted to the holy woman Jutta, and soon there was a sizeable community with Jutta as *magistra* or abbess. In 1136, when Jutta died, Hildegard, at the age of thirty eight, was elected in her place to lead the community. Thus as Abbess of the nuns in a double monastery, Hildegard entered on the great experiment that would be central to one of her significant contributions to the history of philosophy and anthropology – the study of women and men in interaction, based on her acute powers of observation.

Despite her efforts, Hildegard's visions had continued. She was afflicted with constant ill-health and finally her confidant, the monk Vollmar, persuaded her to begin to write down her visions. She is quite specific about the undertaking of this task, as she tells us in the preface to *Scivias*:

> It happened in the year 1141 of the Incarnation of God's Son Jesus Christ, when I was forty-two years and seven months old, that the heavens opened and a fiery light of the greatest brilliancy coming from the opened heavens, poured into all my brain, and kindled in my heart and my breast a flame ... And suddenly I knew and understood the explanation of the Psalter, the Gospels and other Catholic books of the Old and New Testaments ...

It is unlikely that this was Hildegard's first meeting with the scriptures, but she was always insistent that her wisdom came not from herself, but from her divine illumination. She continues in the same preface to describe how her visions worked. They were 'not in dreams, nor sleeping, nor in frenzy, nor with the eyes of my body ... but watching them, and looking carefully with an innocent mind, with the eyes and ears of the interior man ...'[13] Some scholars have described the process as symbolic thinking. As Hildedgard began to write, Vollmar was enabled to discern that God was the source and he entered on a lifetime of recording, interpreting and supporting the visionary. Her health improved, but continued to be one of the major concerns of her life.

In 1147, Hildegard wrote to Bernard of Clairvaux again seeking reassurance and support for her insights: 'I beg you, Father, in the name of the living God, to listen to me and to answer my questions ... I, wretched creature, more than wretched, being a woman ... I saw you in this vision more than two years ago as a man looking at the sun without fear, but with great audacity.

And I wept because I myself am so timid and have so little courage.' This timidity is a constant theme in Hildegard's writing, but her life contrasts so significantly with her words, that one is forced to believe that she is engaged in the expected womanly rhetoric. It was dangerous for a woman to claim heavenly guidance, and even more dangerous to write with a view to teaching. The usual biblical explanation was that God chooses the weak to confound the strong. Hildegard expands on this theme by explaining that the age has become effeminate and that men have abandoned the tasks that are rightly theirs. Therefore God has to depend on 'wretched women' to take up the slack and put the men to shame. Bernard replied with unwonted humility and admiration: 'When inner instruction and the unction which teaches everything already exist, what need is there for us to teach or warn?' Eventually, both the Archbishop of Mainz and Pope Eugenius himself added their words of approbation, and as far as we know, Hildegard sought no further approval. There is a wonderful story, believed by some scholars, denied by others, that in her seventies, Hildegard, by then known far and wide, set out for the University of Paris in order to get her writings and theological teaching included on the university curriculum. Unfortunately, this was the age of Aristotle, and his philosophy, clashing in so many crucial ways with that of Hildegard, won the day.

From this time on, writings poured forth from Hildegard in a never-ending stream. *Scivias* was completed in 1151 and was followed in 1158-1163 by the second book of this visionary trilogy, *The Book of Life's Merits*, dealing with ethics. The third volume, *The Book of Divine Works*, on God's work through science was written between 1163 and 1173. In between were the nine-volume, *Physics*, and the extraordinary *Causae et Curae*, which is a handbook on diseases and their remedies, based on her own observations in the monastery's hospice. Hildegard's efforts to name and categorise herbs is among the foundational documents of western pharmacy. Throughout her whole life, the Abbess had a profound interest in matters liturgical and a constant stream of liturgical and musical texts flowed from her hands for the use of her sisters. Many of these texts have survived and make Hildegard the only medieval figure whose life story must include a discography. Besides, from 1147 on, hundreds of letters flow from her stylus all over Europe to emperors, kings, popes and saints, as well as monastic and lay correspondents. She had become the repository of the widom of the West. In 1155, the almost mythical emperor, Frederick Barbarossa, preparing to depart on the third Crusade, invited her to his palace. In all these interchanges, Hildegard is forthright, critical and unhesitating in condemning the failure of her correspondents to live up to the requirements of their state in life, even though she continues to describe herself as an unfortunate member of the 'frail sex'.

From the time of the papal approval and endoresement of her work, Hildegard had become a celebrity and her monastery at St Disibode was flooded with new members. She determined that a move to new quarters was necessary and, through her family, gained a suitable site at Rupertsberg, across the river from Bingen. The monks of St Disibode, led by their Abbot Kuno, vigorously opposed this plan, entailing, as it did, the loss not only of the prestige but also of the wealth brought by Hildegard's fame. As often happened in the lives of medieval mystics, Hildegard developed a mysterious illness, which she attributed to God's dissatisfaction at the opposition to her plan. Eventually, Kuno was defeated, Hildegard recovered and in 1150 the sisters made their move. Hildegard was now Abbess of her own monastery, and eventually also of a second daughter house at Bingen, though not without a ten year struggle to free themselves from the monks supervision. Throughout the struggle, the Abbess' health fluctuated with the success or failure of her plans. The Abbey at Bingen still exists, and as Hildegard's popularity grows, it has attained the status of a major centre of pilgrimage for scholars, students and admirers.

From 1158 on, Hildegard was engaged in a series of missionary journeys which took her across the length and breadth of most of Europe. She preached monastic and ecclesiastical reform and, despite illness, challenged all who seemed to be backsliders. At Pentecost in 1160, she preached publicly in the great Cathedral at Trier. By 1167, when she undertook her fourth and final preaching tour, she was in her seventies and struggling more than ever with her health. Apart from her major works, the founding of two monasteries, her voluminous correspondence, and the accomplishment of four major preaching tours, each followed up in Pauline style by letters outlining the main points of her message, Hildegard composed several other works of theology and monastic commentary. All agree that her strangest achievement was the composition of a new language which might better express her symbolic and often impenetrable thought. Each contemporary upheaval brought a letter or sermon from the inexhaustible Abbess, including the Cathars, and the stragglers of the Third Crusade. The emperor, Frederick Barbarossa, on whose goodwill she relied for the maintenance of the property at Rupertsberg, was instrumental in the appointment of four anti-popes. This gained him one of her most wrathful letters, calling him an infant in faith and a madman.

In 1173, Vollmar, her life-long faithful secretary, died and the monks refused to replace him. Appeals to Pope Alexander III brought encouragement, but eventually, one of her great admirers, Guibert of Gembloux, who had come to visit, stayed as her secretary till her death. In 1178, aged eighty, Hildegard was engaged in one of the greatest controversies of her life. An excommunicated but reconciled nobleman had been buried in the cemetery at Rupertsberg. The canons of Mainz Cathedral demanded that he be exhumed and given to them. Hildegard adamantly refused, and with her abbatial staff blessed and then destroyed all outward traces of the tomb. The whole community was excommunicated and Hildegard's enemies, in attendance at the third Lateran Council in Rome, insisted that the interdict remain. Another stormy letter was sent to Mainz, condemning the canons for stilling the glorious liturgical music on the banks of the Rhine. 'Together with all my sisters, I felt deep bitterness ... and was overwhelmed by sadness ...we have ceased to sing the

Divine Office, limiting ourselves to reading it in an undertone.'
There follows a spirited defence of liturgical music from Adam,
through David, the prophets and the whole of monastic life.
From the very beginning, the devil has been trying to still this
music. 'And so you, and all other prelates, must be extremely
wary before issuing a decree which closes the mouth of a community singing to God and forbids them to celebrate and receive
the sacraments. Beware in your judgements not to be deceived
by Satan …' The sentence of excommunication was eventually
lifted in March 1179. Hildegard died six months later on 17
September 1179. The wave of miracles and pilgrims grew so
great in the following years that the nuns asked the bishop to
command their dead Abbess to cease her miracles. Despite some
attempts, Hildegard was never canonised, though she is venerated throughout Germany on her death-day.

Everything about Hildegard was and remains unique. Yet
though we have more writing from her than any other woman
for hundreds of years, her personality does not shine through.
One can get glimpses of her indomitable courage, her concern
for her sisters, her utter and even obsessive devotion to her
friends, and the paradoxical mix of humility and defiance which
marked much of her interaction with those in authority, yet she
reveals remarkably little of her own spiritual life. Hildegard's
whole world was ordered, with no boundaries between heaven
and earth, science and liturgy, music and medicine, the living
sap of plants and the gracefilled presence of the Holy Spirit in
the soul. One of her most loved images is *viriditas*, greenness, a
symbol for fertility, grace, life and proof of God's presence. God
is essentially Living Light and life is a kind of cosmic dance in
this light – a dance because the darkness is forever lurking at our
feet. *Scivias* is her most famous work, shorthand for *Scito vias
Domini* or *Know the Ways of the Lord*. It is a kind of visionary
guide to Christian doctrine, covering everything from creation
to marriage, written in ordinary language but in extraordinary
images. It is encyclopaedic in its scope, dealing with 6 visions on
the Father in Part I, 7 visions on the Son in Part II and 13 visions

on the Holy Spirit in Part III. Part III, Vision 13 includes the *Ordo Virtutum*, perhaps the first medieval morality play. Here, all the virtues are feminine and their dialogue illustrates the ongoing working out of God's life in the soul. This drama was set to music and has been recorded in recent times. The combination of Hildegard's music and the brilliant illuminations of her visions (probably done by one of her sisters), adds to our picture of the utter genius of this unknowable woman. During the second World War, these precious paintings were moved to Dresden for safe keeping and have disappeared completely. Fortunately, the sisters had prepared a hand-drawn facsimile and it is from this that all the current reproductions derive. Her vision of the Trinity in Book II of *Scivias* gives some idea of the pictorial nature of her theology:

> Then I saw a most splendid light, and in that light, the whole of which burnt in a most beautiful, shining fire, was the figure of a man of a sapphire colour, and that most splendid light poured over the whole of that shining fire, and the shining fire over all that splendid light, and that most splendid light and shining fire over the whole figure of the man, appearing one light in one virtue and power. And again I heard that living Light saying to me: This is the meaning of the mysteries of God.

For Hildegard the whole world is the playing field of God where every thing and every being is a sign of God's fullness and potential sphere of action. Of all the signs, the human being is considered to be the greatest. It is not an accident then that Hildegard spent so much of her life observing human beings in action. Volumes had been written on human nature and on the inferior space occupied by women, but all this writing was book-knowledge, a mere quoting of ancient authority. She was the very first to base her writing on actual observation of human beings, especially in the monastic infirmary, where she seems to have worked as a nurse-physician. She kept exact accounts of her observations, not only of a huge variety of herbs and how they functioned, but also of the biological composition of the

women and men, and of how their biology affected their personalities and vice versa, and even more, about how these two com-
ponents affected human interaction. *Causae et Curae* is one of the
very first books in the West on the psychology of personality.
Hildegard tried always to support her philosophical views on
human beings by direct observation. She inherited the ancient
wisdom about the four-fold composition of the universe into
earth, air, fire and water, but disagreed with Aristotle on the
way these elements were divided between men and women.
Aristotle had assigned the higher elements of fire and air to men
and the lower, water and earth, to women. Hildegard posited
that men were composed of fire and earth, and women of water
and air, and that our personalities depended on how these elements interacted. Both women and men are created in the image
of God and hence she frequently reflects on the feminine aspects
of the Divine. Conversely, since God contains both feminine and
masculine elements, the images of God, men and women, each
contain both of these elements. Hildegard often encouraged
women to strengthen the masculine elements of courage and
strength in their personalities and likewise the men to develop
the feminine qualities of grace and mercy.

Hildegard was convinced that any advance in the spiritual
life required self-knowledge and so, after describing the process
of reproduction in detail, she proceeded to paint portraits of
four different kinds of women and men. First, she shows how
the experience of intercourse differs for each: 'For as soon as the
storm of passion arises with a man, he is thrown about in it like a
mill. His sexual organs then are so to speak the forge to which
the marrow delivers the fire ... If however the wind of lust arises
from the female marrow, it comes into the uterus ... and stirs the
woman's blood with excitement. But the uterus possesses a
wide and open space ... so that the wind can spread around the
woman's womb; therefore it lets her flow with passion less
vehemently.' A woman's sexual pleasure is more 'gentle and
silent' than that of the man. Men and women are each divided
into four kinds depending on how they live: men can treat

women as a sex object, as an equal in a personal relationship, he can be a wolf and treat women as prey, in reality hating her, or he can be quite indifferent to women. Women can be 'charming and lovely in their embrace', they can be manly and share many qualities with men, the intellectual woman is shunned by men because they don't know how to captivate her and the unstable woman discourages men. Hildegard is the very first writer known to us who attempts to study women in their own right and from observation.

The Abbess in her double monastery was also interested in how men and women, vowed to chastity, should interact. She concluded that, in each case, the second types are best for both marriage and chastity. The first type of man, the fiery and passionate type should never go into a monastery because he would 'find it too hard not to embrace women'. Type 2 men make good monks – they need women, but they know how to treat them as friends, for without female friends they are like a 'day without sunshine'. The fourth type of man could live a chaste life, but he would be too apathetic for a monastery. As for women, type 1 needs a sexual relationship with a man in order to be healthy and balanced. Type 2, the intellectual woman, could live without men, but she is usually unbearable without them. Type 3 gets sick without men and type 4 again is apathetic. It is noticeable that Hildegard is so even-handed in these descriptions. She does not consider the need of women and men for each other to be negative, just part of the self-knowledge necessary in order that creation can be worked out. On the contrary, if women are completely happy to be altogether without men, that is probably a deficiency of character. The ideal is for women and men to have developed all four of the elements.

In all of this, Prudence Allen credits Hildegard with being the inventor of a consistent theory of the principle of complementarity in the West. Traditional teaching had seen the relationship of women and men either in terms of a polarity of opposites, with the woman always inferior, or in terms of identity, based usually on a sexual renunciation, which afforded to

women a manly status. Teachers, such as Augustine of Hippo
had struggled to include the doctrines of equal creation in the
image of God and the final resurrection of the body in their
development of the principle of polarity. Their cultural and
emotional need to see women as inferior clashed with their theological convictions about equal creation and redemption. It was
Hildegard who, based on her actual experience of male/female
interaction in a double monastery, was able to argue the principle of complementarity, which held firmly to an equality of male
and female together with significant observed and documented
differences. As we have seen, these differences extended from
the experience of sexual intercourse, rooted in essential biological role differentiation, to the possibility of chaste relationships
in a monastic setting. While she accepted conventional theories
about women's silence and obedience, her own life was marked
significantly by neither of these qualities. Perhaps she experienced in herself the blending of all four elements in the making
of the balanced person who could transcend all boundaries. The
principle of complementarity still governs most of Roman Catholic
anthropology in its delineation of male and female roles and
virtues, and is seen most significantly in the teaching on the
ordination of women.The concept of a male/female mutuality
of gifts and relationships, which more and more functions, at
least theoretically in the secular sphere, is still impossible of realisation within the ecclesial community.

Hildegard's final secretary and biographer, Guibert of
Gembloux, tried to balance the paradoxes in her life:

> The apostle does not permit a woman to teach in the church.
> But this woman is exempt from this condition because she
> has received the Spirit, and with a heart instructed in wisdon
> by his teaching, she has learned through her own experience
> … by her wholesome teaching she instructs many, pouring
> forth abundantly as if from two breasts the milk of consol-
> ation for the young and the wine of correction for those who
> are stronger. But … she is nonetheless mindful of her own
> sex and condition, and especially of the aforesaid prohibition.

Yet she obeys the Spirit, not him whom the Spirit sends. Likewise, the apostle commands women to veil their heads, partly for decency's sake and partly to commend a certain just submission. But this woman is free ... For she has transcended female subjection by a lofty height and is equal to the eminence, not of just any men, but of the very highest.[17]

As Barbara Newman points out, there are real tensions in the thought of this brilliant woman. Her wholistic cosmology rests uneasily beside her dualistic ethics. She displays a strong and most unusual scientific interest in sexuality, but also demonstrates a moral contempt for sex. She has the most exalted theological view of women's cosmic significance, being one of the very first to study the Divine Feminine, coupled with a very practical view of femininity as a form of weakness. She was a strong advocate of the ecclesiastical and monastic reform movements which were centred on universal obedience to those in authority, but at the same time, insisted on her individual right to ignore elements of this reform and withdraw her obedience from the authorities in her own life. In her theology, *Sapientia*, the feminine figure of Divine Wisdom was central. This theology is optimistic in the awareness that God is always accessible, and that God's healing energy is available and abundant. On the other hand, her worldview was one of renunciation, moral dualism and ascetic transformation. Again, as Newman emphasises in the title of her book, Hildegard calls woman the 'sister of Wisdom' but only when she has rejected sexuality in favour of a life of virginity. No wonder Guibert of Gembloux tried hard to reach a balance in his biography.

Nevertheless, Hildegard never ceases to fascinate because of her extraordinary and unmatched combination of qualities, and because of the unrivalled scope of her writing. Her universe appears as brilliant, full of colour and energy, and brimming with *viriditas*. The next generation of women mystics will turn their attention inward to study the landscape of the soul. None employs the scientific approach to the universe that Hildegard used so brilliantly. Perhaps, she pushed the possibilities of her time to their utmost. It was her misfortune that, because of the prior claims of Aristotle on the hearts of the scholastic world, her work was destined to disappear for centuries. It was never integrated into scholastic theology, which uniformly preferred the pagan philosopher's approach to the essential polarity of the sexes and the view of the female as *mas occasionatus*, an accidental human.

Elizabeth of Schönau

The stories of Elizabeth of Schönau and Hildegard of Bingen have always been intertwined. A twelfth-century commentator says: 'In these days God made manifest his power through the frail sex, in the two maidens, Hildegard and Elizabeth, whom he filled with a prophetic spirit, making many kinds of visions apparent to them through his messages, which are to be seen in writing'.[18] These two women were contemporaries, though Hildegard was born over thirty years before Elizabeth and outlived her by another twenty-five years. Both come from a similar background – the Benedictine double monastery – and each spent some time in the chief leadership position there. Both were counsellors to their own sisters and to much of the surrounding Christian community. Hildegard seems to have disapproved, to some extent, of the trance-like ecstasies experienced by Elizabeth, and this is what occasioned their eventual epistolary communication and possible meeting.

Elizabeth is a transitional figure in the history of women's mysticism. Though rooted in the Benedictine monastic environment, her visions are more akin to those of her later Beguine sister mystics, especially as regards their high emotional intensity, and her very intimate encounters with God, Jesus, the Holy Spirit, Mary and a whole host of saints. Like the sisters of Helfta, Elizabeth seemed to be able to enter into visionary communion with every saint in the liturgical round. Her visions were often in the context of liturgy, as would later usually be the case, and were especially linked to her reception of the eucharist.

Elizabeth of Schönau was born in 1129, apparently from a

family of lower nobility about whom we know nothing. At the age of twelve, she was sent to the convent at Schönau to be educated and she entered the community there at the age of eighteen in 1147. During a religious crisis connected with one of her many bouts of illness around Pentecost in 1152, her visionary life began. Her visions occurred in three different modes. First there was the simple vision, where she saw things in her mind. Then there were the ecstasies where she had more profound mental experiences, and finally were her trances, where she seems to have been 'rapt' from her body, in a way that she often describes in violent fashion. From these last, Elizabeth always needed time to recover, and on these, she was accompanied by a male angelic figure who explained, cajoled, and even beat her, if she did not execute the vision's directions. The trances were also associated with a great deal of bodily suffering, experienced in solidarity with the sufferings of the passion of Christ, and led Elizabeth to be very conscious of the body as a privileged meeting place with God. At the age of twenty-eight in 1157, Elizabeth became *magistra*, that is superior, of the women's section of the monastery and filled this role until her death in 1264. Elizabeth is portrayed as a much-loved, child-like member of a very supportive community.

Elizabeth's brother, Eckbert, has passed her teachings on to later generations. Once a priest of Cologne, he was persuaded by his sister to become a monk at Schönau, and a short time after her death, he took up the post of Abbot. Her writings consist of three books of Visions, a work entitled the *Book of God's Ways*, some letters and other assorted visions, and a short biography penned by Eckbert after her death. These writings were extremely popular all over Europe, in fact more popular than those of Hildegard during her lifetime. For centuries, the *Book of God's Ways* was read in monasteries and convents and was used as a book of spiritual guidance by the laity. One piece of unwanted publicity concerned a prophesy about a major catastrophe which was to occur during the year in which Good Friday fell on the feast of the Annunciation, 25 March. This was to occur in 1155 and occasioned an outpouring of penitential prayer and asceticism. After this, Elizabeth's name was falsely attached to a host of apocalyptic prophesies about the last day and many supposed signs and wonders. This caused her great suffering and plagued her reputation for centuries. It seems to have been in part the substance of her correspondence with Hildegard. Elizabeth was assured that we are all 'earthen vessels' and can do nothing of ourselves. 'O daughter, may God make thee a mirror of Life', was Hildegard's prayer for her.[19]

The teaching of Elizabeth of Schönau centred on the act of prophecy, not in the sense of foretelling future events, but in the sense of being entrusted with a word from God that must be communicated to the designated recipients. Elizabeth was much disliked by the clergy for her strong attacks on the corruption and weakness of the church under their guidance. 'Because in these times the Lord deigns to show his mercy most graciously in the weak sex, such men are offended and led into sin … while the men were given over to sluggishness, holy women were filled with the Spirit of God, that they might prophesy, govern God's people forcefully, and indeed triumph…'[20] The Virgin Mary plays a constant role in these visions and displays joy or displeasure depending on Elizabeth's success. Unlike many later mystics, Elizabeth of Schönau experienced God, Jesus and Mary as harsh guides, who exacted punishment for the non-fulfillment of their wishes. Nevertheless, Elizabeth is quite unique at this period in her womanly attachment to Mary and was instrumental in spreading devotion to the doctrine and the feast of the bodily Assumption of Mary. Elizabeth proposed 23 September as the more appropriate date for the feastday, but apart from the immediate locality of Schonau, the church adhered to the more traditional date of 15 August.

Elizabeth, because of the continuity and seriousness of her sufferings, saw herself as a martyr, and often uses language reminiscent of that of the third-century Carthaginian martyr, Perpetua. Like Perpetua, Elizabeth was launched into an independent ministry in the church by her martyrdom, and seemed convinced that no priest-mediator was necessary for one who had immediate access to God through suffering and the witness of martyrdom. This was the source of her authority and of her sense of prophetic mission.

A unique ingredient of Elizabeth's teaching was contained in the *Book of God's Ways*. Here she describes a mountain, whose peak was approached by many paths. The medieval fascination with various groups and their political and religious reponsibilities is in evidence here, but also the conviction of Elizabeth that God's ways were open to all. The blue path was designed for contemplatives, the green for activists and the purple for martyrdom. Many other paths were designed for the married, the celibate, for adolescents and for children. Each path had its appropriate admonitions. This was used as a spiritual handbook for centuries and assured all that a personal relationship with God was possible for everyone, even the smallest child.

These women came by many different paths, to live the life of Benedictine monasticism. Each was called to demonstrate extraordinary courage in speaking their God-given truth to a mostly hostile church leadership. Nevertheless their role as God's mouthpiece was accepted by many in their own lifetime and for centuries afterwards. Each pushed the role of women much further than current ecclesial and social custom allowed, and each suffered greatly in consequence. All three lived eventually surrounded by loving sisters in highly supportive monastic communities, but one always senses their isolation. Each, in the end, had to stand alone with her God and assume responsibilities that none of them seems to have sought. They stand at a turning point in the history of Christian women. The next few centuries will witness an enormous elaboration in the spiritual gifts and resources of women, and will open out the monastic experience beyond the cloister walls, despite the church's best efforts to confine this experience.

CHAPTER FIVE

Beguine Spirituality

This chapter could truthfully be entitled 'Lost Opportunities'. It describes a women's movement of about two centuries' duration which could have altered the history of Christianity. These women were called Beguines, a name at once belittling and ennobling. The Beguines belong to that undercurrent of Christian history which, known hitherto to a few dedicated experts, is now reaching the light of day in a torrent of scholarly and popular interest. In many ways they attract a similar bemusement today as they did in the twelfth and thirteenth centuries. The Beguines simply do not fit in. They did not fit the careful hierarchical gradation of life in the middle ages and, since this conventional version of history has been accepted in the intervening centuries, it is difficilt for scholars to manouvre the framework in order to make room for them. If, however, one has followed the history of Christianity from the perspective of women, the story of the Beguines will present just one more familiar chapter of the repeated attempts by women to gain a foothold in the Christian church that would respect their unique gifts.

The Beguines were at the centre of a medieval conflict about the role of women, the place – or even the existence – of a group called 'the laity', the nature of monastic and canonical forms of life and their contribution to the Christian church, the relationship between secular and monastic clergy, the nature and usefulness of the *vita apostolica* to the ongoing life of the church, and the breaching of the lay/clerical divide. Beyond that, the Beguines raised questions about the place of the scriptures in the life of the ordinary Christian and the nature of prayer, especially its liturgical and mystical varieties. If all that were not enough, the Beguines belonged to no recognisable group, acknowledged no founding saint and broke down the barriers between the public and private worlds in a way that astonished both their supporters and their opponents. Since conflict was at the heart of Beguine life, almost from the start, and since conflict was anathema to the institutional church, the history of the Beguines has been virtually erased from the common memory with the eradication of the conflict. The story of the institutional church has continued as if the Beguines had never existed. Theirs is, indeed, a dangerous memory, a memory of a time when the structures of the church became porous for a time and, without even a conscious effort by the Beguines, began to look very fragile. As Philip Sheldrake remarks, conflict lets us in on the secrets of the past. It shows us the fault-lines in the ecclesiastical structures, and reveals the fragility of the whole. It is no wonder then that the retrieval of conflict is so useful to those who have lost their histories and so fearful to those who would maintain the old story.[1]

Who were these Beguines? Here we will explore their origins, trace their growth and decline, look to delineate some qualities of their spirituality, and then look at one or two of the key figures. Since the Beguines are one of the rejected groups of history, the retrieval of their story presents us with the same difficulties as other rejected or heretical groups. Those who supported them, usually for their own purposes, are often too fulsome in their praise, and the opponents, especially since the Beguines were women, simply repeat the now familiar list of female propensities to evil and heresy and leave us with little of a specific historical nature. The Beguines, however, were so unique that they raised questions of identity and role that had not been faced before, and so the refrain: 'who are these women?' is usually accompanied by a list of their astonishing new activities. This is of some help to the historian but, in this instance, the existence of an amazing collection of writings by Beguine women adds real insight to the story. Again, it is necessary to add that this writing presents twenty-first century readers with particular problems. Enough is revealed, however, to gain a glimpse of a movement of women who present a wholly new face to the Christian church, and whose loss is only now being fully realised.[2]

> And so, in our days
> In Brabant and the land of Bayern,
> Has the art arisen among women.
> Lord God what art is this
> That an old woman better
> Understands than a man of wit?[3]

This poem by a Franciscan, written around 1250, demonstrates at once both the astonishment and contempt with which this new art of intellect, prayer and the mystical expression of spiritual realities, was being greeted. The poem continues to marvel at how a 'woman becomes good for God'. The amazing powers of these new women seem to surpass even the achievements of the 'divine woman', Hildegard, who some years previously, as we have seen, had elicited the approval of even Bernard and Pope Eugenius. Both Hildegard and the Beguines, though not without some education, seemed to depend more on their inner wisdom and direct contact with the Holy Spirit rather than on the dialectic of the new theology of the schools. It is this element of freshness and depth in the spirituality of the Beguines that continued to astonish their contemporaries.

The Beguines had begun to appear in Belgium, France, Germany and Northern Italy at the turn of the thirteenth century. They consisted of women living either singly, in small groups, or eventually in gatherings of fifty or even more, scattered in buildings which they had bought or inherited throughout the towns and cities in these areas. Their origins are still a source of scholarly debate. Some see them as a development of the women who had clustered with more or less of a welcome around the foundations of the Cistercians, or eventually the newer foundations of the mendicant friars, the Franciscans and Dominicans. Others, such as Jacques de Vitry, the biographer of the 'first' Beguine, see them as an entirely new phenomenon. In any case, one of the constant complaints about them is that they acknowledged no founding figure and followed the rule of no saint. So it is likely that the arrival of the Beguines seemed as much a sudden revelation to their contemporaries as to us. These women from the aristocracy and the new urban merchant classes, gathered together to organise their own spiritual lives with both an intensity and an informality not seen before. Scholars note the likelihood of the prevailing socio-economic conditions as one influence in the appearance of this new movement. It was a time when women seem to have outnumbered men. The fact that the women, by becoming Beguines, deliberately made themselves unavailable for marriage seems to have been particularly offensive to many clerics. The thirst of many for the practice of the *vita apostolica* had been noted since the return of the first crusaders. Their contact with the Holy Land and renewed acquaintance with the simplicity of the story of Jesus and his followers had revolutionised certain groups. The search for a life of poverty and simplicity was in the air, and the inevitable contrast with the wealth and growing complexity of the medieval institutional church was hard to miss. As it happened, it was the ecclesiastical establishment which entirely failed to harness the spirit of the age. Instead all the institutional efforts were eventually devoted to destroying it.

The mendicant friars, Franciscans and Dominicans, attracted hundreds of male followers and both Francis and Dominic managed to integrate their spiritual genius – not always without difficulty – with the ecclesiastical needs of the day. The Cistercians and Premonstratensians were continuing to flourish, but by the opening years of the thirteenth century, all these groups of male religious were increasingly resistant to welcoming and caring for female adherents. The need for an independent community for women is obvious to the observer from today, but the actions of a succession of popes, bishops, and founders seemed to cut off this possibility at every opportunity. At the Fourth Lateran Council in 1215, Pope Innocent III, though somewhat sympathetic to women seeking a spiritual life, began the process of reducing the choices of women even further. It was with him that the

stark choice *aut maritus aut murus* – either marriage or strict enclosure behind convent walls – was delineated for women. Here
were the two areas where women properly were fitted. There
were to be no more religious orders, no double monasteries, and
above all, no unattached females. Even more significantly, the
two strands of religious life, the monastic, rooted in a contemplative and highly regularised life, and the canonical, which had
always included a ministerial dimension, were now melded into
one. There was to be only one kind of nun – the enclosed one.

Nevertheless, despite growing ecclesiastical concern, the
numbers of Beguines seemed to grow. They sought to live a
gospel-inspired life apart from the framework and constrictions
of a canonical rule. Despite their possible links with previous
traditions, most modern commentators are convinced that this
was a genuinely new and spontaneous women's movement.
They lived simple lives, gave a promise of chastity, engaged in
manual labour both to support themselves and to help the poor,
set up and worked in hospitals and leprosaria, read and taught
the scriptures in the vernacular, had a fairly strict regimen of
prayer and led lives marked by ascetic practices. They had no
vows, elected their own leaders, saw their promise of chastity as
temporary while living the Beguine life, understood their spirituality as both contemplative and active (to use later terms) and
looked primarily to the Holy Spirit and their sisters as guides for
their life. Initially, there seems to have been no effort by the
Beguines to criticise the ecclesiastical establishment, but the very
informality and integrity of their life elicited both praise and
blame.

One of those who was overcome with astonishment and
praise was Jacques de Vitry (1160-1240). By his own testimony,
he had been converted by the holiness of the life of Mary, the
leader of a group of Beguines in the town of Oignies. Jacques
abandoned his student life at the University of Paris and became
a disciple of Mary. Two years after her death in 1213, he wrote
her life. He was convinced that the example of these women
could transform the church and be a bulwark against the

Albigensian heresy which seemed to be flourishing at its heart. At Mary's urging, he eventually became part of the anti-Albigensian crusade. Jacques de Vitry was an important advocate of the Beguines, but he wrote with his own anti-heretical agenda for the church. He rose rapidly through the ecclesiastical ranks to the Cardinalate, but seemed to have discerned from the start the innovatory potential of the Beguines. As an important ecclesiastical functionary, he travelled widely and everywhere reported on this new movement of women, insisting always on their orthodoxy. In 1215, he set out for Rome to request the approval of Pope Innocent III for the Beguine way of life, but the pope's death foiled his efforts. Instead, he gained a qualified form of approval from the new pope, Honorius III, but it was not nearly as affirmative as he had requested. An insight into the spirit of the age emerges in the fact that Jacques de Vitry carried everywhere with him the severed finger of Mary of Oignies. He had requested her head and after a rather unseemly row, finally managed to retrieve her little finger.

We know that, in his *Life* of Mary of Oignies, Jacques de Vitry was consciously following the writing of the fourth century monastic supporters, especially Jerome. He saw himself as something of a new Jerome, guiding the footsteps of women for the benefit of the church. He saw the Beguines of his day as the new Mothers of the Church and successors to the great Paula and Marcella of Jerome's day. It remains fascinating to the historian, how movements begun by women are co-opted by men and the women become, for history, part of the followers of the 'great man' while the actual truth is entirely the opposite. The initiative in the case both of Jerome and Jacques de Vitry lay with the women. Nevertheless, Jacques de Vitry's *Life* of Mary present us with a new kind of hagiography. He uses her life as a model, a piece of propaganda, a reproach to those he describes as 'shameless men' who 'howled like mad dogs' in their rage at the Beguines. The area around Liège was rich with religious women in both formal and informal settings, but it is Mary that is the focus of Jacques de Vitry's praise, because, as he writes, she has been dead for two years, and is therefore beyond harm.

Mary was born around the year 1177 into a rich and respected family in Nivelles, just south of modern Brussels, in the diocese of Liège. She was married at the age of fourteen, but preferring chastity, she persuaded her husband to join her in the pursuit of a religious life. From around 1190, the two laboured together in a leprosarium founded on family property in Willambrouk. Mary's holiness began to attract followers and a group of women gathered to benefit from her guidance. In 1207, she obtained permission from her husband and her director to visit the priory of St Nicholas in Oignies, a short distance south east of Nivelles. It was near this priory that she set up her own establishment and remained there till her death. It was here also that Jacques de Vitry eventually joined her group. Shortly after the *Life* of Mary was published, the praise of the Beguines was re-echoed by two other important ecclesiastical leaders, Robert Grosseteste of Lincoln, and Robert of Sorbonne, who remarked especially on the willingness of the Beguines to support themselves. They sought no favours from anyone and rejected all offers of patronage and therefore made very few demands on the clergy. Paradoxically, it was this praise in high quarters which made the Beguines look suspicious. They seemed too holy for their own good and began to sound like the heretics, putting the ecclesiastical establishment to shame by the chastity and poverty of their lives. The church's dilemma when faced with holy heretics was intolerable and the solution of Dominic to produce even holier clergy was extremely welcome.

R. W. Southern's description of the Beguine movement has remained significant for over thirty years. He describes it as a 'series of reactions to the conditions of urban life and commercial wealth, combined with disillusionment about elaborate structures of government and systems of theoretical perfection'.[5] Southern points out that these conditions were to become a permanent feature of the ecclesiastical life of Christendom, and that in the earliest reactions to this state of affairs, women seemed to play a leading part. Southern emphasises the informality and regionalism of the Beguine movement and sets his own sights on the city of Cologne. He quotes Matthew Paris, the chronicler, who was initially no lover of the Beguines, and describes them as growing in numbers beyond all expectation, seeing that their religious profession was such a 'light profession'. He reports that in the neighbourhood of Cologne there are now about two thousand Beguines.[6] The city of Cologne had a population of around fifteen thousand at the time, so the presence of so many Beguines would indeed have been remarkable. Southern worked his way through the records of property transactions in order to verify these comments. He can pin-point the first Beguines as two sisters, Elizabeth and Sophie, who sold small properties in 1223. Between 1250 and 1310, there is a huge in- crease in such property transfers, and thereafter they gradually decrease. Nevertheless, there are still one hundred and sixty- nine Beguine convents at the end of the century, and as we shall see, by 1400, all Beguines were forced to live in convents. The peak in the year 1310 and the subsequent levelling off of the numbers of Beguine institutions can be ascribed to two major events at this time. First, in June 1310 the Beguine, Marguerite Porete, had been burned at the stake in Paris on an accusation of heresy. Secondly, the official repression of the Beguines was gaining momentum around the same time. Already in 1274, at the Council of Lyons, there had been an outcry at the 'unbridled multitude' of new religious groupings, and it was declared that all such groupings founded since the Fourth Lateran Council in 1215, 'which have not obtained papal confirmation, are forever prohibited and quashed, no matter how far they have pro- gressed'.[7] By the time of the Council of Vienne in 1312, the offi- cial hostility to the Beguines is apparent:

> We have been told that certain women commonly called Beguines, afflicted by a kind of madness, discuss the Holy Trinity and the divine essence, and express opinions on matters of faith and sacraments contrary to the catholic faith, deceiving many simple people. Since these women promise no obedience to anyone and do not renounce their property or profess an approved Rule, they are certainly not 'religious',

although they wear a habit and are associated with such religious orders as they find congenial ... We have therefore decided and decreed with the approval of the Council that their way of life is to be permanently forbidden and altogether excluded from the Church of God.[8]

As Southern points out, the Council itself was aware of the ambiguity of such a stance. How could they prevent people from gathering and praying together? Was this not basic Christian behaviour, quite apart from the necessity of following one of the approved religious rules? Therefore, they append a milder statement about what might be called good women who 'live a life of penance and serve God in humility'. What is abundantly clear is that the informal and free life of the Beguines was suspect. It crossed too many clearly defined boundaries. In over one hundred years of life, the Beguine movement had found no official place in the church, nor had it sought one. Its very informality and lack of approbation was its downfall. Besides, the perennial 'woman-question' lurked at the background of every spiritual innovation. As one of the contemporary opponents said: 'I would have them married or thrust into an approved Order.' There was no room in such a highly structured ecclesiastical establishment for a woman-initiated approach to women's spiritual life. Eventually most Beguines were either disbanded or precisely 'thrust' into established groups. It is time now to look at the life of the Beguines and to explore the salient aspects of their innovative spiritual life.

The Beguines, intent as they were on living a simple gospel-centred life, produced one of the most extraordinary bodies of mystical literature in the whole Christian corpus. Their focus was entirely on the humanity of Jesus, and it was their strong belief that, through the imitation of the life and especially the sufferings of Jesus, they would become one with him, and through him with the transcendent God. For the Beguine, the most human aspect of the humanity of Jesus was the fact that he suffered, and their efforts focused on the almost literal imitation of what he endured. To this was added the whole panoply of extreme asceticism as witnessed earlier in the great desert ascetics, namely, fasting, sleep-deprivation, bodily mutilation and the most intense self-mortification. For the modern reader, the most extraordinary aspect of all this is that in the midst of all this horrific self-inflicted suffering, these women are attended by their maids and seem to carry on the most active and involved lives. Such a life, of course, was designed to prepare one for the experience of mystical union with God, and the writings of the Beguines constitute a brilliant exposition of this union. In many instances, the root symbol of this mystical union was an intense personal devotion to the eucharist, where, through the reception of the Body and Blood of Christ, the Beguines experienced their closest union with their Beloved.

As we have seen, the church had felt the necessity of interposing itself, through its reform legislation, between the individual believer and the gospel revelation. The task of the church was to make Christianity liveable and to render the believer accountable, sometimes in very minimalist ways. The whole focus had been on the monastic way of life and this had come to constitute almost the normative totality of the Christian lifestyle. Beyond a more or less regular attendance at Sunday eucharist, not a great deal was expected of the average non-monastic person. The Fourth Lateran Council in 1215 had had to impose annual reception of communion on the ordinary believer, since reception had lapsed almost completely. As mentioned earlier, church reform had come to mean clerical and monastic reform, and even these had not delivered what had been promised. When the new evangelical movements began to proliferate in the twelfth century, it was this new immediate contact with the scriptures, with the story of Jesus and his followers, with the *vita apostolica*, which began to sweep Europe. The Beguines were at the heart of this movement, and as we begin to decipher their writings, we can be overwhelmed at the concreteness of their biblical life, despite its frequent mystical heights. As the Beguines grew in their experience and understanding of the mystical life, they felt an urgent need to share it, primarily with their sisters, and then with the whole church. Since they had touched the face of God, they longed to make this experience available to all. Hence many of the Beguine writings sketch out the stages of the spiritual and mystical journey and become the guides in this journey for hundreds of their followers. It is not difficult to imagine the consternation of the ecclesiastical establishment as these often unschooled women, who had neither received nor even sought a mandate to teach, were now, in effect, running schools of biblical and mystical learning in the vernacular languages. It may even have been this departure from the sacred and exclusive ecclesiastical Latin language that most brought the Beguines to clerical attention. Indeed the Beguine writings are among the earliest and most brilliant examples of vernacular literature in Flemish, German, French, Italian and Dutch.

Elizabeth Avilda Petroff offers, perhaps, the best overview of this new mystical literature, and it is her work that we shall mostly follow here.[10] Individual Beguines, such as Mechtild of Magdeburg and Marguerite Porete will be explored in the next two chapters. Petroff has outlined seven distinct stages of the mystical journey found throughout this literature: purgative, psychic, doctrinal, devotional, participatory, unitive or erotic, and cosmic ordering. It was a medieval assumption that women were better fitted for visionary experiences than men, and so there was a certain expectation that, given the ascetic practices followed by these women, such experiences would be the outcome. What was unusual about this particular period of Christian spiritual life was the abundance of practitioners and teachers available for both the beginner and the experienced. Despite the off-putting nature (from a modern perspective) of the ascetic practices, it is the firm conviction of most contemporary scholars that the Beguines, and their female contemporaries in other groups, did not enter on such an ascetic regime from a sense of women's sinfulness as a daughters of Eve, but rather from a desire to imitate the actual details of the life of Jesus. It is remarkable that where we have both male and female descriptions of the same lives, the male author emphasises the penitential nature of an asceticism appropriate to the weakness and sinfulness of women, while the female author emphasises the evangelical and unitive aspects of this life, often describing internal rather than external suffering. It is a question that the modern reader cannot help exploring: what did these women think they were doing? From all the accounts that we have, it does not appear that they were punishing themselves for being women, as contemporary official teaching might have assumed, but that they were preparing themselves for what they considered to be an inevitable complete union with the Trinitarian God.

The first stage of visionary life, as it had been from the earliest times was the purgative or cleansing stage, where the visionary had to withstand opposition on all fronts, often interpreted as the work of demons. The violence and pain of the individual's inner life at the start of this spiritual journey is externalised in violent attacks on the body. Jacques de Vitry had described this stage in the *Life* of Mary of Oignies in this way: 'From the horror she felt at her previous carnal pleasure, she began to afflict herself and she found no rest in spirit until, by means of extraordinary bodily chastisements, she had made up for all the pleasures she had experienced in the past.' One cannot help wondering when the young Mary had had time for all these carnal pleasures, having entered a chaste marriage at the age of fourteen. It is part of the author's intention to portray Marie in the most expected orthodox light. Nevertheless, from all accounts, many women did impose or fantasise such punishments for themselves, as they were part and parcel of the medieval mindset for the life of a holy mystic. The description of Mary of Oignies goes on to describe how 'in error' she 'cut out a large piece of flesh' and then when she returned to her senses, she was so horrified that she buried it. The story relates that the deed was not discovered until her body was being prepared for burial.

The second stage of the journey leads the visionary to turn from her own concerns to the needs and spiritual welfare of others. Her spiritual life has become more intuitive and less the result of self-initiated ascetic practices. She hears voices, receives commands, has premonitions about others' lives and can often read hearts. She begins to be of help to others in their spiritual dilemmas, and begins to learn the necessary spiritual skills of communicating to her clients information about themselves that they may not like to hear. Several incidents survive in a variety of women's lives about such spiritual dealings with priests, who arrive to celebrate the eucharist, only to be pulled aside and told to repent of quite precise mortal sins before daring to consecrate the host. Such events quickly mark the visionary as a spiritual authority even at this very early stage of her spiritual journey. God seems to speak through her and she is greeted by all with a mixture of fear, respect, and gratitude. Her fame begins to spread.

As Petroff points out, this interaction with others leads the visionary to the third stage, that of doctrinal learning. The spiritual dilemmas of others' lives, not to mention the visionary's own life, would certainly have aroused the need for a deeper rooting in Christian teaching. Whether the visionary becomes more finely tuned to the Christian instruction surrounding her in sermons, the readings of the canonical hours, the admonitions of a spiritual director, or her own access to literature, or whether in fact she was Spirit-taught, as many implied, this is the stage where genuine Christian learning takes place. Since women were universally deprived of the clerical university education in Latin, other avenues had to be found, and these women found them. Hildegard of Bingen's writing on the Trinity is an example of this learning, but it is common to all the visionaries at this period. The extraordinary life of the woman called Christina Mirabilis, who had died and been returned to life, is seen as one long lesson on the recently developed teaching about the sufferings of purgatory. Christina, who lived in trees, recoiled from the smell of human flesh and threw herself in water and flames without injury, at last found peace when these purgatorial nightmares had ended.[11] The women mystics seem to have received visions in answer to spiritual dilemmas, and the solution is sometimes granted in parable or in riddle form, which the suppliants have to work out by themselves.

The fourth stage must have been intensely satisfying for the visionary. It consists of devotional visions of Christ and other heavenly figures. Christ is experienced at all stages of his life from infancy to life in glory, and leads to experiences of love interchanged and a growing depth of contemplation in the visionary. These experiences seem to have had their origin in the liturgical round of festivals and on the meditations practised by all religious people at that time. There is some evidence that a form of meditation that was a kind of directing of the imagination to the various gospel scenes was taught formally by the Franciscans and Dominicans in their public preaching during the thirteenth century. It is also true that such meditation had been a staple of monastic life for centuries. This devotional and emotional form of meditation, as well as repetitive prayer, seems to have been the chief form of prayer taught to laypeople and nuns, especially those unable to read Latin. The Beguines seem to have carried such meditations forward into actual experiences with the *dramatis personae* of their prayer. Jacques de Vitry describes one such experience of Mary of Oignies:

> Sometimes it seemed to her that for three or more days she held Him close to her so that He nestled between her breasts like a baby, and she hid Him there lest He be seen by others. Sometimes she kissed Him as though He were a little child and sometimes she held Him on her lap as if He were a gentle lamb. At other times the holy Son of the Virgin manifested himself in the form of a dove ... He manifested himself to Marie in a form which was in keeping with the feast. Thus he showed himself at the Nativity as though He were a baby sucking at the breasts of the Virgin Mary or crying in his cradle, and then she was drawn to Him in love just as if He had been her own baby. In this way the various feasts took on new interest according to how He manifested himself and each caused a different emotional state.[12]

It is clear that the meditations of the Beguines had become an exciting and affective part of their lives – a reward for their perseverance thus far on the spiritual journey. One cannot help wondering how such meditation would have fared had the women been allowed an education. It is clear that such devotional meditations were common even among the more theologically literate nuns, as we shall see when we explore the extraordinary school of prayer at the convent of Helfta in the next chapter. Such homely meditations must have gone a long way to healing the visionaries of previous emotional deprivation, just as the vision of the 'good mother', Mary, seems to have healed Christina of Markyate of some of the wounds caused by the cruelty of her own mother. Such devotional meditations extended also to the experience of the passion and death of Jesus, although at this stage, the visionaries seem to have been able to concentrate more on the love of Jesus than on the pain.

These visions led naturally to the experiences of participatory love and compassion in the life of the woman mystic. Experiences of participating in the suffering of Jesus now take on a redemptive value and the mystic experiences herself as contributing to the good of those around her and of the whole church. The process of identification with Christ is deepened as the focus of participation moves from the experience of human suffering to that of identification with Christ in divine love. One of the human and visible effects in the life of the visionary was a deep sense of expanded love and compassion which often revealed itself to the world in floods of tears. The weeping of the women mystics was recognised by all as a further step on the road to sanctity. Margery Kempe, as we shall see, was something of an exception here, as her tears were generally accompanied by loud shouts and groans to the extent that the devotions of everyone else were rendered impossible. Mary of Oignies 'would sometimes moderate her sorrow and restrain the flood of her tears and, leaving behind His humanity, would raise her mind so that she might find some consolation in His unchangeableness'.[13] These tears were greeted occasionally with frustration by clergy, especially if they interrupted the celebration of the liturgy. De Vitry tells the story of one such priest who rebuked Mary of Oignies for her weeping so that she felt it necessary to leave the celebration and retire to a secret place to pray for the priest. Her prayers were answered. 'It happened that "The Lord opened and none shut".' The priest was so overcome with floods of tears that 'he almost suffocated. The harder he tried to restrain this force, the more drenched he became and the more soaked did the book and the altar become.'

Such participatory visions often take on an erotic overtone which, with the frequent use of the Song of Songs as one of the favourite medieval biblical texts, was not unfamiliar in the religious circles of the age. The experience of mystical union was often, though not always, articulated in the language of erotic love. At any rate the pierced body of the crucified Jesus became the focus of the mystic's longing and seems to have been the liberating image for the launching of the woman mystic back into the life of the community. As Petroff remarks, this was the moment when these visionaries pushed the barriers which secular and ecclesiastical culture had erected between the male and the female, and the woman mystic felt so Christ-identified that no societal barriers could restrain her. Often the visionary experineced a kind of mystical marriage at this stage, which was then the occasion of her most active period of work in the wider Christian community. For these women, the height of mystical union did not lead them to seek the life of a recluse, but rather the life of active involvement in work for the poor and the alienated. As we shall see specifically in the life of Marguerite Porete, this is the moment when the dualistic divisions of culture and theology resolved themselves in the life of the mystic and they learned to 'live without a why'. The barriers between the contemplative and active life had been removed through the experiences of mystical prayer and the life of the women visionaries was seen to be capable of delegitimating the whole of ecclesiastical culture and theological teaching.

As the lives of these women take on a sometimes frantic pace as word of their sanctity spreads, and thousands begin to turn to them for healing and guidance, it is very often the experience of eucharist which sustains them on an ongoing basis. The story of these women's lives has focused often on the earlier stages of the journey, especially on their horrific acts of penitence, as though this were all that constituted the life of holiness for women. Even with such women as Christina of Markyate, as we have seen, the story fades away as she moves on to the most important aspect of her life's work, namely the founding and maintaining of a very powerful monastery. The same is often true with the Beguines. The story of women's bodily mortifications seems to have been heard more easily by the church as somehow appropriate for women's sanctity. It is when the women follow the inevitable logic of the spiritual journey that difficulties arise. There is no doubt though, that the devotion of the Beguines to the eucharist changed the attitude of the church and opened the way for a larger participation of the laity in this central worship ritual. Juliana of Mont Cornillon (1193-1258) is credited with having been ordered in a vision to have the feast of Corpus Christi instituted. After a turbulent life resulting from a major upheaval in her convent life when a male prior disenfranchised the nuns, she took refuge in the Beguinage at Namur. She died here, after leaving a eucharistic festival to the Catholic Church which for centuries was the primary focus of lay eucharistic devotion.

Mary of Oignies was nourished literally and figuratively by the eucharist:

> The holy bread strengthened her heart; the holy wine inebriated her, rejoicing her mind; the holy body fattened her; the vitalising blood purified her by washing. And she could not bear to abstain from such solace for long. For it was the same to her to live as to eat the body of Christ.[14]

This is in the words of Mary's biographer, but we have volumes written by women themselves throughout the thirteenth century on the centrality of the eucharist in their lives. Caroline Walker Bynum who has done extensive research in this area, testifies that women in every area and every walk of life were 'inspired, compelled, comforted and troubled by the eucharist to an extent found in only a few male writers of the period'.[15] Exclusively female eucharistic miracles include the ability to distinguish between consecrated and unconsecrated hosts, (often a test set the mystic to ascertain her authenticity), the experiences of sweet odours and honey-like tastes coming from the hosts, and the appearance of Jesus, often in the shape of a beautiful baby.[16] It was especially the theme of union with Christ in the reception of holy communion that was central to these women's lives. Desire for the eucharist dominated much of their spiritual experience and the metaphors of tasting and drinking God and even nursing and being nursed by God are frequent in the literature.

Throughout the thirteenth century, devotion to and the theology of the eucharist was changing dramatically. Partly arising from the Gregorian reform of the clergy and the emphasis on their new purity which was a prerequisite for their new eucharistic power of consecration, and partly from the new centrality of the elevated host, often stamped with the features of Jesus, the Mass and the reception of holy communion had now become one of the commonplaces of everyday lay life. It was not that the laity received more frequently – they did not – but devotion to the eucharist was in the air. The doctrine of transubstantiation and the real presence of Jesus in the consecrated host added not only to the attraction of the eucharistic celebration, but also to the awe in which the host was held. In fact, the host itself was often seen as having a centrality of its own, apart from the Mass, and we know that in many convents, holy communion took place after the Mass was concluded. Within the convent structure the frequency of reception of holy communion was a frequent topic of debate. Daily reception was rare, but women could be excluded for several reasons, including being considered too holy, too lax, or too ill. Besides, many followed St Augustine's view that a less frequent reception out of awe and reverence, might be preferable to too much familiarity. We know also of lepers who were not allowed to approach the altar. In this way, reception of communion led to a heightened sense of privilege and expectation. Just as Hildegard of Bingen had dressed her nuns as brides in preparation for communion, so too many women mystics saw communion as a meeting of bride and bridegroom. To receive communion was to receive Christ. Christ had made himself available to all in the form of this holy food. For many, communion itself represented the height of mystical union.

Many women, however, were known for other paramystical experiences. The moment of reception was the herald of an ecstatic state. The mystic experienced complete divine union and felt as if they were 'eating God'. The flesh of the woman and the flesh of Christ were mingled, whether it was the infant form of the child Jesus, the manly form of the youthful male, or more frequently the suffering form of the crucified Jesus. The women felt thay they were holding him, bathing him, playing with him. Indeed we hear of women who refused to let him go. Women were often betrothed to him in a form of mystical marriage. The physicality of the presence of Jesus seems to have been central to the experience. God was with them in human form, and this became so much part of the women's experience that some seem to suggest that the humanity of Jesus was especially made present for women, whereas the divinity was for men. At any rate, God was felt to be supremely accessible to these women in the experience of receiving communion.

Bynum considers this intense womanly experience to be an alternative experience to priestly authority. Just as the power and authority of the priest was being elevated, women were increasingly excluded from even the most minor clerical tasks, such as handling the sacred vessels. In many ways, then, eucharistic devotion became a substitute for priesthood. There is no doubt that these women claimed a new kind of power through their eucharistic experience. They were enabled to bypass the clerical monopoly of the sacrament and often received the ministry of Jesus in person. Their distinctly non-clerical status received its own affirmation as it was endowed with a new and special spiritual significance. Christ could replace the priest altogether, and in fact, it was often the reception of the eucharist that empowered women to take on their own special mission of rebuking corrupt clerics. Mechtild of Magdeburg, in one such eucharistic vision, saw the lower circles of hell peopled with men only, most of them clerics. The reception of communion in the eyes of many women surpassed even the importance of the consecration in spiritual significance. It was not through worldly or ecclesiastical power that the women received their mission and were united with Christ, but by the direct ministration of Christ himself.

Bynum and others also draw attention to the significance of the eucharist as food in the lives of these women.[17] Even though all warn against transposing social and psychological categories from one era to another, nevertheless, all see some correspondence between the modern phenomenon called *anorexia nervosa* and the experience of the medieval women mystics. Many became simply incapable of tolerating any food at all, especially meat. Many claim to live on the eucharistic food alone. Almost universally, food is divided into holy and unholy varieties. All the metaphors around the experiences of eating and non-eating appear in all the literature. Women who are unable to eat themselves spend a great part of their lives feeding others. Food was the one area of a woman's life where she was perceived to have any power. The refusal to eat was an act of power which totally disconcerted both family and society, and gave the woman an authority not available elsewhere. This experience often coincided with the onset of puberty and the deeply emotional dilemmas of vocation. It is striking that food is so much more central to the writing and experience of these women than sex was. The women had little or no control over their sexual lives and the disposition of their bodies within a married relationship. But food was an area of womanly control – they gathered it, prepared it, cooked it and served it. When they refused these tasks as well as the partaking of food, a new power was apparent in their lives. The choice for the renunciation of food was the one area where they could make personal decisions. Holy eating replaced the intake of normal food, and once the break was made, who would return to ordinary food after the experience of eating God?

Even though some of the events in the lives of these women

seem truly bizarre now, and probably also then, nevertheless, these experiences are one form of womanly response to the new theological teaching about the real presence. Many official teachers affirmed the eucharistic experiences of these women as support for the doctrine of transubstantiation and a direct attack against the Cathar heresy, especially in its reliance on dualism. The experiences of these women were a direct contradiction to the Cathar dualistic emphasis on the evils of the flesh as contrasted to the purity of the soul. In medieval mystical experience, the body became central. It was the humanity of Jesus in all its physicality that these women experienced. The women also moved beyond the dualistic strand in traditional official teaching, which often wondered whether or not women were made in the image of God. These women personally experienced their own creation in God's image. God was emblazoned on their inner selves. They knew God's likeness in and through their own bodies. These women ignore centuries of negative teachings about women and their supposedly evil sexuality and embrace femaleness as a special sign of closeness to Christ. As Bynum says: 'Women drew from the traditional notion of the female as physical a special emphasis on their own redemption by a Christ who was supremely physical because supremely human. They sometimes even extrapolated from this to the notion that, in Christ, divinity is to humanity as male is to female.'[18] All of this points to a major change in medieval eucharistic theology from the earlier notion of the eucharistic as spiritual refreshment and the bread of heaven, as a pledge of the church's unity and the one unbroken body of Christ, to the sense of the eucharistic as body of Christ broken for all.[19] Women seem to have felt that broken bodiliness gave them a special entrée to the presence of Christ in the eucharist. There is also a predominating sense of compassion in these writings which extends not only to the brokenness of the body of Christ but to all broken bodies. It is in this way that their experience of eucharist propelled these women into works of mercy and initiated an involvement of women in the social ministry of the church which was essential to church life for centuries.

Hadewijch of Antwerp

It would be impossible in such a small volume to include specific writings from all or even a small number of these Beguine mystics. The following chapters will explore in some detail the writings of Mechtild of Magdeburg and Marguerite Porete, but before leaving this chapter, we shall take a brief glance at the writings of one of the writers about whom we know almost nothing, but whose writings are universally acknowledged to reach the heights of medieval or any literature, Hadewijch of Antwerp. Hadewijch's writings were known to some later medieval mystics, such as John Ruysbroeck, but they disappeared, to be discovered again only in 1838. Identification was not easy as there are over one hundred women known to us with the same name, but recent scholarship has cleared up many of the questions about her identity. Hadewijch came from the aristocracy and had received an exemplary schooling. There is abundant evidence in her work that she knew Latin and French well, was familiar with the whole range of patristic literature and also with the theological, canonical and spiritual writers of her own day.[20] Her poetry is also so full of references to the contemporary genre of courtly love poetry that some scholars speculate that Hadewijch might have been a musician or troubador before her conversion to the Beguine way of life. She has left us a corpus of some forty-five poems in stanzas and sixteen in couplets, thirty-one letters and fourteen visions, all of which seem to have been written between 1221 and 1240. She seems to have been the mistress of a group of Beguines and in charge of the development of a number of younger members along the paths of mysticism. The whole group seems to have incurred the wrath of some official because eventually the Beguinage was disbanded and Hadewijch herself was evicted and apparently forced into exile. All these details have to be gleaned from her writings, as well as the hint that it was her teaching about living Love that was the cause of her troubles.

Letter Six to a young Beguine is seen as something of a manifesto for the Beguine way of life, especially the life of Love. 'To live in perfect accord with the will of His love ... longing always to be all that love asks of us, that even if we wished we would choose and ask nothing better than what pleases love, whether the world should curse us or bless us for it ... And knowing this we must always know that for us life is a loving service and a longing exile. For so Jesus Christ lived as a man upon this earth.'[21] In the more autobiographical Letter XI, she says: 'in the end, I cannot believe that I have loved him best, and yet I cannot believe that there is any living man who loves God as I love Him.'[22] Hadewijch's whole focus then was the mysticism of love and what Bowie calls an experiential radicalisation of the theology of love.[23] Love becomes her spouse, her Lady, her God and her companion. Since she uses the Dutch word *Minne*, which is grammatically feminine, for Love, there is a particularly womanly aura about her writings.

Hadewijch employs all the conventions of courtly love in her spiritual writings, especially that of the faithful lover and the fickle and demanding Lady. In her writing, the fickle Lady is God. Love and suffering are almost synonymous for Hadewijch, for without the suffering of love there is no union. Such suffering is not seen as penance for sins or for human frailty but suffering is union. 'Love causes more sorrows than there are stars in heaven.' In Letter 6, she had written, 'We all wish to be God with God, but God knows there are few of us who want to live as man with God's humanity.'[24]

All through Hadewijch's work, this divine love is called Lady Love. It is a Love that gives herself wholly but yet always remains beyond the clutches of the beloved. This inability to return love fully is what causes the mystic's suffering, but this is called a 'single rejoicing' because God, in Christ, suffers along with us. The beginner on the journey of love starts by being delighted with the gifts of love, but she is eventually led to a deeper appreciation of her own insufficiency and this can lead to a sense of despair. Her desire to love wholly stirs up in her a rage of insufficiency.[25] But this Love is always recreating her again, always new and always ready to make all things new, because newness is simply part of the infinity that Love is. Humans can feel utterly lost in such a vast sea of Love and must proceed without any map or guide. What Hadewijch teaches her young students is the need for absolute trust and an unreserved commitment to the one Love that governs the whole of one's moral life.

Hadewijch experienced the same eucharistic union with Christ as so many of her Beguine sisters. In Vision VII, she describes the growth of this eucharistic relationship. Christ came first simply as the species, then in person in the whole of his humanity, and she feels his presence throughout her whole body. Then the human Christ fades away, but she has become wholly assimilated to him and 'it is as if we were one without any difference'. Hadewijch, like all Beguines, is driven by this love to act as Christ toward all others, and so her eucharistic devotion drives her out to help the poor. She is human and has to act out of her humanity. She must live on earth in exile and misery and a constant sense of forsakenness, but knowing at all times that she possesses the fruits of love. She teaches her charges that our task on earth is to find that unity with God, that state of pure being, which we had before we were created. We can feel the presence of this uncreated being in the depths of our souls, if only fleetingly, but we must allow ourselves to be re-created by God: 'If you wish to attain your being in which God created you, in all nobleness, you must not refuse any difficulty; with all hardiness and pride you must neglect nothing, but valiantly seize the best part, I mean the totality of God, as your own wealth.'[26] There is an inner inevitability in the soul that leads us unceasingly back towards this original destiny. Christ is our model in the working out of the unspeakable desires which thrust us into the infinite spaces of divine love. Her poetry is centered on the sense of agony that this unceasing desire arouses in her. It is a journey that cannot be halted, just as one might try in vain to stop the labour of a woman in confinement. As one continues this journey, one's life on earth is also lived more in harmony with others, especially through the works of mercy.

Like so many other Beguines, and despite her own education and, in fact, her insistence that her young Beguines get a strong education and study hard, Hadewijch insists on the primacy of love over reason and intellect. She explains that reason can touch God only in what he is not, that is, it has to work through symbols, images, and arguments about God. Love, however, touches the very Being of God and plunges the lover into the abyss of God's life. Her spiritual doctrine is summed up well in the saying: Love God with God's love so as to become God with God. In every other relationship, it is often the face that reveals love to us. With God, however, or 'in the case of Love, it is the face that remains most secret, for this is Love Herself in Herself'.[27] Our journey towards God is like a re-integration of all our powers in the searching mind, the trusting heart and the loving soul so that we can say, 'I have integrated all that was divided within me.' The soul has been widened out to take on the dimensions of God.[28] When this state is reached, then the ordinary virtues are no longer of any use to the mystic. They are part of the beginner's path, but once Love has been attained, the virtues are just a distraction, keeping our attention focused on the self rather than God.

One cannot but be amazed at the confidence of these women in their love relationship with God and, even more, that so many of them remained active workers for the poor and abandoned, in what they thought was the natural consequence of this love. It can be observed that other forms of mysticism, especially the male forms, tend to draw the mystic away from the world. The Beguines, however, are propelled into the world to help others gain the same benefits. They do not consider their gifts to be unique, but wish to make them available to all in a kind of de-mocratisation of mysticism. With Hadewijch, it is especially in her letters that her own loving personality shines through. She addresses her charges with great affection: 'Ah dear sweet child, may you be wise in God, for you have great need of wisdom, as has anyone who wishes to become like God.' It seems almost second nature to them to work out ways of handing on their learning and to lead others along the pathways of mystical life towards becoming God with God.

We will see many of these themes in the writings of Mechtild of Magdeburg and Marguerite Porete. It may be well to enumerate them here, if only to demonstrate the cumulative effect of Beguine teaching. Though the Beguines had antecedents, it seems that their spiritual doctrines were worked out by themselves with very little help or encouragement from the official church. Their writings give us a glimpse into a version of Christianity far removed from the official and supposedly traditional form. The women reach back, consciously or unconsciously, into an other stream of Christian tradition, rooted in the gospels and in the life of the human Jesus and his followers. It is here that they discover their devotion to poverty, simplicity, a ministry to all who are marginalised, a thirst for the imitation of Christ in and through his sufferings, but focusing primarily on their loving and unifying force. Devotion to the eucharist as the main avenue to a total union with God is a new thirteenth century expression of the journey of love, expressed, as we have seen, almost exclusively by women. It is strange indeed that the men who daily performed the miracle of the eucharist, as the thirteenth century saw it, did not seem to have evolved a similar eucharistic devotion. What is also new in these women is their ability to move beyond the cultural and ecclesiastical understandings of who they were and what they were capable of, to discover depths and heights of spirituality unimagined before. In the process, they seem to have moved beyond a dualism which has bedevilled the church almost since its first meeting with Greek thought, and united their whole being, body and soul, in a sense of personal integration into divinity that all theology denied them. They managed to prove in their own persons the shortcomings of a reason which could only argue and not experience. It is surely one of the greatest gifts of this women's movement that they found themselves able to prove from their own experience that they were created in the image of God.

CHAPTER SIX

Two Remarkable Convents: Helfta and Assisi

The height of the medieval papacy was achieved during the reign of Innocent III from 1198 to 1216. Innocent benefited from two centuries of reform efforts and was able to actualise the claims which previous and, indeed, succeeding popes were able to make only on paper. For about one thousand years, popes had seen themselves as successors of Peter, presiding in the holiest of cities where the bones of the founding fathers, Peter and Paul, were deemed to lie. By Innocent's time, this claim had been elevated to new heights, vicar of Christ. The pope alone spoke for Christ and ecclesiastical power was thus centralised in the pope's own person. Because this *plenitudo potestatis* or fullness of power did not last – in practice – beyond the first few years of the thirteenth century, the actions of Innocent III have had an extraordinary influence throughout the remainder of Roman Catholic history. The Fourth Lateran Council in 1215 still influences church practice in a variety of ways, and can be said to have laid the foundations for the Roman Catholic tradition. With the growth of papal power went a certain decline in episcopal and monastic power, but a vast increase in the clericalisation of the church.

The growth of the universities added greatly to the character of the thirteenth century. From the middle of the twelfth century, the university of Paris had become pre-eminent for the study of law and theology, though it had been preceded by the already century-old universities of Salerno and Bologna. At Paris, students were divided into nations and colleges and there were three faculties – arts, theology and canon law. By the beginning of the thirteenth century, there were almost three thousand students there, all clerical. Oxford and Cambridge followed in the next few years, and eventually most cities had their own university. The fortuitous rediscovery of parts of the Aristotelian corpus aided the universities enormously in the formulations of the new theological conundrums and provided the world with two new figures of power, the theologian/intellectual and the bureaucrat who had become expert in canon law. The universities were now the avenue to all positions of significance and even popes were chosen from the ranks of university professors and masters.

As we have seen, the monastic life of the church had been extraordinarily diversified throughout the twelfth century. Even greater innovations were at hand. In 1209, Francisco Berhardone, son of an affluent Assisi merchant, renounced his heritage and wealth and founded the Franciscan Friars, to be followed in 1216 by a young Spaniard called Dominic Guzman, who founded the Dominicans. Collectively known as the Friars, these two groups, though initially quite different, provided similar ministries throughout the thirteenth century. The Franciscans were devoted to poverty and a more pastoral ministry, the Dominicans saw themselves as working primarily, through preaching and example, to rid the church of heresy. These two groups were town and city based and had shed, not without difficulty, the ancient stability of the monastic orders. In the Franciscans and Dominicans, the church now had a mobile and obedient body, who would go anywhere at the pope's command. They were to be enormously influential for the future history of the church, perhaps especially in the new accessibility of the ordinary people to evangelisation through good preaching.

The disastrous fourth crusade had been initiated in 1202, again in the early years of the reign of Innocent III, in an effort to remedy the failure of the third crusade to regain control of Jerusalem. Despite the participation of Richard the Lionheart of England, Philip Augustus of France, and the Emperor Frederick Barbarossa in the third crusade, the whole enterprise had fizzled out through internal disputes. The rise of the nation state played havoc with the notion of a papal universal army. The fourth crusade was an even greater trauma to the church, allowing itself to be deflected from its original purpose, the freedom of Jerusalem, and proceeding instead to Constantinople. The scandal of the sacking of this most ancient Christian city and its great church, Hagia Sophia, has never been erased from the eastern mind. The wealth of Constantinople was too tempting for the crusaders and the wrecking of one of the greatest places of worship in Christianity seemed irrelevant to them. The murderous and deeply intolerant attitude of the crusaders has stained the soul of western Christendom ever since.[1] The crusading idea, though initially giving rise and responding to some religious feeling among western knights, degenerated rapidly into a military machine which did untold damage. Once the idea took hold, however, it remained a constant temptation as a quick solution to ecclesiastical problems on the home front. Crusades were mounted against groups of dissenters, the most horrific being the crusade against the Albigensians, who were slaughtered in their thousands. This crusade also represented the failure of the Domincan ideal of holy preaching against holy enemies, and this failure was eventually compounded by the institution of the Inquisition by Pope Gregory IX in 1233. We shall explore this institution further in other sections of this work, because although women were not the only victims of the Inquisition, it was widely held that women were more prone to heresy because of the weakness of their intellect and their emotionality.

As church centralisation progressed into growing clericalisation, the laity descended once again to the bottom of the agenda. The rapid success of many heresies, based on the re -interpretation and dissemination of the scriptures, showed up the needs of the ordinary people for some spiritual nourishment in the turmoil that was the thirteenth century. The Cathar heresy became rooted in the area around Albi and whole generations of people grew up believing that this was Christianity. It must have been extremely difficult to distinguish heretical movements from their more orthodox cousins as many shared the same commitment to the *vita apostolica*, the cult of poverty and, inevitably, anti-clericalism. In general, lay people were presented by ecclesiastical reforms with two new possibilities. The first, the sevenfold sacramental system, not new but newly organised, and secondly, the popular devotion which grew up around the eucharist. The new power of the celibate clergy gained even more lustre from the power of consecration, and clerical control was spread to the life of each individual through the new sanction of confession as the necessary pre-requisite to the reception of holy communion. The rulings of the Fourth Lateran Council about annual confession and communion backfired, in a sense, on the church, as the people focused their attention on the consecrated host. The feast of Corpus Christi tended to give official approval to such devotion and it remained a powerful lay influence until recent times. Finally, the new insistence on confession with its resultant penances gave rise to new pastoral problems. What happened to people who were penitent but who had died before their assigned penances had been completed? The notion of purgatory had been growing in importance and now the need of people to shorten the purgatorial time of their loved ones, not to mention their own, was answered by the institution of indulgences. The stockpiling of indulgences henceforth came to be a standard part of church practice, and kept the laity busy for the next several centuries.

The thirteenth century then presents us with a series of responses to the growing power and wealth of a clericalised church. Despite the beauty of the great gothic cathedrals which furnish us with some of the greatest medieval imagery, the century must be remembered for an increase in savagery and a splitting of the church even further along clerical and lay lines. Women and men of the laity leave barely a record in ecclesiastical archives. As a group, they are a constant pre-occupation, however, and are perceived as an ever present threat in the bosom of 'Mother Church' as she came to be called at this time. Individual clerics appear in their hundreds, so that we have some sense of the ecclesiastical goals and devotions of the ordained male. The re-discovered lives of the Beguines, as we have seen, open a door to the spiritual aspirations and sometimes mighty achievements of some women. This chapter will look at two remarkable groups of women, confined in a sense to the ecclesiastical margins, but managing to achieve intense religious lives in religious enclaves that cannot fail to strike us as remarkable. These are the women of Helfta in Germany and Assisi in Italy. Neither group escaped entirely the ravages of the century, but their lives are marked by a serenity that can only be attributed to their own spiritual genius and to the wisdom of their Dominican and Franciscan advisors.

Helfta

For over fifty years the convent at Helfta was a centre of remarkable spiritual activity by women, and for forty of those years, it was presided over by one woman, the Abbess Gertrude of Hackeborn. Most of what we know of her has to be presumed from the richness and liveliness of the convent she ruled, but we know that she was born around 1232, was given as an oblate to the convent at the age of five, and was unanimously elected as its abbess at the remarkably young age of nineteen in 1251. Gertrude died in 1291 and we have very few other concrete details about her life. We know that she maintained high standards of educational excellence, that she attended to the growth of the convent library and to the excellence of its scriptorium. The course of studies consisted of the trivium and quadrivium, the standard university course in the liberal arts, and to this was added theology and the study of mystical prayer.[2]

Helfta was the third and final site of the convent founded by the Count and Countess of Mansfield in 1229 for a small group of nuns who intended to practise the Cistercian way of life. Helfta was never recognised as officially Cistercian, but is a good example of women who looked after their own interests, in the absence of other spiritual support. The move to Helfta in Saxony was made in 1258, and shortly thereafter, we find the convent supported and guided by the local Dominicans. Helfta itself was the gift of the two powerful brothers of the Abbess Gertrude. It grew to be a large and prosperous convent, housing as many as one hundred nuns, and attracting both welcome and unwelcome attention because of its prosperity. Helfta was occasionally pillaged by local brigands, but it survived under the good government of the Abbess and the protection of her brothers and of the Archbishop of Magdeburg. It was even able to found a daughter house in 1262. Helfta was destroyed in 1343 when it was caught up in a local dispute about episcopal succession.

The most extraordinary aspect of Helfta was the witness of its intense intellectual and mystical life, centred on the celebration of the liturgy, under the direction of the Abbess. We have no writings from Abbess Gertrude herself, but the writings of three extraordinary women have come down to us. These are the sister of Abbess Gertrude, Mechtild of Hackeborn, a younger contemporary and close friend, Gertrude of Helfta, and finally, the aging Beguine, Mechtild of Magdeburg, who retired to Helfta at the age of sixty-three. We shall look at the work of each of these in turn, and then make some concluding remarks on the influence of Helfta.

Mechtild of Hackeborn

Mechtild of Hackeborn followed her sister, Abbess Gertrude, into the convent at the age of seven in 1248. The story goes that the family was visiting Gertrude and that Mechtild refused to go home. She spent the rest of her life there and died in 1298 after a three year illness. Mechtild became the novice mistress and the *Donna Cantrix* or choir mistress of the community. She is reported to have had the voice of a nightingale and to have had all the sweetness of personal disposition to accompany her voice. For some years before her death, Mechtild had been the recipient of visions, often quite explicit directions about the conduct of the liturgy and also confirmation for her extensive involvement as a spiritual guide to many. She confided these visions to some of her sisters in the community, one of whom was probably the younger Gertrude of Helfta, and they were written down in a kind of biographical memoir, called the *Book of Special Graces*.[3] As Director of Novices, Mechtild would have been the teacher of these nuns and apparently she was quite distraught when they decided to write down her story of 'special graces'.

The whole of Mechtild's life was rooted in the liturgical round of the convent, the chants and hymns of the Divine Office and the daily and seasonal festivals celebrated in the eucharistic liturgy. Her whole life seems to shimmer through the exceedingly beautiful and highly colourful writing of her memoir. She was noted for bringing an intelligent piety to the prayer-life of the community. Her singing thrilled everyone; indeed the angels are said to have joined the community in reponse after Mechtild's intonation of the anthems. Whenever her voice failed her, angels took over her task. She was the community chantress for forty years and was known far and wide as the 'nightingale of Christ'. Mechtild also experienced Christ as a beautiful singer and one of her names for him was *cantor cantorum*.

Mechtild was also a learned teacher for the nuns of the community and a spiritual guide to multitudes who sought her help. Her advice is always colourful, sometimes homely and written in the most brilliant language: 'The Lover of your soul holds your hands in His, His fingers entwining yours, that He may show you how He works in your soul and how you ought to follow Him by imitating His example.' She then goes through the entwined fingers explaining the significance of each. To another correspondent she writes in an image familiar to every householder:

> When a powerful king is coming to lodge, one cleans the house immediately. But if he is so near that there is no time to throw out the dirt, one hides it in a corner till later. So, if one has the sincere desire to confess her sins and never to commit them again, they are erased from God's sight.

She continues her homely images, describing one vision of Jesus:

> My kitchen is my heart which, like unto a kitchen that is a

common room of the house and open alike to servants and masters, is ever open to all and for the benefit of all. The cook in this kitchen is the Holy Ghost, who kindly without intermission provides things in abundance.

Several devotions find their origin at Helfta, especially the devotion to the Sacred Heart. Mechtild of Magdeburg and Gertrude of Helfta are particularly known for this, but it seems a common part of the devotion of all the Helfta nuns. One Sunday, as the community was singing the *Asperges*, Mechtild asked the Lord to cleanse her heart:

> Straightway the Lord with love unutterable, bending to her as a mother would to a son, embraced her saying: 'In the love of my divine heart I will bathe thee', and he opened the door of his heart, the treasure house of flowing holiness, and she entered into it as though into a vineyard.

She goes on to describe the vineyard with twelve kinds of fruit and ponds full of fish with golden scales and dozens of other delights. It is obvious that for Mechtild and her sisters, there was no doubt about the beauty and colour of the heavenly realm, nor, as the quotations show, did she have any qualms about seeing Christ as female and herself as male. Besides singing and teaching, she speaks of spinning, weaving, dyeing, cooking, mending clothes and tending the sick. The convent was Mechtild's whole life, and the community regarded her as having a special advocacy with God. During the last few years of her life she was overcome by ill-health, but her community mediation continued. When there was word of marauding soldiers, she would not cease praying until Jesus assured her: 'You will not see a single soldier.' Like so many other convents, the sisters had to take sides in times of crisis, and Helfta also was put under interdict for choosing the wrong side. The silencing of all music and ceremony at Helfta must have been a particular torture to Mechtild. She died in 1298 shortly after their liturgical life was restored.

Gertrude of Helfta

One of the most extraordinary pupils of Mechtild must surely have been Gertrude of Helfta, also known as Gertrude the Great, and as all commentators add, not to be confused with Mechtild's own sister, the Abbess Gertrude of Hackeborn. The younger Gertrude seems to have been an orphan, or a casualty of one of the periods of turmoil in Germany. We have no information whatever about her except that she was brought as an oblate to the convent at the age of five in 1261. She was a brilliant student and was so musically gifted that she often replaced Mechtild as choir-director and community chantress. During her early life, though, she tells us that she found the convent an uncongenial place. Like so many other mystics, she is quite specific about the turning point in her life: 'I was in my twenty-sixth year. The day of my salvation was the Monday preceding the feast of the Purification of your most chaste Mother, which fell that year on the 27th of January. The desirable hour was after Compline as dusk was falling.' Gertrude is one of those women for whom we have both an autobiography and a biography. Both are contained in the *Herald of Divine Love*, a compilation of the Helfta community about Gertrude. Her autobiography is contained in Book II, written in her own voice and addressed directly to God. Books I, III and IV are written by another hand.[4] It seems that the major temptation of her early convent life was the seduction of the intellectual life and she felt as if she were a nun in appearance only. Her conversion was occasioned by the appearance of Jesus as a handsome youth of sixteen, questioning her grief and announcing that her salvation was at hand. With the promise, 'I shall make you drink from the torrent of my delights', her spiritual journey took off and never wavered again. In 1289, she wrote her autobiography, thus providing us for the first time with a personal account of the life of a most unusual Helfta nun. Gertrude is recognised by all as one of the most balanced of the mystics. She is highly emotional, but her faith is rooted in a God who balances justice and love in equal measure. In many ways, her life is more rooted in past patterns; for example, she insists more on the traditional virtue of obedience as the mainstay of monastic life, rather than on the new practices of voluntary poverty.

Gertrude is a counseller and mediator *par excellence* and sees this as the essence of her monastic life. She is absolutely convinced about her teaching role and knows with certainty that her authority comes directly from Christ. Despite her emphasis on obedience, Gertrude often bypasses monastic structures on Christ's authority and does not hesitate to see herself in clerical roles and with clerical authority. Gertrude's God is king, but is addressed too as mother. Christ is lover and bridegroom. Mary is mother, but also the marshaller of the forces of heaven. Like her Helfta sisters, Gertrude has little difficulty in transposing gender categories. The humanity of Christ is central to her spirituality because he is what we are and that is the source of union. Our humanity is in him, and in him it is joined to divinity. The great symbol of this is the eucharist, mystical union and, Gertrude's own favourite image, the Sacred Heart. Our ability to enter into the humanity of Christ means that our salvation is already accomplished. Our task is to unite ourselves to this humanity and Gertrude uses a host of images for this union – eating, drowning, swimming – in a union that has already taken place.

Gertrude's favourite image, besides the eucharist, is that of the Sacred Heart. Here the emphasis is not on suffering, but on the glory and triumph of a love which is never exhausted. Gertrude is at her most lyrical when she writes of this heart. It is her food, her shelter, her place of refuge, and the constant instigator to a love which will communicate the love of Christ to all. Though aware of the possibility of damnation for sin, Gertrude tends to emphasise the possibility of ever progressing toward God, confident of God's salvific love. She pays remarkably little attention to the devil or to the story of the Fall and certainly has no sense that, as a woman, she is presumed to share the fault of Eve. Gertrude's ascetic struggle is with obedience, but she writes gloriously about the goodness of all things. Her visions are dominated by a sense of the person on the move towards God rather than on the corruption of the world. For Gertrude, humanity is already wedded to divinity. In this, her spirituality has a definite eastern tinge. As Bynum points out, Gertrude's strong sense of community and of the necessity of obedience is rooted in her entrance to the convent at the age of five.

The lifestyle and spirituality of the new friars had penetrated Gertrude's consciousness about monastic life. If it is a hidden life, it must always be vicarious. She is there for the good of her sisters and for others. When she translates the scriptures or works of theology, when she prays or composes prayers, when she counsels or preaches, all of this is for the sake of others. She is simply Christ's channel of guidance, information and forgiveness to others. She has complete certainty about the priority of service. Together with her own teacher, Mechtild of Hackeborn, Gertrude provided years of guidance to the monastery. There is no doubt that they saw themselves as taking on priestly roles, at the direction of Christ. These women had no official administrative roles in the community – it was their visions that empowered them to become the mouth-pieces of God. When Gertrude hesitated one day about the roles she was assuming, Jesus in a vision assured her that he personally would give her all seven sacraments:

> For I baptise you in my precious blood; I confirm you in the power of my victory; I take you for my spouse in the pledge of my love; I consecrate you in the perfection of my most holy life; I absolve you from all chain of sin in the piety of my mercy; I feed you with myself in the superfluity of my charity, and satisfy you with delights; and I penetrate your entire being like ointment by the sweetness of my spirit ... that you may grow in sanctity and aptitude for eternal life.[5]

The spirituality of Helfta is a sacramental spirituality, but with a difference. Though not engaged in a critique of the clergy, as Mechtild of Magdeburg was, Gertrude did not hesitate to take on priestly roles. At the command of Christ, she was free to pass on the forgiveness of Christ to her sisters and to enage in the act of 'binding and loosing' as the priest did. This sense of authority seemed to come so naturally to her that we do not hear of any questioning by the community, or by the Dominican advisors of the community. On the Sunday after Easter, Christ came to Gertrude in a vision and breathed on her, saying: 'Receive the Holy Spirit. Whosoever sins you remit shall be remitted.' Gertrude challenged Christ: 'How can this be since the power of binding and loosing belongs only to priests?' Christ responded: 'Those whom you, discerning through my spirit, judge to be not guilty, will surely be accounted innocent before me ... for I will speak through your mouth.' Gertrude wonders why it is necessary for her to receive these gifts so often and Christ responds, showing that he is familiar with the current theology of priestly ordination: 'When anyone is consecrated to the diaconate and then into the priesthood, far from losing his office as deacon he just acquires a greater honour from the priesthood; so when I give a gift several times to a soul, truly it is established in it more firmly by repetition and its blessedness is thereby increased.' It is clear that Christ had yet to learn that the Sacrament of Orders could be administered only to men.

The eucharistic regulations of the Fourth Lateran Council seem to have created some kind of crisis of conscience in those preparing for holy communion. All through the writings from Helfta, we hear of the sisters and the laity coming to the nuns with scruples about their worthiness to receive. This kind of scrupulosity has not appeared before. One could say that the bulk of the counselling done by both Gertrude and Mechtild had to do with reassuring and challenging the scrupulous. The mixture of awe before the real presence and the threat to receive worthily seems to have placed many in a quandary. Gertrude has endless examples of people producing ever new reasons for abstaining from communion. Gertrude, apparently wearying of this, questioned their intention and then 'constrained' them to receive. Then she herself began to lose confidence. In response to a query, she was assured by Christ: '... never will I let anyone whom I judge unworthy of the vivifying sacrament of my body and blood ask this of you.' Christ went on to assure Gertrude that just as the universal church could rely on the promise once made to Peter about binding and loosing sins, so could Gertrude. 'And touching her tongue he said, "Behold, I give my words into your mouth …".'[6]

Though Gertrude hesitates about using the priestly power given her by Christ, she never raises the question of her gender. There was no doubt whatever in the thirteenth century about the ineligibility of women to preach and teach and to be ordained. Nevertheless, Gertrude's visions project her into a priestly role, which she exercises for the benefit of the community and all who come for help. Apart from the information about Gertrude in her own writing and the other books of the *Herald*, we also have a book of spiritual exercises composed by her for the benefit and instruction of her sisters. This book can be compared, both in spiritual depth and value, to the work of Ignatius of Loyola a few centuries later. The seven themes include exercises on conversion, renewal of the monastic profession, stirring up God's love and preparation for death. Her instructions are always balanced and yet inspiring. Gertrude herself tells us that she once asked Jesus to suggest to her a practice to commemorate his passion. Jesus suggested praying with her arms extended, and Gertrude responded immediately that such practices were not suited to the life at Helfta, nor were they part of their spirit. We are told that God loved her for the freedom of heart she displayed, which meant that he always had access to her.

The writings of these Helfta women are full of the joys of nature. Their awareness of and joy in their surroundings fill every page of their writings. Space does not allow a full exploration of this, but one quiet moment in the life of Gertrude is described thus:

> I had gone into the courtyard before Prime and was sitting beside the fishpond absorbed by the charms of the place. The crystalline water flowing through, the fresh green trees standing around, the birds circling in flight and above all the freedom of the dove gave me pleasure …

She went on to meditate that if she allowed the 'flowing streams' of God's graces to flow through her, she would grow like the trees with a 'fresh flowering of good works'.[7] Gertrude died in 1301, still singing the praises of the loving heart of Christ and filled with assurance that the moment of her death was the entrance to the life of total union she had always sought.

Mechtild of Magdeburg

One cannot help but be struck by the serenity and beauty of the life of the nuns at Helfta, as communicated in the memoir of Mechtild the nightingale and in the writings of Gertrude and her biographers. The third of the great Helfta mystics known to us had come to Helfta for precisely this peace and tranquility, little of which had been known to her in her previous life. Exhausted, going blind and fleeing the hazards of the life of a Beguine, Mechtild of Magdeburg arrived at the convent, aged sixty three, sometime in 1270. She had already completed the first six books of her famous mystical work, *The Flowing Light of the Godhead*, and was able to dictate the seventh book to one of her new sisters. In fact, it seems to have been the twelve-year stay of Mechtild of Magdeburg which turned the Helfta community into an amazing group of writers.[8]

Mechtild was born around 1207 and seems to have grown up in a family of lesser nobility. She was familiar, as we know from her writings, with the protocol and paraphernalia of court life and also with the conventions of the poetry of courtly love. Her first inkling of a call by the Holy Spirit came when she was twelve, but it was not until the age of twenty-two that she headed for Magdeburg to join the Beguine community there. Her writings, consisting of poetry, prose, hymns, allegories, letters, and visionary dialogues, seem to have occupied most of her life. Mechtild was a strong, argumentative and critical woman and she seems to have been heart-broken and deeply ashamed at the lack of fidelity of which she accuses the church of her day. Her writings were re-arranged by her Dominican guide, Heinrich of Halle, and he professes his astonishment at what he calls her 'masculine' style. Mechtild wrote in Low German, but that text is not extant. Nevertheless, she has always been recognised not only as the greatest German Beguine, and an extraordinary spiritual genius, but also as one of the most important lyric poets in the German tradition. What differentiates her specifically from her sister mystics at Helfta is the constant sense of danger and persecution that pervades her writings. She seems to have felt under threat both as a Beguine and as a contemplative and prophetic mystic, and despite Dominican support and protection, she was an exhausted and almost broken woman when she finally retired to Helfta.

During her forty years in Magdeburg, Mechtild lived an intense life of asceticism and prayer, and seems to have been constantly at loggerheads with the clerics there whom she castigated as 'stinking goats' and 'Pharisees'. She worked ceaselessly and spoke publicly about church reform and refused to cease her efforts despite episcopal rebuke. She seems to have been haunted by the sinfulness of the church and the dilemma faced by a loving God when such sinfulness was punished. Her whole life and writings circled endlessly around the idea and experience of unconditional love and its consequences. The notion of suffering predominates in her work, in contrast also to the Helfta nuns, partly from her own experiences of persecution, and partly from her sense of the necessity of identifying with the sufferings of Jesus. This also gives her writings a driving, anxious and restless quality, which draws the reader into her unending pursuit of divine love. Mechtild's position in the world also reveals a greater awareness of herself as a woman, and she develops her sense of being female in both positive and negative ways. There is a double poisonous sap in the female body as a result of the sin of Eve which designates the woman not only as having a tendency towards sin, but as being designed for suffering. Through her female body she feels she is dragged down toward the earthly temptations of false love and bodily indulgence. On the other hand, females are more available for and gifted with the ability to suffer. In one vision, Christ assured her: 'You will be martyred with me, betrayed by envy, sought out by falsehood, captured by hatred ...' and so on through all the sufferings of Christ's passion, until finally 'you shall rise from the death and ascend into heaven, drawn by God's breath'.[9]

Nevertheless, Mechtild is convinced that, because of the humanity of Jesus, sin is not intrinsic to human nature. In fact, it is this conviction and the abundant appearance to the contrary in her own life and throughout the church, that is the source of her greatest suffering. This agonising sense of sinful inadequacy gives rise to her devotion to the Sacred Heart, and for Mechtild, it is a broken heart. Penitence, then, is more at the heart of her life than in that of her Helfta sisters, as she seems to have borne the weight of a sinful world on her own shoulders. She wished to take the whole of corrupt Christianity in her arms. 'Our Lord said: "Let be! It is too heavy for you!" No, sweet Lord, I will lift it up ....And God let me have my will, that so I might find rest.'[10] The goal of Mechtild's life, then, is to remove not only sin and corruption from the church, but also she wishes to take upon herself the whole punishment. She cannot tolerate the notion of hell or of eternal punishment and feels a personal responsibility for the release of all from such a fate. Hence her enormous belief in the efficacy of prayer.

The sense of the all pervasive love of God underlies her preoccupation with sin and suffering. She cannot equate the notion of eternal damnation with the God she has come to know in her own life. Distance from God she can appreciate and indeed has experienced as a cleansing force, but hell is beyond her comprehension. She challenges Christ on this theme constantly, questioning him sharply about how he can bring himself to leave souls there. Left to herself, she says, she would empty out hell. Despite the contemporary church teaching that souls in hell are beyond the reach of prayer, Mechtild constantly prays for them and harries Christ into responding to her prayers, alms and good works for these souls.[11] Mechtild even offers to go down to hell to see if she can re-unite these poor abandoned souls with their heavenly lover.

Mechtild never blames human beings for their sins, as her opinion of redeemed humanity is linked inevitably with the redeeming humanity of Christ. She even challenges learned opinion on this. If sin were human, Christ would have sinned, she says, and that is simply impossible. Sin, for her, is always demonic. One would find nowhere in the writings of Mechtild anything approximating the expression 'It is only human'. She would find such a thought incomprehensible. For her humanity had been raised once and for all with Christ. Holding such a view, one can understand the constant theme of suffering and anguish in her life. It is no small thing to set onself the life-task of emptying hell. At least, Mechtild could console herself that she had some success in purgatory. On one day alone, she reports that she liberated seventy thousand souls from this prison. Her commentators suggest that Mechtild almost credits humans as having two natures, like Christ, and that it would be possible to be 'held so tightly' by God's love that we need not sin. For at the bottom of all Mechtild's teaching is the absolute conviction of love. She cannot imagine God not loving and she cannot imagine any human being, damned or otherwise, not yearning for God's love. If humans yearn, then it is God's very nature to respond.

Despite this intense longing to save the whole of humanity, Mechtild always seems alone and isolated. She experiences herself as a mediator, counsellor and teacher for others and takes this task on as a heavy responsibility. She sees that compassion is central to the life of Jesus, and indeed to the life of the Trinity, and she herself sets out to act the same way with the compassion of a mother for her children. Mechtild's visions seem to be her only source of companionship and some reveal an extraordinary intimacy with God. On one occasion, no priest has come to say Mass and she challenges Jesus about this: 'Lord! Must I be without Mass this day?' She was instantly provided with everything she needed. John the Evangelist heard her confession, and John the Baptist celebrated the eucharist. When she published this vision, she was criticised for portraying that John the Baptist, a layman, could say Mass. She was not slow to answer: 'No pope nor bishop nor priest could speak the Word of God as John the Baptist spoke it ... Was he then a layman? Instruct me ye blind! Your lies and hatred will not be forgiven without suffering.'[12] As we can see from this event, the eucharist was central to her life and she admits that she has not revealed the depth of intimacy that she experienced at Mass. She marvelled at God's vulnerability in the eucharist: 'Yet I, least of all souls, take him in my hand, eat him and drink him, and do with him what I will! Why then should I trouble myself as to what the angels experience?' Mechtild even challenges God about the fact that he has not made her a 'learned priest', but almost immediately reflects on the consequent temptations of power. As Book 6 of her writings begins, 'Great danger lies in power.'

It is the lack of power that is the greatest benefit to women. This is what saves most women from hell – in her visions, she saw only princesses there. On the other hand, the lower reaches of hell were filled with men – clerics in particular. The freedom of women from power is loved by God because it liberates the female soul and allows God unlimited access. In Mechtild, God is nearly always male, and the church and souls are female. Her sense of reality in this area is much more stereotypical than many other women mystics. Her position as a Beguine in the world made her much more conscious of the disqualification of her gender, even though in God's eyes, being female was a major blessing. Mechtild, as bride, had a hunger for God and, like other women mystics, needed to see, hear and touch God. Eventually, her mystical path led her to the experience of the no-thingness that is at the core of God. Like Marguerite Porete, she learned to peel back the 'things' that we affirm of God and find the no-thing at the core:

> This is the nature of great love, it does not flow with tears, it rather burns in the great fire of heaven. In the fire it flows swiftly, and yet remains in itself a great stillness. It rises almost up to God, yet remains small in itself ... Ah most blessed love! Where are those who know you? They are wholly irradiated in the Holy Trinity, they no longer live in themselves.[13]

One can imagine the peace that filled Mechtild's soul when she finally arrived at Helfta at the age of sixty-three. She seems to have lost none of her energy there as her presence unleashed a flood of creativity in that community, already shimmering with life. Mechtild of Hackeborn seems to have formed a special relationship with the 'ancient sybil of the Rhine', as Hans Urs von Balthasar christened her. This is where Mechtild was to die. While she was still at Magdeburg, she had asked God about death:

> Lord, I still have a great dread as to the way in which my soul shall pass from my body. Then the Lord said: It shall be thus. I will draw my breath and your soul shall come to me as a needle to a magnet.[14]

When death was drawing near at Helfta, she asked God what to do in her last days and was told to do exactly as she had in her first days, namely, to keep herself in love, longing, repentance and fear. When her time came, she took her leave with her usual sense of self-possession and poetry:

> When I am about to die, I take leave of all from which I must part. I take leave of Holy Church; I thank God that I was called to be a Christian and have come to real Christian belief. Were I to remain here longer I would try to help Holy Church which lies in many sins. I take leave of all poor souls in purgatory. Were I to be longer here I would gladly help to expiate their sins and I thank God that they will find mercy...
> I take leave of all sinners who lie in mortal sin ...
> Of all penitents working out their penance ...
> Of all my enemies ...
> Of all earthly things ...
> Of all my dear friends ...
> Of all my wickedness ... of my suffering body ...

And then she turned her eyes to heaven with its floods of light, where all 'sing for joy and laugh and leap in ordered dance. They flow and swim and fly and climb from tiered choir to choir, still upward through the height.'[15] It seems that after a 'foolish' childhood and a 'troubled' youth, and a life which, according to herself, produced little in the way of 'shining works', Mechtild of Magdeburg had finally reached her heart's desire: 'In loving, to die of love.'

Assisi

Mechtild was the last of the German Beguines and in many ways the convent at Helfta represents one of last great flowering of women's mysticism at this time. The convent did not last much longer and was totally destroyed in the never-ending warfare of the next fifty years. But Germany and the Lowlands were not the only sites of women's lives of utter devotion. Italy was also full of the fire of religious renewal at this time, and among the greatest practitioners of the *vita apostolica* were Francis of Assisi and the woman who was called his most faithful disciple, Clare. For forty years, Clare persisted with an absolutely indomitable will in the effort to have her rule approved by the church. She had to fight against the restrictions imposed by Pope Innocent III and the Fourth Lateran Council on the founding of any new orders. She successfully resisted five other attempts by popes and cardinal protectors to have the Benedictine rule imposed on her community, and eventually succeeded in her endeavour, if only for a short time and for her own convent. On 10 August 1253, Pope Innocent IV visited her on her deathbed, with the approved new Form of Life. Clare received it with joy and also distress that it was so much less than she desired. She died the next day, and the sisters had to resist the Pope's efforts to canonise her even before she died. She was eventually canonised two years later.

The story of Clare has usually been appended as an interesting footnote to that of Francis of Assisi. She deserves attention in her own right, however, because she was the first woman, and remains one of only a handful, to have her own rule recognised by the church. Nevertheless, despite their very different starting points, the lives of Clare and Francis were completely intertwined, and they seem to have been drawn to each other by very strong spiritual and emotional ties. Clare came from one of the noble families of the area, and her birth was proclaimed from the altar of the church in reponse to prayers for her safe delivery. A voice from heaven was heard saying: 'Fear not, woman, for you shall bring forth without danger a light that shall greatly illumine the world.'[16] The baby girl was accordingly named Chiara, the bright one, after her birth in 1194. A few years earler, in 1181, Pietro Bernardone, a rich merchant, had a son, Francis, who seems to have lived a fairly normal life until after being a prisoner of war in one of the local intercity skirmishes, decided to abandon the world and devote himself to the poor. Companions were not slow to join him and, already before he had met Clare, he had a simple rule approved in 1209 by Innocent III.

The merchants of Assisi, including Francis' father, were trying to form a commune and were in constant conflict with the nobility, including Clare's father. Apart from the spiritual turmoil about property and poverty, a huge socio-economic and political change was occurring in the city that was home to these two heroes of poverty. Their spiritual decisions were taken at a time when capitalism was being born. Clare had been dispensing food and money to the poor from the family home, to her mother's approval and her father's intense disapproval. She was reputed to be exceedingly beautiful and a fine marriage to advance the family fortunes was expected of her. Francis had taken a vow of poverty in 1208, and in 1211, he had begun public preaching in the Cathedral of San Rufino. It seemed inevitable that these two would meet, and in fact they communicated frequently throughout the year 1211. Clare realised that she was being asked not just to share with the poor, but actually to be poor, like Jesus, and Francis. In 1212, this is what she resolved to do and she never relinquished this resolve. Her intention was that God, the great Almsgiver, would take care of her. Her sister, Agnes, decided to accompany her in the implementation of this resolve. Together with Francis, they laid their plans for the evening of Palm Sunday. Clare was to attend Mass dressed in her best finery, as befitted a bride. That evening, she escaped from her home and after several adventures with the family in pursuit, she eventually met with Francis. After receiving the tonsure from him, she finally settled in San Damiano, the church which Francis had repaired.

From 1212 until her death in 1253, Clare remained the inspiration and leader of a group of women which, in a very short time, numbered over ten thousand, scattered throughout central Italy. In 1216, she was given the title of Abbess of the convent at San Damiano, though she always resisted titles, preferring that everyone be called simply sister. Clare's one aim in religious life was to practise total poverty, what was called the *privilegium paupertatis*, that is the privilege of owning nothing. This desire put her at odds with the ecclesiastical trends of the time in several ways. The Fourth Lateran Council had forbidden the creation of any new religious orders – even Francis had to struggle not to have the Rule of St Augustine imposed on him. This created considerable and continuous conflict between Clare and the Roman curia. The church's aim for women was that they be enclosed in a monastic setting, according to the Benedictine rule, and that their solemn vows would separate them forever from the world. Clare's aim was that, like Francis, she would work and beg, have no official rule but a simple form of life, and be of constant service to the poor. Begging and enclosure were essentially in contradiction, and the service of the poor conflicted with the church's desired goal for women, which was the daily round of chants and offices in a life of prayer, hidden away from the world. Clare had to make the inevitable compromises about enclosure eventually, and her relationship with Francis seems to have become more distant. But she never let go of her longing for poverty. She was at constant pains to point out the difference between traditional vowed poverty which allowed for communally owned property, and the kind of poverty she desired which was to own nothing communally or personally.

We have some insight into the early life of Clare and her followers from the writings of Jacques de Vitry, who passed through Assisi in 1216, on the way to his consecration as Bishop of Acre. His interest in women's religious lives had not declined

in the three years since he had written the life of Mary of
Oignies, and he has left us one of the few testimonies to Clare's
actual experiences at this time. They lived by their own work or
on alms given to them by the friars or the people of Assisi.
Jacques de Vitry was impressed by the fact that the sisters were
'greatly distressed and perturbed because, by both clergy and
laity, they are honoured more than they would wish to be'.[17] He
further reported that the women lived according to the pattern
of the primitive church and lived together in complete harmony.
This early freedom did not last long, and eventually the communities had to accept a form of enclosure by order of Pope
Gregory IX in 1239. It is said that Clare never went out again, but
the struggle about poverty continued for decades.

Clare's devotion to Francis remained undiminished, but it
seems that they were never as close again in fact. Francis instructed his friars to visit the sisters 'rarely and unwillingly', and
to avoid at all costs the 'snares of female companionship'. She always spoke of him as the 'blessed father' and told her sisters that
he wanted them to 'have no fear of poverty, toil, tribulation, re-
viling and the world's scorn, but rather to hold them as highly
delectable things'. Clare urges her sisters to remain faithful always to these ideals: 'And thus I was ever anxious with my sisters to preserve the holy poverty which we promised to God and
the blessed Francis; and thus the abbesses who succeed me in
this office, and all the sisters, are bound to observe it unbroken
to the end – that is, in not receiving or holding any possession or
property by themselves or through any intermediary, nor anything which can reasonably be called property, save only as
much land as necessity demands for decent provision of the
monastery; and that land shall not be worked except for a gar-
den to serve their own needs.'[18]

This is, obviously, as Bynum says, a vision of a utopian way
of life, but everything we know of Clare's regulations for her sisters is marked by moderation. She was probably anorexic herself and had ruined her own health through excessive fasting in
her early years, but she regulated against any such extremes by

her sisters. She reminded them that they were not made of stone, and that the sick especially should have access to proper food, care, 'wooly socks' and warm blankets. She apparently hated giving orders and urged that every decision be made communally, including the parcelling out of the community tasks. She also hated any kind of hierarchical arrangements and resisted all honours directed towards herself. Thomas of Celano, the prolific Franciscan writer, called her a 'new captain of womankind'. Clare was also much more open than Francis apparently was about male and female interaction. For her, brothers and sisters were meant to live together and share their spiritual gifts. She believed that women were as tough as men and that women should not rely on the service of men. The government of the community by consensus was a complete innovation, and probably understood by nobody except Clare herself. Clare introduced processes to help novices to part responsibly with all their possessions. She instructed her sisters to recite the office rather than sing it, as she saw music as a distraction from the words. It is also a sign of a more humble life and makes allowances for all, even those who cannot sing or read. Clare was always attentive to those considered of least importance and suggested that they often knew best, and should always be consulted. She showed total confidence in the personal decisions of the sisters themselves and urged each one to feel responsible for all. Forgiveness was the hallmark of her community, and it is probably the only convent that does not dwell on the punishment of sisters for infractions. The unity of mutual love should do away with such sanctions.

These ideals of Clare sound very similar to those of the Beguines, though we have little written evidence of internal Beguine life. The church, and most others thought her foolhardy, but what motivated Clare, she shared with all her sisters, whether in Flemish Beguine groups or German convents, a new and remarkable confidence in the ability of women to love and to form communities founded on love.

CHAPTER SEVEN

Women Challenging Church:
Marguerite Porete and Catherine of Siena

When Barbara Tuchman wrote her fascinating book on the 'calamitous' fourteenth century, she discerned many parallels between that distant time and the late twentieth century, not least in the distance that existed between stated beliefs and principles and their concrete expression and implementation.[1] Then it was the church, the aristocracy and the politicians (the latter two being roughly synonymous) who were named as the cause of such discrepancy, especially in their misuse and abuse of power. Today, though the power of the universal church, as it was expresed in the all-embracing role of Christendom, has decreased considerably, nevertheless similar critiques have been appearing more and more frequently. The politicians, of course, now of a less aristocratic variety for the most part, still attract so much heated debate that the end of politics is forecast. What Tuchman was exploring in particular was the ability of a society to recover after a calamity of monumental proportions, in her case the horrendous Black Death. When she was writing in the late seventies of the twentieth century, she was thinking in particular of the ravages of wars in Europe and elsewhere. Both church and politics have been assailed in our day by serious calamities which have damaged their credibility. Perhaps the challenging and reforming efforts of two fourteenth century women have something to teach us on the brink of a new century.

The two women in question are Marguerite Porete, who was burned to death as a relapsed heretic on 1 June 1310, and Catherine of Siena, who was born the year in 1347, the year the Black Death began, and after a life of reforming efforts, died, it is said, of a broken heart on 3 April 1380, at the age of thirty-three.

Both women burned with an intensity of desire for the reform of the church that leaps from the pages of their writings even today. Catherine's efforts were confirmed by sainthood, and more recently, by being named a Doctor of the Church. Marguerite Porete's efforts were vilified, condemned as heretical, and she paid the ultimate penalty of death by burning at the stake. This chapter will explore, all too briefly, the lives of these two women, beginning with Marguerite Porete, whose star is beginning to rise again in our day, if only in the pages of historians and analysts of medieval spirituality.

Marguerite Porete

Despite the arrival of a new generation of scholars interested in the work of Marguerite Porete, we still know hardly anything about her. She is thought to have been a Beguine of Hainaut who wrote her book, *The Mirror of Simple Souls*, sometime in 1296.[2] It was addressed to the general public and women in particular, and seems to have achieved instant popularity. Soon afterwards, however, it was condemned by the Bishop of Cambrai and burned in the public square of Valenciennes. Its use was prohibited under pain of excommunication.[3] Marguerite refused to stop teaching and may even have added the final, most clearly autobiographical section in the ensuing years. She also took the precaution of seeking a second opinion, and sent her book to three theologians, who approved of her work but suggested that it might not be for 'simple' souls. Eventually, she was reported to the chief inquisitor, and on her refusal to appear before the court, she was imprisoned in Paris for eighteen months, the legal interval required for consideration of one's position. While in prison, Marguerite seems to have maintained a total silence; at least she refused to meet with the inquisition and take the required oath to tell the 'truth' and retract her teaching. Twenty-one of the most renowned theologians of the age were assembled from the University of Paris and on 31 May 1310, she was condemned and handed over to the secular authorities. On the following day, 1 June, she was burned at the stake in the Place de Grève in Paris, in the presence of the civil and religious authorities. The dignified and serene demeanour of Marguerite Porete is said to have converted many to her teaching. At any rate, that was not the end of her book. It enjoyed a wide circulation and eventually entered the mainstream again as the supposed work of a Carthusian monk. As such, the work was greeted as a holy testimony to the work of God in the soul of a mystic. When the author, in this century, was once more recognised as the woman, Marguerite Porete, it was again greeted as an outlandish and heretical document. It was only in 1946 that the Italian scholar, Romana Guarneri, definitely recognised *The Mirror* as Marguerite's work, and in recent decades there has been an intense interest in the book, especially by scholars of spirituality and mysticism, as well as literary critics. Marguerite Porete is now recognised as one of the greatest vernacular authors of the Middle Ages, as well as one of the most influential mystical writers of any period.

Marguerite Porete happened to live what must have been an extraordinary mystical life at precisely the wrong moment in the history of the church. From the middle of the thirteenth century, as we have seen, there had been growing ecclesiastical suspicion about the Beguines. The Council of Lyons in 1274 reiterated the decrees of the Fourth Lateran Council banning new religious orders and focused especially on groups such as the Beguines. All such unenclosed groups of women were lumped together as semi-heretical in their disobedience and teaching, and popular opinion began to turn against them. There was, nevertheless, great confusion. In some areas, the Beguines continued undisturbed. The great Beguinage in Paris, founded by Louis IX in 1264, had over 400 members, and was protected by both the papacy and the royal house. Philip the Fair became King of France in 1285, and set himself up as the sacred and most pious guardian of the faith in a holy and faith-filled country. This was partly as a result of his piety, but also was intentionally directed against the centralising efforts of the papacy and the papal requirement of tax revenues from France. The loyalties of the

French clergy and people moved gradually from the pope to the king, and Philip the Fair used every opportunity available to cement this loyalty and change ecclesiastical revenue into royal revenue. One of the test-cases was that of the Templars.

The Templars were a military religious order, founded early in the twelfth century as part of the crusading effort. They developed into a huge international organisation, with banking and property interests across most of Europe and beyond. They were a power to be reckoned with and the King of France decided to expel them from his territories. In 1307, the property of the French Templars was confiscated, and to justify such actions, they were charged with the usual scape-goating offences of homosexuality, theft and heresy. The pope was deeply affronted by these actions against men whom he considered his protegés, but his protests were ignored. Early in 1310, fifty-four Templars were burned to death in a field outside Paris and two years later the Order was suppressed.[4]

Ill-feeling remained high between the papacy and the French throne and the trial and execution of the heretic, Marguerite Porete has been seen by scholars as a way for this most Christian king to curry the pope's favour. The documents of both trials have survived and present a fascinating account of the harsh-grinding wheels of inquisitorial justice. A strange character called Guiard de Cressonessart, also known as the 'Angel of Philadelphia', had presented himself as Marguerite's defender. He was imprisoned and also went to trial, but recanted at the last moment and escaped the stake. The trial records make it clear that Marguerite Porete did not recognise the Paris Inquisition as having any authority in her life. She refused either to ask for or accept absolution. William of Paris, the Dominican inquisitor, assembled his collection of twenty-one theologians and canonists and had first to decide whether the case was theological or legal. Disparate propositions were excerpted from her book and treated as propositional truths in a way that directly contradicted Marguerite's whole theological intention. Perhaps her silence indicated that she knew that she did not stand a chance, or perhaps she had reached the heights of mystical serenity as described in her book. Marguerite Porete, this single apparently homeless Beguine, was seen as an enormous threat to the power and security not only of the French kingdom, but also of the security of the church itself. She was a solitary and itinerant Beguine, apparently travelling through the towns of northern France disseminating her message. She wrote in the vernacular and, more than any other woman we know, insisted on the authority of her own voice. Marguerite appealed to no vision, no witness of great asceticism, and no surrounding religious community. She stood alone preaching when she could, and when this was no longer possible, she maintained an eighteen-month silence till her appalling death. The content of her teaching gives some indication why she caused so much fear in the hearts of churchmen and royalty alike.

The medieval world of Marguerite's time was bustling with theological ideas and fervour. Three particular kinds of theology dominated the field. First of all, and the newest theological stream was the theology of the schools, called ever since scholastic theology. This theology had developed from the seeds sown by Abelard and Peter Lombard and used the art of reasoning to solve the dilemmas of faith caused by the disagreement of patristic and other authorities. The newly discovered works of Aristotle raised even newer questions, but also provided the logical and philosophical tools to resolve them. In a patristic sense, this theology was also a development of the work of Augustine of Hippo and his followers, and the dictum, *credo ut intellegam*, 'I believe that I may understand' was key to the whole enterprise. The more traditional brand of theologising represented by the monastic tradition, still continued, but its last great practitioner, Bernard of Clairvaux, had been dead now since 1153. The tradition still continued in the monasteries and was taken up by the new religious orders, especially the Franciscans. This monastic theology could be said to focus on the dictum *credo ut experiar*, 'I believe that I may experience'. As a scholastic education came to be a requirement for all clerics and monks, however, theology of the scholastic variety seemed to command the field. A third major theological contribution was now being offered in the vernacular, by both male and female mystics, but the women mystics were central to this strand, both in numbers and popularity and in the spiritual genius displayed in their works.[5] This spiritual and theological strand was an almost entirely new creation, and was a direct challenge to the other theological streams, not only in its content, but in the insistence of the mostly women practitioners on preaching and disseminating their insights through their writing. Thus questions were raised about the roles of women and men that had seemed settled for centuries, and also about the respective roles of clergy and laity, and their right to preach and teach. To add to the difficulties, vernacular mystical theology presented itself in quite different ways. It spoke through poetry and dialogue instead of through the monastic medium of biblical commentary or the new scholastic medium of the *summa*, a systematic and scientific presentation of Christian teaching. The new vernacular theologians used letters, sermons, face-to-face counselling, visionary accounts and hagiography to present their teaching, and precisely because they used the vernacular rather than the traditionally sacred Latin language, their work was all the more widely disseminated.

To add to this, the new vernacular theology focused on love as the primordial Christian value. Everything was directed to the experience of divine love, even in the secular world of everyday life. This transferral of the possibility of holiness from the monk and theologian to the ordinary person was an entirely new addition to the medieval scene. The practice of mysticism had been seen as an exclusively monastic, and even there rare, phenomenon. Now, mysticism was being democratised and the refrain that is a constant in church tradition was being repeated more and more frequently, the 'simple faithful' are being confused. There is no doubt whatever that the work of many of the women mystics is quite difficult to comprehend. Scholars who have spent a life-time studying these texts warn against the assumption that we can grasp them fully. So it is quite possible that many would be potentially confused. Nevertheless, that was not the intention of the mystics. It was to spread abroad the love of God that they themselves had experienced.

As the thirteenth century dawned, new themes appeared in the writings of the mystics that gave them a totally new direction. What was being explored was the very nature of mystical union. What kind of union with God is possible to us in this world? This was a fairly esoteric question even within the monastic walls. When it was being formulated in convent parlours and on the streets, it caused many a ripple on the theological landscape. Traditional mystical union had been formulated in the imagery taken from the Song of Songs, an imagery of the lovers' embrace and the hunger and seeking by lover and beloved for each other. The goal was a union of wills in love, never forgetting the unbridgeable gap between the divine lover and the human beloved. Medieval women, starting from their own mystical experiences, began to speak differently about this union. They spoke of a union that removed all differences, a union of identity between God and the soul, a union that eventually led the believer to look in the mirror and see not the human face but the divine face. Marguerite Porete was one of the main articulators of such a mysticism in her aptly named book, *The Mirror of Simple Souls*. Even the title gives an indication of her intention – she was offering such a mirror, where even the simplest woman could experience this absolute indentity between the divine and her own soul. One would have to agree, initially, with the theologian chosen by Marguerite, Godfrey of Fontaines, who gave his approval to the work, but suggested that it might not be for the simple.

Based on the translation of Ellen Babinsky, an attempt will now be made to communicate the direction and intention of the thought of Marguerite Porete, followed by a brief analysis of its importance and an even briefer exploration of the influence of Marguerite on one of the greatest medieval mystics, Meister Eckhart, the Dominican. Until recently, it was believed that

Marguerite and other Beguines took their teaching from
Eckhart, the Master. Now it seems certain that the influence was
entirely the other way. *The Mirror of Simple Souls* is a spiritual
handbook for all who want to venture on the greatest spiritual
quest of all – union with God. It is designed around a dialogue
between several symbolic figures, of whom the most important
are Lady Love, Reason, the Far-Nigh (Marguerite's wonderful
name for the Trinity) and the Soul. The object of the discussion is
to penetrate the relationship between the discursive and willing
faculties of the soul, or the role played by knowledge and love in
the journey toward God. Marguerite shows herself to be quite
cognisant of the scholastic method, but it is obvious from the
start that Reason is not going to stand a chance in the dialogue
with Love.

For Marguerite, there are seven stations along the road to the
place where God and the soul are one. Along the way, she describes three deaths that the soul must undergo and two different kinds of soul. Only the most general overview of her work
can be offered here, but enough, hopefully, to give a flavour of
the radical and uncomprising nature of her thought.[7] The first
four stages correspond, more or less to the usual mystical path –
that of the commandments, the evangelical counsels, the works
of perfection which enlarge the space for love, until finally, in
station four, the soul feels itself consumed in an ecstasy of love
and is convinced, for a time, that this is the end of the journey.
Indeed, in traditional mysticism, this was the high-point where
the two wills of the Lover and beloved become united in one
transport of loving union. It is the next transition and the next
two stations which constitute the truly innovative part of
Marguerite's experience and teaching, and it is here precisely
that the inquisition focused its attention.

This is the move beyond will, where the soul must 'depart its
own will' and render itself back to God.[8] At creation, each soul is
given free will and with this free will, the first act is to will differently than God. Now is the time to return this free will to its
creator. God gave the soul this free will gratuitously, 'without a

why', and that is how the soul must now live, 'without a why', because 'one has the why within'.[9] This intriguing phrase is central to Marguerite's mysticism. Hers is not the calculated path of the virtues, where in fact one's will is focused on oneself and one's own perfection. Speaking of the virtues, she says: 'Whoever serves a poor Lord a long time becomes poor in waiting for a small wage. Thus it is that the Virtues ... do not grasp anything about the being of Noble Love'.[10] Now as she lives 'without a why' the mystic is enabled to move beyond the virtues, and beyond all mediation, for she has become identical to and lost in Lady Love. 'I am what I am, says this Soul, by the grace of God. Therefore I am only that which God is in me, and not some other thing. And God is the same thing that He is in me for nothing is nothing. Thus He is Who is.'[11] God cannot take the will; it must be freely given. This is the special task of the fifth station and once it has been accomplished, the soul is described as annihilated, brought to nothingness. Marguerite uses the metaphors of iron burning in the fire and taking on the qualities of fire to illustrate this nothingness, and in a beautiful image, the river that runs into the sea.

> Thus she would be like a body of water which flows from the sea, which has some name, as one would be able to say Aisne or Seine or another river. And when this water or river returns into the sea, it loses its course and its name with which it flowed in many countries in accomplishing its task. Now it is in the sea where it rests, and thus has lost all labour.[12]

It is now God who wills in the soul. It is also at this station that love and knowledge become one, as the intellect is no longer directed merely to created things. Reason is now the servant and Love reigns supreme. Reason has done its proper work together with the virtues through the first four stations. Now, its presence has changed definitively. Now the soul reaches true understanding and is focused only on divine truth, and has left behind the lower forms of intellect represented by Marguerite as knowing and perceiving.

At station five, the true nature of her soul is revealed to the mystic, and it is here that the apophatic nature of Marguerite's thought becomes evident. Michael Sells calls this the 'language of unsaying'. When faced with the transcendent, one has a choice of three responses, silence, kataphatic speech or the need to explain, make distinctions and what we might call 'theologise', or finally, apophasis, or the recognition that the transcendent is beyond all names, and that God is 'no-thing'. In apophatic speech, no single statement about the divine can stand on its own as a meaningful proposition. It becomes a language of double propositions and meaning is found in the tension between the two. In this way, as Sells points out, the essentialism of being and gender is undone.[13] This is accomplished by Marguerite when she reconceptualises the God of Christianity as male and female, but speaking through the female voice of Lady Love. It is at this point that Reason takes leave because it cannot bear the paradoxes of Love:

> Reason cries: 'How can anyone say such things? I do not dare to hear them. I fail, Lady soul, in hearing you. My heart has failed. I live no more.'[14]

What has caused the death of Reason? It is the new speech adopted by Marguerite as she comes to an understanding of her own nothingness:

> Lord, you are One Goodness, through overflowing goodness, and all in yourself. And I am One Wretchedness, through overflowing wretchedness, and all in myself.
> Lord, you are, and thus everything is perfected through you and nothing is made without you. And I am not, and thus everything is made without me, and nothing is made through me.
> Lord, you are all power, all wisdom, and all goodness without beginning, without being contained, and without end. And I am all weakness, all ignorance, and all wretchedness, without beginning, without being contained, and without end.[15]

When Marguerite describes the Soul's arrival at this point of the

journey, she depicts the falling away of all other mediation.
'And one sole encounter or one meeting with the ultimate eternal ancient and ever-new goodness is more worthy than anything a creature might do, or even the whole Holy Church, in a
hundred thousand years. His farness is greater nearness'.[16] As
the soul becomes annihilated, the Holy Spirit rushes in to fill it
with love, like air rushing into a vaccuum. The Holy Spirit now
fills the soul and generates the Trinity within her.[17] The mystic
then experiences the fulness of divinity and is lifted into divine
existence. Now the soul has truly become a mirror. God sees
only Godself in the soul. In conventional imagery, the mirror
represented the falseness and vanity of women. Here, Marguerite,
as with so many other images, reclaims the image of the mirror
as the deepest sign of truth and humility. The soul has become
completely transparent to God. This divine seeing of the divine
in the soul of the mystic is but a flash, a spark, the brief opening
of an aperture, which signals the arrival of station six. It lasts but
a moment, but brings the soul back to her pre-created state,
'where she was before she was'.[18] Now the soul has become established in this new state of being. It moves between stations
five and six, but never falls back. The mystic has achieved
supreme peace of soul which cannot be taken from her. One
would like to hope that that is precisely what Marguerite Porete
was experiencing during her imprisonment, trial and execution.

It is at this stage that Marguerite makes many of the statements which cut her off not only from the theologians of the
Inquisition, but even from others pursuing a similar mystical
journey.

> This Soul … no longer seeks God through penitence, not
> through any sacramnets of Holy Church; not through
> thoughts, nor through words, nor through works; not
> through creatures here below, nor through creatures above;
> not through justice, nor through mercy; not through glory of
> glory … Such a Soul neither desires nor despises poverty nor
> tribulation, neither Mass nor sermon, neither fast nor prayer,
> and gives to Nature all that is necessary without remorse of

conscience. But such nature is so well ordered through the transformation by unity of Love ... that nature demands nothing which is prohibited.[19]

Marguerite always points out that God is not made subject to his sacraments. We cannot treat God as if we were 'merchants', buying and selling the things of God. Marguerite's God is not an 'object' God. We cannot have God as if God belonged to us. We cannot own God. God must be truly God, without being encumbered with our projections of who God ought to be. Everything is at God's initiative at this stage: 'Thus she has from God what He has, and she is what God is through transformation of love, in that point in which she was, before she flowed from the goodness of God.'[20]

Marguerite Porete, then, engages in a boldly gendered mysticism. All her metaphors for God are female, except for the Far-Nigh, which generally represents the Trinity. There is little sense of the body-awareness of other Beguine mystics, and she rejects self-inflicted suffering as part of the mystical path. Marguerite is a speculative mystic, immersed in her experience of God, but light years from the human physical relationship with Christ in the eucharist, which marked the nuns at Helfta.[21] As we shall see, she is likewise most unlike her contemporary, Catherine of Siena. Marguerite, whether in practice or only in theory, had moved beyond the experience of a fragmented self to a new unity of being with the God beyond God. It is here that comparisons with Meister Eckhart become apposite. Eckhart (1260-1327) was a German Dominican mystic, from the same area in Thuringia as Mechtild of Magdeburg. In 1302 he acquired his master's degree in Paris, hence the title 'Meister' by which he has always been known. He lived in Paris on at least three separate occasions, and was teaching there in 1311, the year after the execution of Marguerite Porete. It is said that he lived in the same Dominican house as the chief Inquisitor of Paris, William. The assumption is that his contact with the writings of Marguerite Porete happened at this time, but even a short time after her death, her writings seem to have been in wide circulation, despite the danger of being reported to the Inquisition. In 1313, Eckhart returned to Cologne which, as well as Strasburg, seems to have been his base hereafter. He became an extremely popular preacher and teacher. During Eckhart's life, there had been three condemnations of the writings of his brother Dominican, Thomas Aquinas, so condemnations were in the air at that period. Nevertheless, Aquinas was canonised in 1326. The same year Meister Eckhart was denounced to Rome by the Archbishop of Cologne. Eckhart appealed to the pope, now at Avignon, and actually journeyed there to speak in his own defence. He died before the result of the appeal was heard, having made his peace with the church. In 1329, Pope John XXII condemned seventeen of Eckhart's propositions. Eckhart accused those who judged him as treating as error 'whatever they fail to understand and also regard all error as heresy, whereas only obstinate addiction to error constitutes both heresy and the heretic'. Most scholars today agree with Eckhart rather than with his accusers, and with the revival of interest in the writings of Marguerite Porete, a new wave of interest in Eckhart has emerged, noting now his dependence on her.[22] While there are many similarities between the writings of Meister Eckhart and Marguerite Porete, there seems to be an attempt at a summary of her apophatic teaching in Eckhart's fifty-second sermon. Here, Eckhart describes a really poor person, who wants nothing, has no attachment to penances or other external exercises, who knows nothing and has nothing. This person can even be said to have 'no God', because he or she is one with God in a kind of precreated existence. Eckhart, in his famous prayer, asks God to free him of God, that is to be free of the created relationship with God. For both mystics, no 'relationship' with God is necessary because they have returned to the 'self-sufficient source or ground of Being'.[23]

The study of both mystics is likely to go hand in hand for the next few decades. Each traverses the same mystical path, though the earthly term of the journey ended in such spectacularly different ways for them. The courage and brilliance of Marguerite Porete still speaks across the centuries. Eckhart continues to

inspire generations of those who wish to move beyond the mer-
chandising of an 'object' God. It is unfortunate that both mystics
seem to belong now to a small group of experts, since it was the
prime intention of both, in their lifetimes, to open this way to
God to all 'simple souls'. At this vantage point, there is very little
that is simple about the teaching of either one. The church made
its choices, signalled in the canonisation of Thomas Aquinas and
the burning of Marguerite Porete. One represents the way of
faith and reason, the other the way of faith and love. It was
Marguerite who named these two paths as Holy Church the
Greater for the church of Love, and Holy Church the Less for the
church of Reason. The great hidden church of the lovers of God
was seen by Marguerite as the saviour of the 'lesser' church,
stained as it was with all the signs of power, intellect, wealth and
authority. Perhaps the calamitous fourteenth century of Barbara
Tuchman's history can speak to the calamitous twentieth and
twenty-first centuries of our time, not only in how to re-assume
life after calamity, but also in how to let God be God. This was
precisely the motivation of another great fourteenth century
woman, whose heart was broken in her efforts to reform the
Christian church. This was Catherine of Siena.

Catherine of Siena
Catherine Benincasa was borh on 25 March 1347, the twenty-
third of the twenty-four children of Monna Lapa and Jacopo
Benincasa. She was the twin who survived the ravages of the
great plague which just then was beginning to devastate the
lands of Europe, and apparently the only one of the children to
be breast-fed by the mother. This singular characteristic may, as
we shall see, provide a small clue to the frantic and driven nature
of Catherine for the brief thirty-three years of her life. It is a life
that moves under divine direction from an imposed three-year
silence as a reclusive teenager to a life that sped along the high-
ways of Europe in pursuit of delinquent popes, kings and
queens. Catherine, born in Siena, spent parts of her life in Pisa,
Avignon, Florence and Rome, where she eventually died. Though

Catherine was one of the first two women named as Doctor of the Church, together with Teresa of Avila in 1970, because of the depth and catholicity of her teaching, here we shall concentrate mostly on her public life poured out in astonishing energy for the reform of the church.[24]

Like many another mystic, Catherine recognised her visionary calling early in life, maybe as early as the age of six, and thenceforth this calling was the central motivating factor of her life. Jacopo Benincasa occupied an important place in the life of the thriving commune of Siena, and Catherine figured in the family plans for the promotion of family prosperity and reputation. Catherine, however, resisted all marriage plans, and as a punishment, was treated as a family servant and deprived of the main joy of her life, the privacy of her own room. At the age of seventeen, Catherine was afflicted with smallpox and suffered a severe facial disfigurement. Despite her age, and perhaps because of the disfigurement, Catherine was allowed to join a group of widows called *mantellati*, who were a kind of third-order Dominican group. A mystery hovers still over Catherine's choice to remain at home, as these women did, and not to join a religious community. At any rate, for the next three years, 1364-1367, Catherine took a vow of silence and lived in her restored private room in the family home. It seems to have been during this period that severe fasting and sleep-deprivation came to be the hall-marks of her penitential life. She slept unwillingly for about thirty minutes every two days, and fasted so severely that she was never again able to eat properly. She learned to read and write during this period and this phase of her life – the most private as it happens – ended with the experience of a mystical marriage to Christ, marked by a ring formed from the foreskin removed at the circumcision of Jesus. This marriage was accompanied by a directive to change the whole direction of her life by taking up a public ministry in Siena. Catherine began to tend the sick and needy of Siena, visiting prisons, hospitals and the poor. Eventually, she was joined by a group of women and men who became her constant co-workers and companions, and who, almost immediately, began calling her 'Mamma'. Before long, her mother joined the group also, thus healing something of a rift that existed between the two for years. This arrangement was so extraordinary that the Sienese did not know what to make of it and sarcastically christened the group 'Caterinati'. The name was adopted by the members as a badge of honour and still exists among devoted followers of Catherine. After three years of Sienese ministry, Catherine experienced a mystical death from which she arose with a further ministerial call. This time she felt herself directed to expand her arena considerably in order to 'save souls'. The next few years are marked by extraordinary activity including travels over much of Europe, extensive correspondence, of which almost four hundred letters survive, and involvement in mediation at every level in the church. In 1374, at the age of twenty-seven, Catherine was summoned before the Dominican General Chapter in Florence and assigned as Director, Raymond of Capua, who became her closest friend and eventually wrote her biography.

Henceforth, Catherine turned her attention more to the state of the Catholic church and its politics. In a vision where she received the stigmata, she was also given a fore-warning about the great schism which would tear the church apart. This vision seems to have stimulated the amazing burst of activity which characterised the remaining years of her life. In 1309, Pope Clement V happened to be in France when elected. He decided to remain there – he did not have a great deal of choice – and eventually the new papal operating centre was set up at Avignon. The situation in Rome deteriorated rapidly into a battlefield of vicious and seemingly unending feuds. This set the scene for Catherine's work until her death in 1380. It entailed travelling as ambassador from Pisa and Florence to Avignon and back again, sometimes as papal representative, sometimes as spokesperson for the cities. In 1378, during a respite in Siena, Catherine had completed the dictation of her major visionary work, *The Dialogue*. Eventually, Pope Gregory IX returned to Rome in 1378 and towards the end of that year, Catherine was summoned from Siena to Rome to be at the pope's side, the pope now being the hated and probably insane Urban VI. It was his election and uncontrolled behaviour which precipitated the election of a second pope and the setting up of a rival papacy at Avignon. Catherine was seen as partly to blame for this turn of events, and in the closing months of her life, with a body that suffered at least two strokes, her pro-papal activity reached a crescendo of prayer, pleading, letter-writing, papal bullying, and endless attempts to summon a coterie of saintly people to Rome to act as advisors to the pope. She died on 29 April 1380 and was canonised by the Sienese Pope Pius II in 1461. In 1939, she was named patroness of Italy and on 14 October 1970, she was named Doctor of the Church, a laywoman representing laywomen, as Teresa of Avila, Carmelite founder, created a Doctor at the same time, represented nuns.

Before entering a little more deeply into Catherine's life of ministry and prayer, it is necessary to explore briefly the world and church in which she lived. Throughout the twelfth century, the major battle of the papacy had been with German imperial claims. As the power of the papacy grew, it seemed incapable of tolerating any opposition. Unfortunately, in successfully reducing the power of the emperor, its only worthy rival for temporal power, the papacy left itself without a protector and partner. Instead, it had to choose between a variety of masters, and from the late twelfth until the sixteenth century, this master was usually the French monarchy. Every effort of the papacy to increase its temporal power ended in disaster. One of these disasters was heralded in 1296 by the publication of the Bull, *Clericos laicos*, by Pope Boniface VIII, claiming that the taxation of the clergy was the sole right of the papacy. All monarchs reacted by closing their financial borders and, in general, responded to spiritual threats by temporal measures. Philip the Fair of France was particularly targeted by Boniface and, eventually, in a fit of total frustration, the pope himself was charged by the King of France with simony, immorality and unlawful seizure of papal power. Soldiers of the king then seized the pope at Anagni in September of 1303, and though released within three days, the pope never recovered and died within a month. The death of Boniface represented the outer limit of papal claims to temporal power.

In 1305, the French Clement V was elected pope at Lyons. He decided to remain in France and eventually the papal centre was established at Avignon. The common cant of the day gives some idea of the disintegration of centralised power in Europe: 'The pope is French, but Jesus Christ is English.' It was said that between 1159 and 1303 every notable pope was a lawyer. Equally it could be said that for the next seventy years, every single pope was a businessman. In 1300, hundreds of thousands of pilgrims had flocked to Rome for the jubilee indulgences. Rome had a sacred mystique going back to Peter and Paul and despite the worthiness or unworthiness of the occupant of the papal throne, pilgrims were drawn there. Only businessmen journeyed to Avignon, however, and it must be said that it provided the popes with a safe and secure place to do business. It is interesting that one of the first acts of Clement V in Avignon was to forbid the use of excommunication because it had completely lost its effectiveness from over usage. For seventy years, the papacy functioned as a well-oiled business machine with little or no Roman contact. Avignon flourished as each cardinal built his own palatial dwelling and filled it with 'nieces and nephews' and other relatives and hangers-on. It was a brilliant court, still with tentacles in every village, but totally without spiritual atmosphere or any pretence to one. When Catherine of Siena finally arrived there toward the end of the Avignon interlude, she provided only entertainment for the ladies of the papal court as they clustered around her during her prayer and prodded her with needles to see if her trances were genuine. The great Italian poet, Petrarch, gives some idea of the ordinary person's horror:

Here reign the successors of the poor fisherman of Galilee. They have quite forgotten their origins ... there is no piety, no charity. No faith, no reverence, no fear of God. Nothing holy, nothing just, nothing sacred. All you have heard or read of perfidy, deceit, hardness of pride, shamelessness and unrestrained debauch – in short every example of impiety and evil the world has to show you, are collected here … Here one loses all good things, first liberty, then successively repose, happiness, faith, hope and charity.[25]

Avignon, however, simply mirrored the general situation of the church of the period where clergy represented about 1% of the population but owned up to 50% of the wealth and property. The constant necessity of maintaining and supporting this wealth was already driving the church toward its ruin through the creation and sale of indulgences. It was the same thirst for wealth, this time on the part of the French monarchy, that had led to the horrific destruction of the Templars in 1307 just as the papacy settled into its new home on French soil.

Two further tragedies of almost unimaginable proportions contributed to the disintegration of Europe during the four-teenth century, both in terms of its unfortunate populace and of what Petrarch had described of goodness and normal human feeling. These two events were the great plague and the battle for the papal states. In October 1347, the first signs of the Black Death were seen in Europe when trading ships pulled into the harbour of Messina in Sicily with dying sailors on board. In fact, it was two forms of plague at once, which was one of the main reasons why the death rate was so horrific – up to one half of the population died in many places. By January 1348 the plague was entering France through Marseille, and Italy through the Adriatic ports. By August, it had crossed the channel to England and was spreading eastward through Hungary. The whole of Europe was involved. Pope Clement VI reported from Avignon that the dead numbered almost twenty-five million. As the plague hit each community, it accomplished its deadly work in about four months. It would then recede and the survivors would attempt to resume some semblance of normal life. Then the plague would return with seemingly increased ferocity. No wonder the people thought that God was about the work of the last days. Whole cities, towns, villages, castles, convents, monas-teries, prisons and even papal palaces were emptied. The people

rushed to the churches for shelter but this plague was no re-
specter of sanctuary. The poet Petrarch's brother, a Carthusian,
buried his whole monastery, sometimes three a day until only
he and a dog were left. Then he fled. In Kilkenny in Ireland, a
young member of the Friars Minor, left alone among the dead,
began to write down what he could remember of the world, as it
seemed as if the devil were winning the battle and the world
was lost.[26] The plague had approached Italy from several sides
at once so it seemed to have suffered the most, with cities like
Florence, Genoa, Venice, Rome, Naples and Siena losing up to
two thirds of their population. In Siena, more than half the population died, including the twin sister of Catherine of Siena, and
work on the cathedral which was designed to be the largest in
the world had to be abandoned. The truncated cathedral still
bears witness to the unbearable grief of the survivors. The
plague seemed to wipe out the humanity of the survivors also,
as the chronicles repeat story after story of interpersonal cruelty.
Lawyers would not come to make wills, nor priests to hear confessions. Parents abandoned children and children their parents.

There were some nuns, however, who braved the horrors at
the Hotel Dieu in Paris, for example, with new nuns constantly
standing in for their dead sisters. They 'seemed to have no fear
of death [and] tended the sick with all sweetness and humility'.
It is extraordinary to read these adjectives to describe nuns who
were exhibiting the most extraordinary and unusual courage.
Later, in another outburst of plague in Siena in 1374, Catherine
showed the same courage and took part in the nursing and burial of three siblings and eight nieces and nephews. Some of the
rich were able to flee to their country manors and sat out the
plague surrounded by fresh air, 'wells of cool water and vaults
of rare wine'. Many a chronicler noted that it was the poor and
the youth who died in the greatest numbers. Some just dropped
down in fields. A canon of Leicester Abbey in England reported
seeing five thousand dead in one field alone. It is no wonder that
the survivors were struck with despair, apathy and even madness. Ignorance about the cause of such a horror increased people's

dread, and for most there could be only one cause, the wrath of an angry God. Even the pope spoke of 'God's pestilence'. Eventually, survivors looked for a scapegoat closer to hand, and in a long-standing tradition, the poisoning of the wells was named as the cause and the culprits could be none other than the Jews. This led to new horrors, such as the burning of the whole community of Jews in Basle on an island in the Rhine on 9 January 1349. Another response was seen in the flagellants who travelled through Europe in groups of about three hundred at a time, engaging in self-flagellation in town squares and fomenting all kinds of anti-Jewish and anti-clerical responses. By 1350, the plague was receding, the Jews were quietly returning to the towns and the pope, still in Avignon, felt able to respond to the Roman request for a declaration of a Jubilee Year. In a fatal move, Pope Clement VI linked the Jubilee indulgences with the payment of monies, so that in the end the church, or more correctly the papacy, emerged from the plague much richer but even more hated.

Despite the ravages of the plague in Italy, there was another battle to be fought which added even more to the suffering of the ordinary people and the greed of the supposedly great. The central political fact in Italy in the middle of the fourteenth century was the battle for the papal states. The Avignon popes, safe in their palatial surroundings, knew that a return to Rome would be forever impossible without some temporal protection. Hence the battle to maintain the papal states, which occupied about one third of central Italy. With quite ominous effect, there was a ring of hostile cities on the edges of the papal states, who intensified their anti-papal depredations as the century progressed. Among the most hostile of these were Florence and Milan. In 1367, Pope Urban V had crept back to Rome to try to remedy the situation, mostly at the urging of another famous pro-papal woman, Bridget of Sweden. Bridget, mother of eight, had, after the death of her noble husband, moved to Rome to found a convent of nuns, under the direct instructions of Christ. This new order of women was, Bridget was told, the direct plan of Christ to reform the church. He dictated a rule to Birgitta which was complete in every detail, even down to the nuns' habits and the archictecture of the convent. It was to be a double monastery with lay brothers serving the nuns. Jesus did not seem to be aware that there was a whole series of papal decrees forbidding such an arrangement. Jesus even gave meticulous instructions for the erection of grills and entrance and exit doors to facilitate this dual arrangement without scandal. Finally, Jesus lost patience with the pope's delaying tactics:

> I am the Son of God. This rule which you have heard must be confirmed by the Pope, my vicar, who has the power of binding and loosing. I am He that told Moses I am that I am. The one that was pleased to enter into the body of a human virgin. I am the one who said that I came not to break the law but to fulfill it. I want this rule which was not dictated by any man to be confirmed as were other rules which were composed by men under the same inspiration.[27]

This is the extraordinary situation of Jesus trying to assure the pope of his orthodoxy and right to be heard and obeyed. Part of Bridget 's vision assured her that the return of the pope to Rome would be a sign of the authenticity of her visions, so the return in 1367 seemed like such a confirmation. In 1370, Urban V allowed her to build two Augustinian convents, one for men and one for women and to add some modifications from her visions for the women. Thereupon the Virgin Mary appeared to Bridget and gave her a letter for Urban, warning him that he would suffer a stroke should he attempt to return to Avignon, and Jesus appeared to Bridget to assure her that she could wear his specially designed religious habit in heaven. Despite the pope, the daughters of Bridget, the Bridgettines have always called themselves the Order of the Most Holy Saviour. Nevertheless, in fulfillment of the prophecy, Urban returned to Avignon and died before the end of the year to be succeeded by Gregory XI.

From 1370 on the battle for the papal states intensified, often known to history as the war between the Gwelfs and Ghibellines. The papal legate in Rome was Robert of Geneva who was reputed to be related by blood to half the royal houses of Europe and by marriage to the other half. With such vast uncertainty about who might continue to be a papal supporter, he was forced to hire mercenaries to fight on the pope's behalf. One of the most feared mercenary leaders was the Englishman, Sir John Hawkwood. This man, with the encouragement of the papal legate, Robert of Geneva, was involved in one of the most horrific acts of these papal wars. The mercenaries had been defeated in Bologna and again in Florence and the papal forces humiliated. Robert of Geneva was outraged and directed that an example be made so that all would fear the papal armies. The small town of Cesena between Ravenna and Rimini was chosen. The mercenaries had arrived at Cesena and stolen whatever they could lay their hands on. The populace of Cesena complained to the pope's representative. Cardinal Robert took a mighty oath on his cardinal's hat to protect the town. He persuaded the men to lay down their arms and give him fifty hostages. As a token of his Christian generosity, he then released the hostages. Then, with the hostility of the townspeople eased, he commanded his mercenaries under Hawkwood to massacre the unsuspecting inhabitants. It is said that even Hawkwood demurred, but was urged on by Robert shouting 'Blood and more blood'. Starting on 3 February 1377, with the town gates closed, the people were slaughtered in the pope's name.

Hawkwood then left the pope to fight for Florence on the other side, and at better pay. Robert of Geneva became known as the 'butcher of Cesena', and the people's hatred for the church grew to unheard of levels. The pope excommunicated the Florentines, an ineffectual act, but was gradually coming to realise that if anything of the church were to be salvaged, a return to Rome was inevitable. It is here that Catherine of Siena returns to the picture. In June 1376, Catherine, aged twenty-nine, had been commissioned by the Florentines to go to Avignon to plead their cause and begin the process of peace-making and removal of the interdict. Catherine's main intent was the return of the pope to Rome, but that was but the means to her life-long burning desire, the return of all humanity to the loving rule of Jesus Christ. Catherine had been bombarding the pope with letters as she criss-crossed Europe attempting to rouse someone, anyone, to side with the pope.

> I have been to Pisa and Lucca until now, urging them as much as I could not to join the [anti-papal] League with rotten members who rebel against you. But they are greatly perplexed, because they have no encouragement from you ... I have heard that you have created cardinals. I believe that it would be more to the honour of God and better for yourself if you would always take care to choose virtuous men ... I beseech you, do what you have to do manfully and with the fear of God.[28]

Catherine found the atmosphere of the papal court at Avignon to be profoundly offensive. As we have seen, she was just a figure of fun to the court ladies, but she felt oppressed by the whole atmosphere of sensuality, and the 'stench of sin' was everywhere. She wholeheartedly agreed with the judgement of Bridget of Sweden that at Avignon, all the ten commandments had been reduced to one: 'Bring hither the money'. She showered the pope, whom she called 'my sweet Babbo', with letters in between the countless public and private audiences. She would not have survived the atmosphere of the court had it not been for the presence of her *famiglia* and her advisor and interpreter, Raymond of Capua. Charles V of France argued against her that Rome was wherever the pope was, but Catherine continued with her favourite papal admonition: 'Be a man, Father.' Catherine, usually quite practical in her advice, seemed to lose her perspective as she urged the pope back to Rome:

> I tell you, sweet Christ on earth, on the part of Christ in heaven, that if you act thus (that is, with forgiveness and mercy), without quarrel or tempest, they will all come and put their heads in your lap, with sorrow for their offences ... And then, my sweet babbo, your holy desire and the will of God shall be fulfilled in making the great Crusade ... Peace, Peace, Peace! So that the war may not delay this sweet time.

One of the reasons that Catherine wanted the pope back in Rome was to initiate another crusade against the infidel. It is interesting to see how much a child of her time Catherine was. She longed for peace in Europe, but argued strongly for war against the infidel. The whole picture continued to deteriorate rapidly. By March, both Pisa and Lucca had turned against the pope. Finally, ambassadors from Florence arrived at Avignon and, to Catherine's amazement, they totally rebuffed her, indicating that her influence was worthless in their eyes. The pope refused to meet them, thereby exacerbating an already intolerable situation. Eventually Gregory XI and Catherine left Avignon the same day in September 1376 and the pope, after a series of misfortunes, finally reached Rome in January 1377. Catherine meantime had returned to Siena, and it is here that the final work on her great mystical treatise, the *Dialogue* was completed. Then, amid a storm of letter-writing, she waited to be summoned to the pope's side in Rome, to assist in restoring some peace to the church. The final letter that we have from Catherine to Gregory gives some indication of her frustration. She adresses the pope with all the authority of Jesus Christ and tells him that if he is not going to use his authority, he might just as well lay it aside. Early the following year, the pope asked Catherine to return to Florence in one more effort at bringing this bloody war to a conclusion. Another tragedy soon dominated the scene, however, as the pope died unexpectedly in March 1378.

The confusing conclave need not detain us here, but Urban VI was elected pope amid rumblings of vast discontent in Rome. They were weary of French influence and cried out for a Roman pope. On their part, the cardinals thought they were electing the humble Archbishop of Bari, but once elected, power seems to have gone to Urban VI's head and he has since been called everything from raving lunatic to power-mad despot. He regularly shouted 'shut up', and 'You liar' and 'You stupid blockhead' at his cardinals, and was so unrestrained in his behaviour that even Cardinal Robert of Geneva, the 'butcher of Cesena', tried to calm him. Eventually, a group of cardinals, greatly regretting their election of Urban VI, and trying to make a case that his election was invalid because of the pressure of the Roman populace, withdrew from Rome and elected another pope. To everyone's astonishment, and Catherine's despair, the new anti-pope, Clement VII, was none other than the Cesena butcher himself. Pope Urban VI was inundated with letters from Catherine, and finally she received the summons to go to Rome and she set up her house outside the city. Several of her *famiglia* accompanied her, including after a time her mother. By this time, however, the schism was complete and the world had gone mad. Each pope excommunicated the other, so that the whole world was under interdict from one pope or the other. There were two sets of cardinals, two abbots in religious communities, and the Christian world divided on more or less national lines. To Catherine's immense sorrow, the turmoil tore even her beloved Dominicans apart. Each side, the Urbanists and the Clementines called the others' Mass a blasphemy and in many places the Mass was discontinued completely. Catherine varied between a complete loss of hope and feverish activity. Despite intense bouts of illness, she walked the one mile into Rome every day. She suffered a series of strokes, but always seemed to rally with the least sign of hope. Catherine's final spiritual struggle was coming to terms with the complete failure of her work. To add to her profound sorrow, she found herself blamed for the schism, as many said it would not have happened if the pope had remained in Avignon. It was her misfortune, however, to have to take the side of a man who was considered the most hated man ever to occupy the papal throne.

In January 1380, Catherine had been felled by a serious stroke from which she never fully recovered. She declined over the next several months and it was obvious to her companions that a spiritual struggle of immense proportions was taking place. On Sunday 29 April, one of her closest friends in the *famiglia*, Alessa, noticed a change and took her in her arms. She blessed her friends, and with a final cry of 'Blood, blood, blood', she died. She was buried in Santa Maria sopra Minerva and some time later, her head was returned to Siena, where it is still venerated.

It remains to look briefly at Catherine's spiritual teaching, which is the cause of her elevation as Doctor of the Church, and to examine one of the central features of Catherine's life, her *inedia*, or inability to eat. The central core of Catherine's life was her intimacy with Jesus Christ and the fulfillment of the commandment to love which flowed from this intimacy. Catherine was a most unlikely activist, but her desire to help and care for people was based on the necessity of loving them first. She firmly believed that one can only help those one loves. Ever since her teen years, she emphasised the need for a secret cell where one could retire, a cell in one's heart, from which one gained the self-knowledge which was another of her constant themes. Her thoughts constantly returned to the saying of Jesus: 'I am the Way, the Truth and the Life', and one of her favourite images of Jesus was as a bridge for humanity over the chasm of sin. The soul's guides across this bridge were memory, understanding and will. Catherine rebuked her followers for having a 'false memory' in remembering only their sins and faults. She had little patience with false humility or a false show of holiness. Like so many other mystics, she could easily read hearts.

The deepest form of truth for her was the crucifixion, and in entering into this mystery of suffering, one could move toward wisdom. The sign of wisdom was the ability to live without judging others in a 'sea of peace'. In a very homey image, Catherine likened this peace to the sleep one has after a night of drinking. Catherine's struggles for the church gave her an opportunity to practise her own spiritual teaching. The more she prayed and worked for the church, the worse it seemed to get. When she was at peace, she could remark casually to God that he seemed to be in love with what he had made in her. Towards the end, however, she seemed overwhelmed with the blood-stained world. One hopes that her own analysis of death as 'the moment when love seizes its prize' was indeed a reality for her.

Catherine's life-long inability to eat had excited both praise

and blame from her contemporaries. She seems to have eaten almost nothing for most of her life, and her intense activity can be
explained only from the strength of her will and profound devotion to the sufferings of Jesus Christ. From the age of sixteen, she
restricted her diet to bread, water and raw vegetables, but seems
to have been incapable of digesting even this minimal diet. From
the age of twenty-five, she is reported to have eaten nothing. She
said herself that grace and the eucharistic food transformed her
stomach. Her energy astonished her companions, and on their
travels, she could outride and outwalk all of them. In obedience
to spiritual direction, she tried occasionally to eat, but she simply vomited it immediately. As Rudolf Bell comments, what had
begun as ascetic fasting eventually escaped her conscious control.[29] Bell and others are convinced that Catherine's inability to
eat is much more complex than an ordinary medieval ascetic
practice. He returns to the earliest stages of Catherine's life to
look for an explanation. Catherine's twin had been sent out to a
wet-nurse while Catherine had been kept at home to be breast-
fed by her mother. Catherine lived, the twin died. Catherine was
surrounded with death and destruction all her life, including the
tending and burial of several siblings, nieces and nephews during the Sienese plague of 1374. At the same time, Catherine was
consumed with a hunger for God and her biographer tells us
that she suffered constantly from pain in her own breasts. Other
commentators link Catherine's determination not to join a religious community and her devotion to her family, as well as the
creation of a new family, with a special call she had received to
save her family and heal the brokenness of the family group.
Catherine had been weaned during the worst year of the Black
Death when the 'dead outnumbered the living'. Catherine wrote
about the deception involved in weaning, where food that was
formerly a matter of life and death is now poisoned for the infant. Whatever the exact reason for her *inedia*, Catherine always
suffered from the guilt of being the survivor. It appears that she
may have been the only surviving daughter of the family.
Catherine's pact with God to save her family, the church and

then the world met with untold obstacles. Bynum points out the extent to which Catherine became food for others, but it is doubtful that Catherine would have seen this as her mission. Catherine's aim in life was to become one with her Lord, and if we are to believe the testimony of Raymond of Capua, that is what happened:

> Then her face became that of a bearded man, gazing at me and filling my soul with awe ... It was an oval face of a man of middle age, with hair and beard of a wheaten colour. The stamp of majesty was on his countenance.

Raymond of Capua had no doubt whatever that Christ had now come to take over the one who was so devoted to him during her life.

CHAPTER EIGHT

Women on the Edge: Heresy and Prostitution

From the earliest days of Christianity there had been a clash of ideas and teachings, but the middle ages began to pride itself on being in possession of the Truth, as the papal throne was occupied successively by canon lawyers and university masters. From the time of Irenaeus, there had been a perception of one mainstream orthodox teaching which could easily be recognised by all, and therefore deviation from this could only be a sign of willfullness and hardness of heart. Thus the heretic, the deviant was always seen as committing primarily the sins of pride and ignorance. It was Irenaeus, too, who had laid down the signs of orthodox teaching: rooted in the gospels, handed on by the bishops as chief teachers in union with the church of Rome, and adherence to the credal statements. Even then there was a sense that the scriptures were dangerous for the ordinary believer and that the minimalist, but fairly comprehensive credal statements would be much safer. Even so, as we know, the early centuries of Christianity were torn apart with Trinitarian and christological heresies until the Councils of Nicaea, Constantinople and Chalcedon gave the church its official doctrinal foundation. There were other dissenters in the moral and ascetic arena like Helvidius, Jovinian, and especially Pelagius, but the powerful teaching of Ambrose, Augustine and Jerome silenced these disruptions, sometimes with their own exaggerated versions of truth.

It is generally observed that the five hundred years from 500 to 1000 were devoid of heresy – indeed the church then was more concerned with survival. The ninth century iconclastic crisis in the East touched the western church only at the highest levels of pope and emperor. The first medieval heresy concerned the two differing interpretations of the eucharist inherited from Ambrose and Augustine. The Ambrosian tradition emphasised the changing of the bread and wine into the Lord's body and blood, but without specifying how this change occurred. The Augustinian tradition stressed the dynamic symbolic unifying power of the sacrament, incorporating all into the mystical body of Christ. The medieval debate among early scholastic intellect- uals was initated by Berengarius and utilised the new meta- physical categories of Aristotelian philosophy. The debate ling- ered on until the doctrine of transubstantiation was finally made official at the Fourth Lateran Council in 1215.

From the twelfth century on, new waves of heresy rolled through the church, with the emphasis this time being almost al- ways the reform of the church from within. Traces of the ancient heretical enemies re-emerged in new interpretations of Donatism, Manichaeism and Docetism, but this time most of the 'heretics' were lay-people without theological training, almost all of whom were initially bent on reform. The genuine reforming cry of a return to the true sources of Christian faith in the scriptures was a common feature of all these movements. That meant a re- emphasis on the evangelical practice and principles of poverty in imitation of Jesus and his followers, and a questioning of the whole clerical, canonical and sacramental structures which seemed to have overlaid the original true message. The public perception that the leaders and members of these movements were holier and closer to true Christianity than the current ecclesiastical rulers added an edginess to these debates that kept emotions at fever pitch. In general these movements can be di- vided into three groups, though there was much overlap. First were those who revolted against the rich established hierarchi- cal church and the increasing clerical control through law and sacrament. Their aim was to return to the *vita apostolica*. The fact that some of these, such as the Franciscans and Dominicans, were incorporated into the church as the front line against heresy only added to the confusion of many. Other groups such as the Waldensians, the followers of Peter Waldes from Lyons, survived various efforts at repression and eventually became part of the reformed church. A second group included those who resurrected the old dualistic Manichaean categories which were always lurking beneath the surface. The re-connection with eastern thought in the crusades may have been the initiating factor here, but it was this group which challenged the doctrine of the church at its most basic levels. Groups such as the Cathars taught that there were two Gods and thus questioned the very basis of Trinitarian and christological thought. Nevertheless their ascetic tendencies growing out of a total contempt for the body, which was considered to be the creation of the evil God, seemed not unlike, in fact even better than, the best monastic practice of the day. Finally, there were a few well-thought out programmatic heresies of a few highly gifted people, such as Joachim of Fiore, as well as some extraordinary, though marginal systems which only serve to illustrate the diversity of thinking in what has always appeared to be a highly monolithic and centralised medieval church.

One of the major common denominators of all these systems was an ingrained anti-clericalism, and therefore a rejection of all mediation with God through the clergy. Accompanying this was the assumption of such roles by ordinary people who felt called through direct communication with God to preach and lead the people toward a more biblical practice. Those who followed the old dualistic systems also despised the clergy for their immorality and in fact dis-countenanced all who practised marriage. The ultimate sin for them was the increase in this world of the offspring of the evil God through procreation. The avoidance of all forms of sexuality, the rejection of meat, and harsh lives of repentance and asceticism led to groups who saw themselves as pure and perfect. Thus alternative authority structures were set up and, to add to the difficulties of orthodox Christianity, many of these groups accepted women leaders.

The response of the church, initially, was to charge the bishops to perform their recognised authoritative teaching role, as had been the case since Irenaeus. The numbers and variety of the dissenting groups, however, and the lack of theological acumen of some bishops, indicated that other remedies were necessary. The apparent holiness of the dissenters eventually led to the idea of forming a group who would beat them at their own holiness game and thus call them back to the fold through conversion and repentance. This was the platform of the Dominicans and later the Franciscans. The entire failure of this method also, led the church to fall back on the old Augustinian solution of force, and in 1207, the crusade against the Albigensians, that branch of the Cathars grouped around the city of Albi, was launched. It was a vicious and horrific affair with unimaginable atrocities. Thousands of men, women and children were hunted down and exterminated through various forms of slaughter. One of the worst massacres took place in the church of La Madeleine at Béziers when seven thousand women, children and elderly people, who had gone there for shelter, were burned to death. Ignorance was not accepted as an excuse and the very fact of living in a particular area was sufficient to decree that one was heretical. The crusade came to a bloody end in 1229 with a treaty that ceded much of the Albigensiañ territory to the French crown. The following year a permanent ecclesiastical tribunal was set up by Pope Gregory IX in order to root out any heretical traces village by village. This was the Inquisition, set up by the Synod of Toulouse.

The legal basis of the Inquisition was found in the discovery that ancient Roman law had decreed the death penalty against the Manichees for acts of treason, and since heresy in a total Christian society was seen as treason, the law was adapted for the current church difficulties. The tribunal was a travelling tribunal before which everyone from the age of reason had to appear to vouch for the orthodoxy of their belief. From 1229, torture had been allowed as a means of getting at the truth and inspiring repentance. Initially, the inquisition was seen as a restraining instrument against the atrocities of marauding mobs. The results, however, were even more chilling. Once accused before the tribunal, there was little means of escape, with the least penalty being the wearing of a yellow star or circle to mark one as an outlaw. The accused became a non-person on the principle that error had no rights, and malcontents of all kinds used the opportunity to accuse the innocent as well as the guilty. From 1215, all Jews and Muslims were required to dress differently, to indicate that they were always under observation. Individuals brought before the court were exhorted to confess and repent with a promise of mercy. Torture was almost inevitable and confessions obtained by this means were treated as evidence. Torture was also the means for obtaining the names of other guilty persons. Heretics who confessed were condemned to life imprisonment. Those who refused to confess or who lapsed into their old ways were handed over to the secular arm for execution by burning.

Women played a prominent role in many of these groups – in fact the presence of women, and especially their leadership roles only added to the horror of the church. There were a few women, however, who, influenced to some extent by these movements, created their own systems. We have space to examine only three of these, but the extraordinary circumstances of their lives indicate the diversity of church life and practice during the later middle ages.

Guglielma of Milan

The first of these is Guglielma of Milan, who was seen by her followers as the incarnation of the Holy Spirit, whose presence now on earth inaugurated the third age. This notion, associated with Joachim of Fiore, was in the air almost everywhere, with the first age being that of the Father, and the second that of the Son. The age of the Son, that is the age of the current ecclesiastical arrangement, was now over. The new age of the Spirit issued in a new time of freedom and justification. We know little else of Guglielma herself except that she died in 1282. After Guglielma's death, her closest follower, Mayfreda, declared herself the first pope of the new age and elected a body of female

cardinals. The details of the group's teachings are available to us
from the inquisitional records and from them we learn the extraordinary events of the group's life. Over thirty individuals were
examined from 19 April 1300 to 12 February 1302. The group's
main teaching was that the existing church had obviously failed
to convert many people, especially the Jews and Muslims. A
new female saviour was needed and this was Guglielma's heavenly appointed role, since from henceforth only women could
save humanity. The second church had had its chance and failed.
Guglielma and her followers were treated as utopian fools and
she was called the 'high priestess of pagan orgies'. Much of the
response is simply the projections of the male inquisitors, as the
simplest way of blackening the name of a group of women is to
accuse them of sexual immorality. As we shall see, this was also
attempted, though with a singular lack of success, with Joan of
Arc.

It emerges that part of the teaching left by Guglielma included
instructions that Mass be celebrated at her grave by Mayfreda,
thus inaugurating the new Jerusalem. The rites of the old church
would be abolished, as well as its scriptures, which originated
from the Son for the second church. There would be new clergy
and new religious orders and all Jews and other outsiders
would be welcome and baptised. Guglielma was believed by her
followers to have the same flesh as Jesus and to carry the *stigmata*.
Her life followed the details of the life of Jesus including miracles and teachings. Guglielma, however, was born on the feast of
Pentecost and her birth was announced by the Archangel
Raphael. While Pope Mayfreda awaited the new Pentecost, she
was to write the new gospels and see that commemorative
meals were celebrated.

Meanwhile Milan had been under interdict from 1262-1277
in yet another Gwelf and Ghibelline row over the appointment
of the archbishop. It was a strife-ridden church and many believed that the reigning pope, Boniface VIII, had not been properly elected. In disgust with the turmoil in the Milanese church,
many turned to the new groups for spiritual comfort and guid-

ance. Among the main groups in Milan were the *Humiliati*, a
well known poverty group who practised the *vita apostolica*.
These sheltered Mayfreda after her leader's death. In the house
of the *Humiliati*, there were paintings of Guglielma enthroned
with the Trinity, and pitchers containing the mixture of water
and wine which had been used to wash Guglielma's body. This
was used, reportedly with great effect, to anoint the sick.
Mayfreda assumed the office of priest and celebrated Mass frequently. Not all Guglielmites were women, but only women
could hold office. The local Cistercian community of Chiaravalle,
just outside Milan, took up and promoted the cause of
Guglielma. Her body was translated to their monastery with
great ceremony, and that day and the day of her death became
the principal festivals. New frescoes and altars were created and
new Masses and prayers written in her honour. The cult of
Guglielma ended, however, in 1300. Mayfreda and two other
followers were condemned and burned to death and the corpse
of Guglielma suffered the same fate.

Na Prous Boneta

Another woman who was victim of this new hard-line inquisitional policy was Na Prous Boneta, who was burned at the stake
in 1325. She was a spiritual Franciscan and a follower of Peter
John Olivi, but also a leader in her own right.[2] The records of the
inquisition give us some of the details of her life. She was born in
1290 and seems to have had a connection with the spiritual
Franciscans from about 1315. The leader of the spiritual
Franciscans in southern France – that is, those who claimed the
greatest fidelity to the teaching and example of Francis – was
Peter John Olivi, who had died in 1297. His teaching was apocalyptic and his practice of poverty led to radical social teaching.
His followers saw him as the second Christ, though he died at
peace with the church. Pope John XXII, 1317-1334 declared the
teaching of the spiritual Franciscans to be heretical, though they
had been spasmodically persecuted for decades before that. Na
Prous was imprisoned briefly in Montpelier for her connection

with them, but she was released. The Spirituals, though, were under siege. In 1317, four Beguines were burned at the stake at Narbonne, and the following year, four friars suffered a similar fate at Marseille. They were venerated as martyrs, but many of their followers, including Na Prous and her sister, Alisette, retired to Montpelier for shelter.

From 1320 on, Na Prous reports many visions, including being carried to heaven where she spoke directly with Jesus Christ. On Good Friday 1321, while she was in the church of the Franciscans in Montpelier, where she had lived on and off since she was seven, 'Christ transported her in spirit, indeed in her soul, up to the first heaven. When she was there she saw Jesus Christ in the form of a man as well as in his divinity ... he showed her his heart, perforated almost like the little openings in a lantern.'[3] The rays of light accompanied her for a long time afterwards. On the following day, Holy Saturday, God the Father appeared to her at the time of the elevation of the host. God was always present to her from this time on and the Holy Spirit was given as fully to her as to Virgin Mary. She was told that she was to be the 'herald of the Holy Spirit'. Her entrance into prayer often took the form of crying out 'Friend, friend, friend' and God always came on the third cry to see what she wanted. Once she asked him to 'have mercy on all the sins of the Jews, the Saracens, and all the peoples of the world'. God replied: 'I know whom I have chosen.' On another occasion, God told her: 'The blessed Virgin Mary was the donatrix of the Son of God and you shall be the donatrix of the Holy Spirit.' She was told that the third age was about to dawn and that the 'everlasting gospel' would be fulfilled. Olivi had received the Holy Spirit before his death, and this marked the end of the power of Christ in this world. Henceforth, there would be no further need for popes, sacraments, with the exception of matrimony, or confession to priests. Penitence would be internal, and poverty would be a mark of the truly faithful. Na Prous professes herself to be unable to believe any pope who declares a life of poverty to be heretical, as John XXII had done. During the years 1321 and

1322, there had been mass burnings of lepers in France. The spirituals were horrified and seem to have been the only group to have opposed this slaughter. Na Prous compares the act to the slaughter of the innocents by Herod, the pope being the new Herod. When the writings of John Peter Olivi were burned, the pope became for her truly the Antichrist. His sin was as great as that of Adam when he ate the apple and 'lost all the grace earlier given to him by God'. Na Prous wanted more for her visionary church. Christ told her that clerics and lay people should love each other spiritually in that very same spiritual friendship with which 'Christ and the apostles loved each other'.

Anyone who believed in her words would, according to Na Prous be given two gifts by God, namely, 'he will forgive the sins of the believing person, and he will give him the Holy Spirit'. The absolute conviction of this woman in her own beliefs is astonishing. She told the notary: 'if this Pope John XXII, and the cardinals, prelates, and doctors of the sacred page should say to her and demonstrate by reasonings and by the authority of holy scripture that the aforesaid things, which she holds and claims herself to believe and hold, are erroneous and heretical, and if they were to warn her to revoke the aforesaid errors, she would neither believe nor obey them'. From now one, for Na Prous, Christ will be the one head and the papacy will be 'annulled for perpetuity'. Excommunication would make no difference to her, for she was certain of Paradise. Finally, 'having been warned, called, and urged many times in court and elsewhere, to revoke and abjure all the aforesaid things as erroneous and heretical, she persevered in them, claiming that in the aforesaid, as in the truth, she wishes to live and die'. In this unshaken belief, Na Prous Boneta went to her death at the stake in 1325.

Joan of Arc

The story of the final woman heretic to be briefly explored here is much better known, because a mere twenty-five years after her death by burning, she was 'rehabilitated' and finally canonised. This is Joan of Arc. Her story is well known and dramatists and film-makers continue to be fascinated by its drama. Most of what we know of Joan we know also from the records of the Inquisition.[4] Her story is familiar and need not be retold here – the restoration of the Dauphin to the throne of France and his coronation at Rheims Cathedral. It is not the victories of Joan that have caught the imagination, but her subsequent betrayal by the French, Burgundians and English, and her sham trial at the hands of the Inquisition. Bishop Cauchon was the chief architect of her downfall, urged on primarily by the English. Many of the legal requirements of the trial were ignored, most especially the requirement that during the trial she be held under church auspices, where she could receive the appropriate ecclesiastical warnings and opportunities for repentance. Instead, Joan was held in a secular English jail and subjected to endless indignities. The official inquisitor rarely even attended the proceedings, but was among the first to excuse his actions in the subsequent overturning of the court decision. Then it was twenty-five years too late for Joan.

It seems that the legal systems of several nations, not to mention the learned men from the University of Paris, were all arranged against Joan. She was held in chains in the English prison at Rouen, and after lengthy interrogations, the University of Paris, on 14 May 1431, met in full session to deliberate the charges which had been brought against her. They concluded by finding her guilty of 'being a schismatic, an apostate, a liar, a soothsayer, suspect of heresy, of erring in the faith, and being a blasphemer of God and the saints'. They added to their judgement the appeal that 'very diligently this matter be brought swiftly to an end, for verily length and dilation is most perilous and it is very necessary to make in this matter notable and great reparation for that the people who, by this woman, have been mightily scandalised, be led back into good and holy doctrine and belief'.[5] Bishop Cauchon gathered his court on Saturday 19 May, to get their final approval on this judgement. All agreed with very few demurrals, the most notable being the young friar Isambart de la Pierre, who had often tried to bring some religious comfort – if only an ecclesiastical warning – to Joan. She was brought before them on Wednesday 23 and after their lengthy speeches, said: 'The way that I have always spoken and held to in this trial, that will I still maintain.' By now, Joan was tired of their trickery. She knew, as well as they, that the circumstances of her detention made of this a political and not a religious trial. Over and over she replied to taunts and trick questions, 'You will get no more from me on that.' They tried to get her to say what games she had played as a child in order to trick her into a confession of witchcraft. Likewise, as she placed her whole confidence in her voices, they tried to find a sexual element there by constantly quizzing her about whether the angels and saints were naked or fully clothed when they came to her. The utter dogged patience and ingenuity of this nineteen year old uneducated country woman far outstripped the best that the church, the university, the military commanders and the politicians had to offer.

Finally as the trial was reaching its inevitable conclusion, the charges were reduced to one – the wearing of male clothes. Joan asked one more time: 'Come now, you men of the church, take me to your prisons and let me be no longer in the hands of the English.' Bishop Cauchon replied abruptly: 'Take her to where you found her.'[6]

The final acts of the trial were utterly unprincipled. The wearing of male clothes was a deliberate ploy to force Joan into being a relapsed heretic. She agreed to sign a short recantation of about six lines that included the agreement to put on appropriate women's clothing. When Joan returned to her cell and asked for such clothing, she was told to undress and surrender her male clothes and proper clothing would be given her. What was given, however, was a bag with exactly the same garments she had just discarded, making her, in Cauchon's eyes, just as he wished, a relapsed heretic. The signed recantation vanished and another much more complicated one with a false signature was entered into the records. The young Isambart de la Pierre visited Joan in her prison cell and for the first time we see signs of despair and helplessness. 'And in fact I saw her tearful, her face covered with tears, disfigured and outraged in such sort that I had pity and compassion on her.' A special trial for the relapsed heretic was now rushed through. When the whole panoply of judges went to visit her in prison to conduct these proceedings, she was ready for them. 'God has sent to me by saints Catherine and Margaret great pity for the mighty betrayal to which I consented in making abjuration and revocation to save my life, and that I was damning myself to save my life.' The notary added a marginal reflection: 'fatal answer'. Joan added that if they wished, she would resume women's clothes, 'but for the rest I will do nothing about it'.

On 29 May, Cauchon summoned as many as forty assessors and rushed them through a decision about Joan's fate. It was announced that on the following day Joan would be taken to the Old Market Square in Rouen to suffer the punishment of being a relapsed heretic. When Joan was informed of the decision, it is said that she 'complained marvellously'. Bishop Cauchon eventually went to her cell and she told him: 'Bishop, I die by you.' The records give detailed accounts of Joan's last moments. By this time, it is obvious to many observers that this was a false and terrible result to a false trial. The Canon of Rouen was heard to murmur: 'I would that my soul were where I believe this woman's soul to be. We have burned a holy woman.' Several others testified to the same thing, including some of the members of the Inquisition who had been reponsible for her death. Even one of the English was overcome by Joan's demeanour as she died: 'One of the English, a soldier who detested her extraordinarily, and who had sworn that with his own hand he would bear a faggot to Joan's pyre, in the moment when he was doing so, and heard Joan calling upon the name of Jesus in her last moment, stood stupefied and as if in ecstasy, and was taken thence to a tavern near the Old Market, so that, drink helping, he might regain his senses.'[7] The executioner was devastated by what he had done and feared that he 'might never obtain indulgence from God for what he had done to that saintly woman'.

Eventually a series of enquiries was held into the execution

of Joan, initiated, it seems by her mother and her brothers. The
first was a royal enquiry, which did not seem to interest the king
for too long. This was followed by an ecclesiastical court, which
started proceedings on 2 May 1452, twenty-one years after
Joan's death. Joan's mother went as far as the pope to have her
daughter rehabilitated and was rewarded finally by being able
to read herself, in Notre Dame Cathedral, the Bull demanding
that the Inquisition reverse its decision. She was accompanied
by dozens of people from Joan's village of Domremy. A whole
new set of testimonies was now begun and the court travelled to
every part of the country where Joan had been during her short
life. On 7 July 1456, the decree was read in the great hall of the
episcopal palace of Rouen, with many of the same cast of characters present who had condemned her in the first place. It is such
an unusual document that it deserves to be quoted in part:

> In consideration of the request of the d'Arc family against the
> Bishop of Beauvais (Cauchon), the promoter of criminal pro-
> ceedings, and the Inquisitor of Rouen ... We, in session of our
> court and having God only before our eyes, say, pronounce,
> decree and declare that the said trial and sentence of con-
> demnation being tainted with fraud, calumny, iniquity, con-
> tradiction and manifest errors of fact and of law, including
> the abjuration, execution, and all their consequences, to have
> been and to be null, invalid, worthless, without effect and
> annihilated. ... We proclaim that Joan did not contract any
> taint of infamy and that she shall be and is washed clean of
> such ...[8]

One of the copies of the original verdict was then symbolically
torn to shreds and the whole cavalcade moved to the Old
Market Place, the site of Joan's execution, where the process was
repeated. There were celebrations all through France, and especially in Orleans at the end of the month. With Joan's mother,
Isabelle Romée and her family, friends and neighbours present,
a huge banquet was served with 'ten pints of wine ... twelve
chickens, two rabbits, twelve pigeons ...' It is said that Isabelle
died happy on 28 November 1458.[9]

At the time of her rehabilitation, Joan would have been forty five years of age. She was finally canonised on 9 May 1920 and her feast day, a national holiday in France, is celebrated on 10 July.

Before leaving the question of heresy, it will be appropriate to take a brief look at the question of witchcraft. The fullscale witch-craze did not occur until the sixteenth and seventeenth centuries, in what we are pleased to call the modern era, but the beginnings of the witch-burnings go back to the twelfth century. By the end of the thirteenth century, most of the 'theology' of witchcraft was in place and widely believed by everyone. In the year 1275 in the city of Toulouse, a woman called Angela was burned as a witch, after 'confessing' under torture to having had intercourse with an *incubus*, that is a fallen angel, and consequently having given birth to a monstrous creature who was part wolf and part snake. This creature terrorised the area, devouring children, for two years. Angela was put on trial and quickly convicted on these charges. Belief in magic, both good and bad, and in all kinds of superstitions was prevalent long before this, but for reasons about which scholars dispute, the whole fantastical world coalesced into a dogmatic and officially taught belief in witchcraft throughout the thirteenth century. The attack on witchcraft followed the same principles as the Inquisition into heresy and before the end of the fifteenth century, witchcraft itself was declared a heresy. Approximately three-quarters of those executed were women; in some places, whole villages were left with only one or two women remaining. This fact, and its subsequent cover-up by historians who actually believed until quite recently that this was just a case of a few garrulous old women upsetting the neighbours, has led to a thorough, initially feminist-initiated investigation of the circumstances of the witch trials. This exploration has been complicated by the rise of the modern witch movement, who believe that these women represent the remnant of an ancient goddess-worshipping sorority, who were fiercely and unjustly hunted by the Christian establishment. The truth, however, is even more chilling. These women were Christian. There was no such phenomenon as witchcraft as described in the *Malleus Maleficarum*, the witch-hunters manual which was published in 1484 by the Dominicans, Kramer and Sprenger. This extraordinary and influential document pulled together a mass of superstitious and magical stories into a theological and legal framework as a guide for witch-hunters. It is astonishing today to think that everyone, including popes and emperors, not to mention saints and theologians, believed this amalgam of rubbish. On the other hand, the underlying attitudes, if not the actual beliefs, persist in some quarters today. The comment of an Anglican cleric, widely reported after the 1992 vote in favour of the Anglican ordination of women, shows that some solutions to the problem of women's ecclesial role remain an attractive option: 'We burned them before, we can burn them again'.

The devil was everywhere present in the medieval world, and nowhere more obviously than in the 'sisters of Eve', women. As we have seen throughout the search for a possible medieval solution to the spiritual demands of women, the society, church and state found the demands of women for a public spiritual role reprehensible. Women had been a constant preoccupation of the ecclesiastical authorities since the eearliest years of Christianity. Now as the turbulent medieval world unfolded, women were assuming public roles in many areas, including healing. Every village had its healer and these, usually older, women lived at the centre of village tragedies of sudden unexplained infant death, unknown diseases of human and beast, infertility and the accidents of human procreation. It was relatively easy to accuse such women of deliberate intent and the misuse of herbs and spells since such means were widely accepted. The imputed will to harm a neighbour easily upset the balance of village working relationships, and long-standing feuds could come suddenly and viciously to a head.

These are some of the possible explanations for the beginning and increasing malevolence of the witch-craze.[10] By the time witchcraft came to be defined as a heresy, women were seen to be Satan's special minions on this earth. It was clerics themselves, who, in the context of obtaining 'confessions' by ordeal or under torture, disseminated the supposed content of witchcraft, including the witches' sabbath, Black Masses, night-flying, the accompaniment of black beasts like cats or large dogs, and the presence on the body of strange marks, which revealed definitively, in the Inquisitors' minds, the presence of the devil. All this circled constantly around the witches' supposed ability to cause impotence, shrivel and even steal penises, the killing of babies and the use of their ashes for a variety of spells and potions. The fact that many women 'confessed' to these actions with their own variations, added to the accumulation of 'facts'. The *Malleus Maleficarum* pointed out the four characteristics of every witch: she renounced her Christian faith, sacrificed unbaptised infants to Satan, devoted her whole life to the devil and finally engaged in intimate sexual relations with the devil and/or *incubi*. The Inquisitor was instructed to use any means to obtain a confession, since canon law required this for conviction and execution. Throughout the thirteenth century, as various women confessed, under torture, to the details of such witch-like actions, the groundwork was laid for the later witch-hunts.

Perhaps the real reason for such a savage social and ecclesiastical attack against the elderly male and mostly female members of society was the growing fifteenth century fear that witches were beginning to focus on the homes of the rich and leave the homes of the poor in peace. The fear expressed itself in a growing horror that an uprising of the poor was at hand, and that the witches were actually organising a rebellion against unfair social and economic conditions. Such fears were, of course, confirmed by torture. The case of the town of Langendorf illustrates that, at the end of the fifteenth century, the fever was only getting into its stride. In the year 1492, the same year that new worlds were about to be discovered in order to bring European faith and civilisation to a heathen world, the clerics and rulers of Langendorf claimed that there were only two women in the whole town who were innocent of witchcraft. It is impossible to know what exactly they were referring to, but most scholars today believe that there never was any such thing as organised witch covens or sects, nor of course any of the fantastical activities described by the deluded minds of some clerics. On the other hand, there is no doubt whatever that traditionally it was to women in particular that people turned for healing and potions for a variety of ailments, physical and mental. What Hildegard of Bingen had done with admiration in the safety of her convent surroundings was now the stuff of the heresy of witchcraft. The fact that similar fantasies have occurred all over the world has only added to the fascination of scholars and, nowadays one would have to add, practitioners of witchcraft. The existence of an abundance of trial records, which are now available from many parts of Europe, helps to put a face and location on these unfortunate victims of social and clerical delusion.

The Prostitutes

The final group of outsiders to occupy us here has left no record whatever in their own voice, but an abundance of theory about their presence, usefulness, wickedness and possibility of salvation. These are the prostitutes. Much of medieval sexual theorising was rooted in St Paul's dictum that 'it is good for a man not to touch a woman', and in the voluminous reflections of St Augustine on this topic. Marriage continued to be seen as a concession to those who could not achieve celibacy, and within marriage, the absence of any kind of pleasure somehow mitigated the necessary sinfulness of the act of intercourse. For Augustine, lust did not take away the 'good' of marriage, but marriage mitigated the evil of lust. Intercourse by itself was an example of animal lust, but the good of procreation made the intercourse between wife and husband acceptable, even though it was the means by which original sin was transmitted. The medieval world differed greatly from the world of Augustine, and the main preoccupation of the medieval theologians and canonists was to adapt the huge variety of sexual practice to the teachings of the church. In the event, each influenced the other. The imposition of strict Augustinian principles on such a diverse population was practically impossible. Nevertheless, the idea that marriage, the licit and, in fact, sacred, context for the expression of the sexual impulse was gradually being received, despite the complications of the divided heart theories of both Paul and Augustine.[11]

If such was the hesitant attitude to the inevitable reality of marriage, one would suspect that attitudes toward prostitution would be harsh and unforgiving. That is not the case, however. A huge change is noticeable in the medieval attitudes to prostitution. In Roman practice and in Roman law, the prostitute was the lowest of the low, beyond redemption and of legally imposed non-personal status. In medieval law, the Roman attitude towards the prostitute as a necessary evil to keep men from adultery continued, but the prostitute herself was seen more as a weak and straying member of the flock rather than a depraved person beyond hope. The old Roman hostility to the prostitute herself was softened in medieval law by the possibility of her reformation and salvation. Essential to both Roman and medieval law, however, was the definition of the prostitute contained in the word *meretrix*, one who uses sex for money. Even Augustine feared the consequences of banishing prostitutes altogether, and even though the reason is rarely expressed in so many words, it is obvious that Paul, Augustine and their medieval descendants had little confidence in the possiblity of male sexual chastity.

The greatest of the medieval theologians, Thomas Aquinas, agreed. While teaching that fornication is always and everywhere evil, nevertheless, prostitution had to be tolerated. It was, he said, like a sewer in a palace. If the sewer were removed, the whole palace would stink. Kept in its proper place, the sewer served its purpose; likewise the prostitute. The banishment of prostitution would lead to sodomy and other sexually deviant sins. Furthermore, the practice of prostitution by women was explained as being almost inevitable, since women, who were not made in the image of God, were sexually weaker than men. It was still taught as true that even married women who showed a desire for sex were prostitutes at heart. Nevertheless, the

prostitute was still of low status, in fact beneath the law's contempt. She could never accuse others of a crime, the crime of
rape, for example, inherit property, or be a witness for another
before the courts. Nevertheless she was entitled to the earnings
of her trade, and no one could deprive her of this. Indeed, she
was legally advised to make sure that she got her money first,
before engaging in sex, since after the fact, she could not advance her right to the earnings.

There was also a new realisation that women could be
trapped in a life of prostitution through poverty, abandonment,
or the exploitation of unscrupulous pimps. In this sense, prostitutes were more to be pitied and prayed for than blamed. One
major reason, apart from the development of law, for this
change of attitude was the newly spreading devotion to Mary
Magdalen, widely believed to have been converted from a life of
prostitution by Jesus. The medieval Magdalen was a combination of the woman taken in adultery in John's gospel and the
various stories of women penitents in the other gospels, with the
necessary ingredients of long hair, tears and a changed life after
her encounter with Jesus. Over the years Mary Magdalen had
acquired a biography, again as confused with Mary of Bethany,
the sister of Martha and Lazarus. Her shrine at Vezelay was one
of the major pilgrimage sites. The story of Magdalen will be examined more completely in Chapter Ten. There were also several
other exemplary tales of saintly women who had begun their
lives in prostitution. St Mary the Harlot and St Mary the
Egyptian were well known, and Hroswith of Gandersheim's
dramas had popularised the tale of Abraham who had gone in
search of his wayward niece, another Mary. Convents had stories
about nuns who had fallen from their lofty vocations to spend
years in a life of prostitution, only to return to the convent to discover that they had not been missed at all, since the Virgin Mary
had taken their place and concealed their absence. Despite the
fact that these stories might almost seem like an encouragement to
give the life of prostitution a try, they illustrate the medieval love
of the notion of the reformed and eventually saintly prostitute.

Throughout the twelfth century, cities and towns throughout Europe took care to institutionalise the practice of prostitution. Houses of prostitutes were formed, on the model of convents, with Abbesses in charge, and regulations about health, hygiene, and fees. The assumption was that prostitution as a permanent feature of society should be regulated for the good of society and the good of the practitioners. Innocent III took care to establish asylums for reformed prostitutes in 1198, and these were turned into a kind of religious order by legislation in 1224. By 1227, Gregory IX passed further legislation for these houses as the Order of Mary Magdalen. They wore white habits and were often known as the White Ladies. Such houses were also seen as places from which the reformed prostitute could marry. Several such marriages are recorded. Besides, men who were seeking to repent of a life of sin or to engage in good works were encouraged to save these prostitutes by marrying them. Such marriages were greeted with great ecclesial approval. While prostitution continued to be condemned, the salvation of the prostitute became a medieval challenge. The worst women could become the best, and biblical precedent for this became a commonplace.

One of the ongoing difficulties for the legal experts, however, was the continued practice of concubinage. This was more or less stable non-marital sexual union. Again, Augustine of Hippo provided an example here, and his fidelity to his concubine throughout the lifetime of the relationship was eventually used to distinguish this form of relationship from the more serious fornication of prostitution. The prostitute was essentially promiscuous, whereas relationships of concubinage were judged by Gratian (1140) and others to be relatively stable and often exclusive. Concubinage was canonically defined as an imperfect marriage, with pleasure and affection, but not children as the primary goal. Concubinage was seen as a temporary halting site en route to the practice of a canonically sound marriage. The promiscuous prostitute was now defined, in Jerome's language, as a whore who 'is available for the lust of many men'. She is described as a dog, being indifferent and indiscriminate in her sexual partner. Nevertheless, she is to be protected from exploitation. The canonists continue to be in a major dilemma about prostitution. They want to insist on the moral offensiveness of the act, but also allow for its inevitability. They were also aware that a double standard was necessary, and that more had to be demanded from women than from men, given their belief about the tempting, deceptive and Eve-like nature of women's sexuality. In principle, the whole thing should be forbidden, they continually fulminated, but the consequences would be disastrous.

A further complication arose from the necessity of all to pay tithes, that is to bestow on the church one-tenth of their income. Aquinas ruled that prostitutes had to pay tithes but that the church could not accept such money until after the prostitute's reformation. This gave added impetus to efforts to provide houses where such reformation could take place. The unstoppable medieval theologians then asked whether or not prostitutes could go on crusade, and officially take up the cross. Some suggested that this would be appropriate since many otherwise unwilling men would follow her. Others thought such an idea abhorrent. Nevertheless there was general acquiescence in the fact that wherever large groups of men gathered, prostitutes would follow. This was true of armies, crusading or otherwise, and even the huge gatherings of clerics that were necessary for the conduct of synods and councils. In these gatherings especially, it was considered necessary to distinguish prostitutes by their dress from all the other women present. Prostitutes came to be confined to certain parts of town and certain areas and they could be arrested if caught outside such areas. In the middle ages, prostitution was usally carried on in a brothel and streetwalkers were not a common feature.

Jacques de Vitry, that ubiquitous cardinal, gives vivid descriptions of the Parisian prostitutes at the beginning of the thirteenth century. They are everywhere in the city, he says, soliciting clerics, especially the clerics, and shouting 'sodomite' after those who refuse their services. He describes one arrangement where a two storey house had students on one floor and a brothel on the other and the noise from the brothel constantly disrupted the students' classes. King Louis IX was so outraged when a prostitute sat beside the Queen in church that he tried to banish them completely. They were eventually banished to a section of Paris known as Clapier, thus leaving the English language with the slang designation 'clap' for the sexually transmitted disease of gonorrhea. Inevitably, once the state took a hand in regulating prostitution, it took a share of the profits, not sharing the church's dislike of ill-gotten gain. Toulouse, for example, shared the profits equally between the city and the university.

Queen Joanna of Naples, Catherine of Siena's nemesis, had sovereignty over the city of Avignon and set up a house for prostitution there in 1347. Outside the house, it was decreed that the women wear a red knot on their left shoulder. A house mistress was to be appointed for a period of one year at a time. Every Saturday the prostitutes were to be examined for signs of illness or pregnancy. The brothel was to be open every day of the year with the exception of the Easter Triduum. No Jews were to be admitted. Joanna sold this brothel to Pope Clement VI and it continued to function under his sponsorship. Rome also had brothels and collected its fees. When the Council of Constance was called in 1414, it constituted one of the largest gatherings of clerics in the middle ages. Hundreds of prostitutes flocked there for the entertainment of the delegates, and two hundred years later, a similar gathering of prostitutes was an essential part of the background scenery of the Council of Trent.

This chapter is entitled 'Women on the Edge', but in many ways, there was no 'edge' in medieval society. It was organised as a total society, strongly centralised, and organised around clear legal discrimination for and against certain groups. The clear legal, moral and theological principles were, however, very difficult to translate into practice, and a huge gap persisted between theory and practice. The Inquisition represents a last-ditch attempt to bring society to heel. It used the ancient Augustinian remedy of violent force when all else was seen to fail. Though popes, inquisitors and canonists tried to ring such violence around with all kinds of precautions, it was eventually unable to control the monster it had created. In the end, prostitutes fared a great deal better than heretics and those deemed to be witches. There is no record of a prostitute being burned simply for practising prostitution. Though the latter were treated as outlaws, in such a society of small towns and villages, it was difficult to outlaw anyone. It is difficult to imagine the effect of endlessly repeated persecutions, executions and burnings on the average medieval person. Despite the violence of the time, the memory of officially church-sponsored violence continues to be profoundly offensive. The established fact that women were by and large the vast majority of the victims, raises many questions in light of the persistence, to this day, of many of the medieval canonical and theological limitations on a woman's ecclesial role.

CHAPTER NINE

Recluses and Pilgrims:
Julian of Norwich and Margery Kempe

This chapter takes us to England where, in one of the greatest periods of turmoil on that island, the practice of anchoretism flourished. There is an abundant record of recluses, expecially reclusive women, in England from the conquest in the mid-eleventh century right up to the Dissolution of religious institutions by Henry VIII in 1539. Throughout the middle ages, there was a variety of options for those who felt called to lead a religious life. We have explored the Benedictine and Cistercian models, as well as the later medieval additions of the mendicant orders of Franciscans and Dominicans. These, within varying degrees of hospitality, offered opportunities to both women and men. The early medieval period had also provided the option of the double monastery, and for about one hundred and fifty years, women had created their own model of religious living in the Beguine way of life. From the earliest monastic ages, the option of total withdrawal (*anachoresis*) from society had always been present. Indeed, the records tell us that this was the earliest form, as witnesed by the life of the first hermit, Antony. These hermits headed for the desert in order to avoid the temptations and distractions of urban life, and sometimes to protest against the distractions of an over-institutionalised or worldly church. There in isolation, they grappled with their own demons, and were often so successful in their quest for sanctity that they were joined by disciples. The practice of this kind of hermit life continued right through the middle ages. The life was informal. The hermit withdrew to woods or mountains, supported himself – by the medieval period, it was almost without exception men –

moved on when the spirit moved him and was treated with the respect due to one who had made such a choice. Sometimes they were known for holiness; sometimes for nothing more than eccentricity.

Though there had been women hermits in the desert in the fourth and fifth centuries, we hear very little of women hermits in the settled land of Europe. By the twelfth century, however, we begin to hear of anchorites throughout Europe, and the records indicate that in this new practice of anchoretism, women outnumbered men. The practice was especially popular in England, where it seemed that almost every town, monastery, hospital or leprosarium had its own anchorite or recluse. The recluses followed no specific rule, but their way of life was still hedged around by many customary regulations. The recluse made a vow of chastity and a promise of stability of dwelling and, after a period of inquiry, entered the anchorhold, never to emerge again. The recluse was either a lay-woman at the early stages of her spiritual journey who did not desire to join an established convent, or alternatively, a mature religious woman who, following an option provided by Benedict and others for the most mature practitioners of monastic life, requested permission to end her days as a recluse. Once in the anchorhold, both women must have seemed the same, as they lived out their lives with 'God alone guiding them'. Some of the records tell us that women lived as recluses for twenty or thirty years, and one for as long as seventy-five years.[1] The life of Christina of Markyate (Chapter 4) told of the years she spent as a recluse in a kind of underground hermitage, but also of her first period of hiding with the recluse, Alfwen.

Even though we do not have a great deal of information about the identities and personalities of the English recluses, there is an abundant literature about their lifestyle. Julian of Norwich is deservedly one of the most famous, but a brief exploration of the guidelines for recluses in the literature of the day will be initially helpful. Since the whole point of the life of a recluse was the spiritual freedom attained through physical isolation, no definitive rule was written for them. The recluse was left to her own devices. The calmness of the life of Julian probably conceals the awesome risk taken by these women and the fact that some at least ended up in varying states of madness.

The Cistercian, Aelred of Rievaulx, wrote a letter to his sister, a recluse, around the middle of the twelfth century. He assures her that what he writes is not necessarily for her, since she is perfect, but for other young women who might be drawn to such a life without knowing the dangers. He mentions a theme which appears again and again in the literature, namely the necessity of an outer rule to govern the daily necessities and format of the life, and the inner rule, which governed the recluse's path to the highest levels of contemplation. The famous *Ancrene Wisse* was written for three sisters around 1228, and is connected with the Franciscan house at Hereford. The first and last chapters deal with the outer rule, the physical details of life, and the intervening six chapters deal with the inner rule, or spiritual journey.[2] It is more of a handbook than a rule and leaves many options to the discretion of the recluse herself. *Holy Maidenhood* is another such text from around the same period, and describes itself as a 'Letter on maidenhood written for the comfort of maidens'. This letter is similar in form to the many such letters written by Ambrose, Augustine, Jerome and others in the fourth century, but its misogynistic tones seem distinctly out of place in twelfth century England.[3] From this literature, we learn a great deal from the male authors about the process of becoming a recluse, as well as the structures, advantages and dangers of the life itself.

Initially, a nun wishing to live the life of a recluse, had to inform the abbess, and there ensued a period of repeated rebuff and request until the candidate had gained the abbess's approval. The next stage was an approach to the local bishop, and it is probably here that someone like Julian who does not seem to have been a nun would have started. In either case, once the request was made, the bishop became the responsible party. The nun would pass from the jurisdiction of the abbess to that of the bishop. He had a six-fold responsibility, which included all the subsequent decision-making, the provision of a dwelling, or ensuring that an adequate one was provided, together with all the necessary financial upkeep. The bishop also performed the rites of enclosure and took on the responsibility of permanent oversight, including the provision of a chaplain/confessor. Almost four hundred years later we have a description of such a ceremony in the newly-founded Quebec City, when Jeanne Le Ber, daughter of a rich businessman, was enclosed as a recluse:

> The feast of Our Lady of the Snows fell on a Friday that fifth of August, 1695. Solemn vespers were chanted in the parish church, after which a procession was formed, headed by the clergy ... Quitting forever the home of her childhood, breaking asunder the last and closest ties that bound her to earth, she followed the clergy, accompanied by her father and several other relatives. It was a striking scene ... Dollier de Casson blessed the cell and, as she knelt before him, exhorted Jeanne Le Ber to persevere therein ...He then led her to the threshold, and she passed calmly into her new abode, closing and fastening the door while the choir chanted the Litany of the Blessed Virgin.[4]

The actual anchorhold was a house of a few rooms attached to the local church or monastery, with one window opening to the church so that the recluse could participate in the liturgy, and one window opening to the street to facilitate visits, counselling or requests for prayers. This street window provided the authors with abundant opportunity to warn the recluse against gossip, money-making or peeping out to enjoy the passing world. The recluse usually had one or more maids and, as in Julian's case, the services also of a scullery boy. It seems that most recluses kept some animals, at least a cat to keep down the mice, but we also hear of cattle, and even of two snakes, who ate from the same bowl as their owner. The recluses were advised to wash when necessary, to keep the cell clean, to have adequate but not fancy food, and to share any left-overs with the poor. There were abundant warnings about unrestrained asceticism, but moderate fasting, flagellation and other penances were encouraged, with the appropriate permission.

The main point of the life of the recluse was, of course, the freedom that was offered to each individual to conduct her interior life as God alone would direct her. The celebration of the Mass of the Holy Spirit often initiated the anchoress' life, and it was under the direction of the Holy Spirit alone that her life of prayer was conducted. Though isolated in her cell, the recluse was united to all in spirit. This was seen to be her life task – to intercede for all. Sometimes she was also a healer and counsellor, and we also hear of two fighting parties in town or family bringing their dispute to the recluse for mediation and reconciliation. Alms was not expected from the recluse, although she could receive alms if offered. Her compassion was to constitute her alms.

The life of the recluse was seen to be one of paradox. She dwelt on the limits of normal life, isolated in her cell, and yet was at the centre of the town's activities and available to all. She was experiencing the 'burial of the resurrection', and though buried alive was yet an example to all of the life of the Risen Christ. She was a sign of mature faith to all, and yet we hear of recluses telling their severe temptations to their confessors: 'Who knows if there be a God?' Though shielded from all outer temptation, the woman of God was prey to the temptations of the heart. She was advised to be like a bird eating and constantly on the watch to be aware of approaching enemies. The inherent contradictions of her life left a strain of unease and caution in the writings, as the male authors struggled to reconcile their centuries-old prejudices with the apparently mature choices of some amazingly courageous women.

Julian of Norwich

In England, between 1100 and 1350, the life of the woman recluse seemed to be extremely popular. We know that they outnumber men by about ten to one. Overall, they seem to be strong, highly motivated women. It is to such a life that Julian of Norwich dedicated herself at some time in the mid-fourteenth

century.[5] Almost nothing is known of the details of Julian's life –
even the name Julian is that of the Church of St Julian to which
her anchorhold was attached. She is mentioned in three wills of
the period, but these just serve to give us an approximate date of
her death, that is after 1415, the date of the last will. She must
have been in her seventies at the time. There is one other external reference to her life and that is contained in the autobiography of Margery Kempe from King's Lynn, who visited her for
spiritual counsel sometime around 1412. Everything else we
know of her comes from her own writing, and it is obvious that
autobiography was the furthest thing from her mind. It is extraordinary to read Julian's book in the context of the 'calamitous'
fourteenth and early fifteenth centuries and learn practically
nothing about the details of everyday life and the widespread
political and social disasters of the time. It is clear that being a
recluse, in Julian's case, meant total separation from the things
of the world.

Julian tells us that on 8 May 1373, on the third Sunday after
Easter and the day after the festival of John of Beverley, when
she was thirty and one half years of age, her earlier three-fold
prayer was granted. On that date, she fell seriously ill and her
mother was in the process of closing her eyes at the onset of
death when she returned to health. Her prayer had been first, for
an experience of the passion such as the Virgin Mary, Magdalen
and the others at the cross would have had; secondly for a severe illness early in life so that she could experience this passion
in her own body; and thirdly for the gifts of compassion , contrition and longing for God. While apparently in the last stages of
life, Julian experienced sixteen 'showings' which, to judge by
her subsequent writing, abundantly answered her prayers.
These revelations lasted for five hours and there were no observ-
able exterior phenomena. It is assumed that Julian was still in
her mother's house at this time and that she had lived there since
her birth in 1343. A second assumption is that shortly after this
event, Julian became the 'recluse atte Norwyche' and wrote
down the first version of her visionary experience. This is

known as the Short Text. After about twenty years of reflection and prayer on the experience, she wrote the longer and more familiar version, that is sometime around 1393. In the text, Julian calls herself 'unlettered', but this is patently not true. There is no information whatever on her education, but Norwich at that time was a thriving centre for religious orders – we know of Benedictines, Cistercians, Carmelites, Franciscans, Dominicans and Augustinians – so there was some opportunity for learning, if only in attention to Sunday preaching. When she decided to become a recluse, the *Ancrene Wisse* and other texts on the life would probably have been made available for her. Julian, however, seems to have entered her anchorhold with a brilliant intellect which had not been idle in the previous thirty or more years.

Julian writes with a vivid and forthright style and her constant and detailed descriptions of clothing, its cut, style, colour and the way it is draped on the body, gives one to understand that her family might have been involved in the cloth trade which was a central feature of Norwich commercial life at that time. Her anchorhold was – and still partially is – situated at St Julian's Church in Conisford, an important ford at a bend in the Wensum. It was not far from the centre of Norwich commercial activity, as we shall see, and not only trade but also armies and rebellions cannot have failed to have passed close by. We know that Dame Julian – she was also called Mother and Lady – had two servants, Alice and Sara, and also a scullery boy. Apart from the visit of Margery Kempe, to be examined below, this is as much as we know of Julian's external life from her writings. Her lifetime, however, was witness to some of the most horrendous and significant events in the history of England.

Julian was born during the fifty-year reign of King Edward III, who in 1330 had put an end to his mother, Isabella's regency. She had, together with her lover, Mortimer, toppled her husband, Edward II some thirteen years after his ignominious defeat at Bannockburn in 1314 at the hands of Robert Bruce. Isabella and Mortimer were in turn deposed by Edward III, and Mortimer was executed. It is known that Isabella held one of her courts at Castle Rising near King's Lynn in Norfolk, and that her presence there was a constant burden on the area. Eventually, Isabella seems to have turned to religion and was later known for her good works. Julian would have grown up, then, during the reign of Edward III, 1327-1377. He was a respected and competent monarch, but his life was given over wholly to fighting, especially against France and Scotland. Two successive popes, John XXII and Benedict XII, tried to inaugurate crusades in order to get the fighting forces of France and England away from the European mainland. Instead, the situation was worsened beyond repair when Philip VI of France diverted his ships towards England, thus initiating the One Hundred Years' War in 1337, a kind of death struggle between the English Plantagenets and the French house of Valois. Despite spectacular English victories at Crecy in 1346 and Calais, and despite the legendary feats of his sons, the Black Prince and John of Gaunt, the fortunes of England and Edward soon declined. The ravages of the bubonic plague in 1348 did not spare England, spreading from Dorset throughout the forties, and with the incessant fighting, the whole of England was practically drained of manpower. Since Norwich was one of the main gateways to the continent, as well as the gateway from the continent to the cities of London, York and Lincoln, it would have been difficult for Julian to have escaped these events, whether in or out of her anchorhold. The Hundred Years' War dragged on until 1453, through the reigns of four more English kings to the reign of Henry VI, lurching through acclaimed events such as Agincourt in 1414, and disastrous events such as the execution of Joan of Arc in 1431.

The cloth trade and the constant travel in and out of England made the port and the streets of Norwich into a hive of activity. The route was also a highway for the flourishing commerce of ideas as religious from all the houses of Norwich constantly plied their theological and educational trades between the European universities and the flourishing schools of England. Julian would have been a child of six or seven when the Black Death hit Norwich around 1349, and in her late teens, when another plague carried off most of the children of the area. Records indicate that about one-third of the population of Norwich died as well as about half of all the clergy of the city. Nothing of this appears in the writing of Julian, but perhaps her prayer for an experience of early death as well as her permanent theological difficulties with the subjects of suffering, punishment and death derive from her experiences at this time. A succession of failed harvests and further plagues led to famine conditions and, eventually, the peasant revolt under Wat Tyler erupted in 1381. It is conjectured that Julian, having experienced her revelations in 1373, had thereafter become a recluse. The peasantry around Norwich rose in revolt around the same time and were viciously dealt with by the Bishop of Norwich, Henry Despenser. This arrogant, extravagant and cruel man would have been the cleric responsible for the commital of Julian to her anchorhold had she entered it in 1373. One wonders whether her constant professions of loyalty to Holy Church were an effort to see beyond the highly suspect activity of her own bishop.

On the other hand, the church as a whole was experiencing its own pit of despair as the Great Schism, starting in 1377, provided the church with first two and then three popes over the next several years. In fact, it was Henry Despenser, the self-same bishop who was called on by the Roman Pope, Urban VI, to lead a crusade against the anti-Pope in Avignon, Clement VII. The promise and sale of widespread indulgences encouraged thousands to join this crusade in the hopes of redeeming the souls of their relatives and children who had died during the plagues without baptism. The whole venture ended in defeat, disgrace and further scandal. It is again to this demoralised and scandal-ridden church that Julian continues to profess her loyalty. Her contemporary, John Wyclif, a professor at Oxford, could not rouse a similar loyalty in himself. He denounced the sale of indulgences, as well as much of the clericalism of his day in rousing speeches and writings. He was denounced at the Synod of Blackfriars in 1382. His followers, the Lollards, professed great devotion to Jesus and were accused of being 'mumblers of prayers'. The first complete English translation of the Bible was made at this time by the Lollards, and published in 1390. Unfortunately, its connection with Wyclif and the Lollards has always made it seem heretical, but its intent was similar to the attempts to provide vernacular translations for the lay faithful since the twelfth century on the continent. From 1385 on, the Lollards were fiercely persecuted, with the Bishop of Norwich leading the other bishops in requesting the death penalty for them. This was granted by Henry IV in 1399. The place of execution in Norwich, known as Lollard Pit, was not far from the Church of St Julian and the anchorhold. By then, Julian's Long Text was available, having been written in 1393. In such an atmosphere, one can understand another reason for Julian's profession of loyalty to the church as a necessary act of allegiance in order to make known her revelations to the world. 'But in everything I believe as Holy Church preaches and teaches. For the faith of Holy Church, which I had before I had understanding, and which ... I intend to preserve whole and to practise ...' (LT 28).

> But God forbid that you should say or assume that I am a teacher, for that is not and never was my intention; for I am a woman, ignorant, weak and frail. But I know very well that what I am saying I have received by the revelation of him who is the sovereign teacher.[6]

Despite Julian's protestations, she has been accepted, especially in recent years, as one of the most profound teachers of the church. Thomas Merton considered her to have 'greater clarity, depth and order than St Teresa'.[7] The central message of Julian, something she had in common with so many other women mystics, was that the meaning of God was love, and that God's love will triumph. This is the meaning of her much-quoted 'All shall be well', called by Merton, her 'eschatological secret'. With this absolute conviction, Julian's central theological problem is the existence of evil. In her lifetime of dealing with this problem, she never mentions Eve, never associates the presence of evil in the world with her own state of womanhood, and never describes sin as pride or pleasure. Neither does she attribute wrath to God in response to the sin of the world. For Julian, sin is the slide into a sense of worthlessness, despair and self-absorption. It is a forgetting of the essence of one's being, and the true nobility of one's creation. It would be impossible to give a detailed outline of Julian's theology which, though complex, is presented in an orderly fashion. Instead, just a brief summary of her main teaching will be presented.

In Chapter 73 of the Long Text, Julian describes the manner in which she received her *Showings*. She had bodily sight of the mysteries of the passion, she heard words which penetrated her understanding, and she had spiritual insights, which she has only partially shared in her book. She spent the rest of her life going over these events in exquisite detail, seeing in every nuance of hearing and sight, some further revelation of God's love. She describes one of the scenes of the passion thus: 'The drops were round like pellets as the blood issued, they were round like herrings scales as they spread, they were like raindrops off a house's eaves, so many that they could not be counted.'[9] Julian saw meaning in every detail and from this reflection on her experience, her theology developed. Unlike the scholastic theologians of the time, she did not begin from abstract principles, but from the very stuff of her own experiences. Her primary teaching had to do with God as Trinity, as God had revealed the divine self to her. Her words spill over each other as she describes the Trinitarian life. God is Maker, Keeper, Lover, Might, Wisdom, Goodness, (Ch. 5); All Might, All Wisdom, All Love, (Ch. 8); Life, Love, Light (Ch. 83). The Father may, the Son can, the Holy Ghost wills, she says (Ch. 31) and the Father wills, the Mother works, the Holy Ghost confirms (Ch. 59). The human being is three-fold as well – a 'made Trinity' of truth, wisdom and love; one who knows God through nature, mercy and grace, and possesses reason, mind and love. Above and beyond all else, however, God is love.

Wouldst thou know thy Lord's meaning in this thing? Learn it well: love was his meaning. Who showed this to you? Love. What did he show you? Love. Wherefore did he show it? For love ... And I saw surely that before God made us he loved us, and this love has never slackened and never will. And in this love, he has done all his works; and in this love he has made all things profitable to us; and in this love our life is everlasting.[10]

Julian is convinced that love will triumph in the end, and expresses over and over again her absolute confidence in God. For this reason, she is puzzled and distressed about the presence of sin, darkness, evil and condemnation. She cannot equate these realities with the God that she knows intimately. She speaks of this God as 'homely' and courteous. 'Closer is he than breathing, nearer than hands and feet.' One of her most original contributions is her long exploration of God, and particularly Jesus as Mother. This idea had been present in the biblical tradition and in other theologians and mystics as a minor theme, but in Julian, it becomes one of the central themes of her work, and one of the ways in which she tries to deal with the notions of God's love and the presence of sin in the world. We shall return to this.

First, we should take another look at Julian's difficulties with sin. At one point she wonders why God did not just stop all sin. At another, and more generally, she sees sin as necessary, even 'behovely'. 'In my foolish way I had often wondered why the foreseeing wisdom of God could not have prevented the beginning of sin ... But Jesus ... answered sin was necessary, but all shall be well, and all shall be well and all manner of things shall be well.'[11] Next Julian struggles with the concept of damnation, which she knows and accepts is the teaching of the church. This dilemma was central to her theological struggle and is compounded by the revelation that there is no wrath in God. (Ch. 13) She believes that in each person there is what she calls sensuality and substance. The substance of the person, the very essence of the person is so much an image of God that it can never sin. There is a part of the person that remains ever untouched. This goes further than the belief that all have been redeemed by Christ; for her, there is a part that is forever pure. Julian knows the teaching of the church about original sin, but clings to the goodness of the central essence of the person.

Julian's approach to prayer is one of glorious confusion. For her, prayer is mainly longing for God. Unlike most male mystics, she seems to have suffered no dark night. She seems to have been an essentially cheerful person and was so convinced of the reality of God's love that the thought of losing it was never a reality for her. Her ongoing reflection on the dilemma of God's unending love and the mystery of human sin led her to articulate what for many is the central element of her teaching, namely the reflection on Jesus as mother, which occurs throughout her work, and the parable of the Lord and the Servant, which takes up the whole of Chapter 51. Julian had begged God to extricate her from her dilemma about sin and love: 'Good Lord, how is it that I cannot see this truth in you ...?' 'And then, in his courtesy, our Lord answered me by giving me the mysterious and wonderful illustration of the lord who had a servant.'[12] Julian tells us immediately that she saw the truth of the parable on two levels, in physical and spiritual outline. The parable tells of a lord and servant who seem to have a relationship of equals. The servant is sent on an errand and sets off so enthusiastically that he falls into a ditch. He cannot get out and as he lies there, he loses heart, and feels that he is utterly worthless. He forgets that he was ever loved or that he had loved in return. This is precisely a description of Julian's definition of sin – forgetfulness about love leading to the self-absorption of a sense of worthlessness. The servant cannot help himself. But the lord/Lord sees the servant at two levels: first, with great compassion, as the servant lies in the ditch needing help, and secondly with great delight as the lord/Lord can see his future state of restoration. The lord reflects that he will not only heal him with grace but also reward him with love.

For the servant is Adam and Christ and each individual person, and the lord is, of course, God. Christ, the Son of God, has taken all upon himself and stands in for all humanity. God can never blame the Son, and therefore cannot blame us. Even more, the Lord, in Christ, has become the servant. God's love has transformed everything, and the soul, the 'made Trinity like the unmade blessed Trinity' can never now be lost.[13] The giver of love cannot be distinguished from the gift of love, nor from the recipient of this love. As so many other mystics had discovered by different routes, God is what we are. This love of God is not a sentimental thing for her, but must always be understood through the passion, which was always her starting point. Everything had to be judged by the 'standard of the cross'. This, however, was never a revelation of pain but of love. Human personhood is a reflection of this divine wholeness and love. Love is not something that God does alongside other actions. Love is all that God does. Our ignorance of God's love is paralleled by our ignorance of our own souls. Therefore the road to human integration is along the path of belief in love.

Julian has a driving need to know who, what and how God is. In the sense that she is always driving her intellect towards an answer, she is not an apophatic theologian like Marguerite Porete. She speaks constantly of our 'kindly' reason, that is the reasoning power that is appropriate to us as humankind. God wants us to know, says Julian, and also wants us to teach others what we have learned. Partly because of the recent wave of heresy, the church taught even more strongly that women were not allowed to teach. John Gerson, the famous Chancellor of the University of Paris, had written in the early fifteenth century:

> The female sex is forbidden on apostolic authority to teach in public, that is either by word or writing. All women's teaching, particularly formal teaching by word and by writing, is to be held suspect unless it has been diligently examined, and much more fully than men's. The reason is clear: common law – and not any kind of common law, but that which comes from on high – forbids them. And why? Because they are easily seduced, and determined seducers; and because it is not proved that they are witnesses to divine grace.[14]

There is never any suggestion that Julian was ever under suspicion, but her teaching arising from the parable of the lord and servant, and even more, her teaching on Jesus as mother, must have raised many eyebrows, as indeed it still does. This teaching is scattered throughout the book, but is concentrated in chapters 58-63. Again, as with all Julian's teaching it takes its direction from the passion. It was a fairly common medieval theme that the struggle and death of Jesus to bring redemption was comparable to the labour of a mother to bring forth her children. Christ is our mother in a two-fold sense: first of the physical person, and then again, as mother, Christ brings about our spiritual birth. Julian uses the image of mother for both God and Jesus, but it is usually the characteristics of the second person of the Trinity that she is at pains to illustrate: 'I contemplated the work of all the blessed Trinity, in which contemplation I saw and understood these three properties: the property of fatherhood, and the property of motherhood, and the property of lordship in one God'.[15] And again she says: 'The second person of the Trinity is our Mother in nature in our substantial creation, in whom we are founded and rooted, and he is our Mother of mercy in taking our sensuality ...' Julian is always operating at the two levels of sensuality and substance when she discusses human beings, but she is always pointing in the direction of the integration of these two levels in the very being of Christ. Julian develops this motherhood imagery in many directions, but a final image here will have to suffice. In the eucharist, Jesus our Mother, nourishes us: 'The mother can give her child to suck her milk, but our precious Mother Jesus can feed us with himself, and does, most courteously and most tenderly, with the blessed sacrament ...' The motherhood of Jesus, in fact, surpasses the skills and love of even the best earthly mother: 'This fair lovely word "mother" is so sweet and so kind in itself that it cannot truly be said of anyone or to anyone except of him and to him who is the true Mother of life and of all things.'[16] Throughout the book, Julian links her mother theology with the doctrines of creation, incarnation, salvation, the Trinity and the eucharist, so for her it is a wide-ranging analogy indeed. This teaching never became part of mainstream theology, which continued, and continues, to be unrelievedly male in its symbolism. For Julian, after decades of contemplation on the mysteries of God and humanity, it seemed the most appropriate symbol for the passing on to all the mystery of God's love.

One final word must be said about another striking image of Julian, and this is the image of the universe contained in the hazelnut:

> And in this he showed me something small, no bigger than a hazelnut, lying in the palm of my hand, and I perceived that it was round as any ball. I looked at it and thought: What can this be? And I was given this general answer: It is everything which is made. I was amazed that it could last, for I thought that it was so little that it could suddenly fall into nothing. And I was answered in my understanding: It lasts and always will, because God loves it; and thus everything has being through the love of God.[17]

Julian here and elsewhere is trying to pass on two essential aspects of her revelation. First is the insight that compared to God, all is as nothing. Secondly, however, is her reflection that the whole of creation is so precious in God's sight that it is held in being in the palm of God's hand at all times. Julian is convinced that God's creative work which initially brought everything into being, is still at work in maintaining everything in being, and with the same creative and transformative love. Conversely, for Julian, it is our understanding of God's original creative action and our reflection on it, that will enable us to admire and even understand God's creative action still at work in our selves and in the world. Her final thoughts on this can be summed up in one of many oft-repeated phrases:

> For God is everything that is good, as I see; and God has made everything that is made, and God loves everything that he has made ... For God is in man and in God is all.[18]

Margery Kempe

Apart from the wills naming Julian, the only other attestation of her life comes in the *Book of Margery Kempe*. Margery was a younger contemporary from King's Lynn, called Bishop's Lynn in her day, and had visited Julian in an attempt to gain assurance about her own mystical state. No two women could be so dissimilar, and yet, similar concerns emerge in their spirituality.

Both have great difficulty with the contrast between their experience of God's love and the presence of evil in this world and the
necessity of damnation in the next. Compared to the rather
stately solitude of Julian, Margery's life seems to be an unending
stream of turbulent and noisy adventures, taking her from
Bishop's Lynn across England and as far afield as Norway and
Jerusalem, with several ports of call in between. Margery was illiterate, but has left us a marvellous book of ninety-nine chapters, which opens a window on the late medieval English world
that in many ways sounds remarkably familiar.[19] As a glance at
the literature on Margery will reveal, much of the contemporary
interest lies in the fact that The Book of Margery Kempe is the first
autobiography in English known to us, and quite apart from her
extraordinary liveliness and deep spirituality, this alone is sufficient to keep her before the eyes of the public. The book itself
came to light again only in 1934, having apparently been in the
possession of the Butler-Bowdon family in York since the fifteenth century. Its first publication was greeted with bemusement on the literary front and ridicule on the religious front, the
summation of her as this 'queer, unbalanced creature' being the
least of the dismissive epithets hurled at her. More recent feminist literary and spiritual interest has led to somewhat of a re-
evaluation of Margery, and though it is clear that she did not
occupy the same mystical plane as Julian or Mechtild of
Magdeburg, nevertheless Margery opens several doors on a
spiritual life that these 'higher' mystics could not possibly have
experienced. The feistiness and homeliness of Margery Kempe,
as well as her tireless perseverance in seeking some kind of
recognition for herself as a holy woman, is amazing in its tenacity.

Margery was born in 1373, the daughter of John Brunham,
who was, as she proudly declares during one of her trials for
heresy, five times mayor of Lynn and a member of Parliament
for the area. At the age of twenty she was married to John
Kempe and subsequently bore fourteen children. With the exception of the first pregnancy and her dealings with a son towards the end of her life, we hear hardly anything about these

children. When she was aged forty, sometime around 1413, Margery finally persuaded her husband to agree to a chaste marriage, and eventually they moved to separate quarters in order to quiet the wagging tongues that were a constant part of her life. The remainder of her life was given over to her attempts to lead the life of a holy woman, and centred around three main concerns – her pilgrimages, her attempts to get approval for the wearing of the white clothing of a virgin which would lend some authorisation and protection to this life of travel, and the most characteric feature of her spiritual life, which was loud and apparently ear-piercing sobbing.

The England of Margery's time was ever on the alert for signs of Lollardy, that is the practices of the followers of John Wyclif, who criticised the sensual and power-loving clerics of their time and many of the beliefs and practices of the institutional church. At least one local priest had recentlybeen burned as a heretic, so the dangers to Margery were quite real. Her life which defied familial, social and ecclesiastical convention, drew constant criticism, to which she always had a ready retort, whether to the Archbishop of York or the Mayor of Leicester. In fact, it is something of a miracle in itself that her sharp tongue did not get her into more trouble than her already noticeably strange behaviour did.

The birth of Margery's first child seems to have precipitated her spiritual journey. She suffered a deep depression, thought she was going to die, was certain that she would be damned for some unnamed secret sin and was further terrified by the insensitivity of the priest to whom she tried to confess all this. To add to this, she mourned her lost virginity and thought that the gates of heaven were forever closed to her as a result. Many of the other women studied in these pages managed to elude the dangers that marriage was seen to place on their spiritual path. Margery seemed not to have felt called to make this journey until she was well and truly married, and her subsequent struggles give some insight into the self-perception of the married woman, who was placed by general spiritual consent at the very

bottom of the scale of holiness. Margery's whole life is about the
refusal of this designation.

The early chapters of her book tell of her madness – she describes it as being out of her mind – for about eight months.
'And also the devils called out to her with great threats, and
bade her that she should forsake her Christian faith and belief,
and deny her God, his mother, and all the saints in heaven, her
good works and all good virtues, her father, her mother, and all
her friends.' (1, 1) She attempted suicide, tried to bite off her
own hand, the cause of her sin, and tore her skin with her nails.
Eventually she had to be restrained. Her suffering was ended by
the appearance of 'Our merciful Lord Jesus ... in the likeness of a
man ... clad in a mantle of purple silk, sitting upon her bedside
... and he said to her these words: "Daughter, why have you for-
saken me and I never forsook you?"' She immediately grew
calm and asked her husband for the 'keys to the buttery to get
her food and drink as she had done before'. Despite advice to
the contrary from all her nurses and keepers, John, 'who always
had tenderness and compassion for her', gave her the keys, and
she resumed her normal life.

From this time on, she felt bound to God, but found it very
difficult to give up her life of fashionable clothing and money-
making ventures. She took up brewing out of 'sheer covetous-
ness', and despite initially producing ale with as 'fine a head of
froth' as any, the whole venture – as well as the beer – soon col-
lapsed. After the similar collapse of her next money-making
venture, a horse-mill, she finally decided to 'enter the way of
everlasting life'. (1, 2) She began to hear heavenly music and the
merry dance of maidens in heaven. This music remained a feature of her spiritual life, sometimes as sweet, she tells us, as the
singing of a robin redbreast. For the next several years she struggled with her husband for the gift of a chaste marriage and entered on a life of serious asceticism, often going to confession
several times a day. She began to speak publicly of her experiences, urging people to repent so that they too could eventually
join in the 'merriment' of heaven. At this time we first hear of

her loud sobbing and also of the scepticism of her neighbours: 'Why do you talk so of the joy that is in heaven? You don't know it and you haven't been there any more than we have.' (1, 3) Margery spent her life trying to negotiate her claim to sanctity in the face of such neighbourly criticism. Her book is full of the colourful turn of phrase which marks the beginning of the language used still as everyday English speech. One of the features of Margery's life was the call to travel. Initially, the ever-patient John accompanied her, but often she went about alone. On one such occasion, a man attempted to rape her, not believing her claims to the special status of the chaste virgin. She rebuffed him vigorously and he retorted that rather than consort with her he would prefer to be 'chopped up as small as meat for the pot'.

Eventually, Jesus comes again, she tells us, and begins to point her life in the proper direction. He tells her to abandon her hairshirt, her continuous praying of 'the beads' and to seek out a local anchorite, a Dominican, as spiritual director. She is directed to sit still and think, an admonition that had to be often repeated. It is at this time that she begins her travels around England to York and Canterbury, with John still in tow. It was on the return journey from York that she finally persuaded him to cease making love to her. While in Canterbury, Margery created such a ruckus, first by her boisterous tears and then by attempting to teach publicly by telling holy fables, that John finally abandoned her 'as if he had not known her'. (1, 13) Margery now received instructions to travel to the great centres of pilgrimage and struggled for the next few years to gain the privilege of wearing white clothes before she set out. She accosted the Bishop of Lincoln to this end, and he sent her to Archbishop Arundel at Lambeth Palace in London. She received moderately good receptions from these ecclesiastics, and finally was directed to Julian at Norwich. (1, 15-18) She told Julian about her spiritual state: 'about the grace that God had put into her soul, of compunction, contrition, sweetness and devotion, compassion with holy meditation and high contemplation, and very many holy speeches and converse that our Lord spoke to her soul, and also many wonderful revelations, which she described to the anchoress to find out if there were any deception in them, for the anchoress was expert in such things and could give good advice.' Julian gave her great encouragement, affirmed her gift of tears, and urged to her to continued perseverance. Shortly afterwards, in another appearance, she received further reassurance about her lack of a virginal state when Jesus assured her that she could join the dance of virgins in heaven: 'Because you are a maiden in your soul, I shall take you by the one hand in heaven, and my mother by the other, and so you shall dance in heaven with other holy maidens and virgins, for I may call you dearly bought and my own beloved darling …'(1, 22) One can sense the growing assurance of Margery in her spiritual journey, and she tells us that even the neighbours were beginning to visit her to ask for prayers. Finally the day came when she asked the priest to make an announcement in St Margaret's Church that all who felt she had debts should come and collect their money. Then she was finally free to go on pilgrimage, having said her farewells to both her confessor and her husband. It was around the year 1413, shortly after her father's death.

The journey took her through Norwich to Yarmouth, across to the Lowlands and finally to the city of Constance. Her companion pilgrims soon tired of her ceaseless crying and odd behaviour, and made her dress in a kind of sack as a fool. The Papal Legate in Constance – it was 1414 by now, and the great Synod of Constance was about to take place – reassured her of her saintly path, and she was provided with an older man as companion for the next part of the trip. After further adventures in Bologna and Venice, Margery finally arrived in Jerusalem, riding, as she tells us, on a donkey. Here, her crying reached unprecedented proportions as she progressed from one holy site to the next. The more she tried to contain it, the more it burst out. Her pilgrim companions were outraged, and after trying reason – 'Our Lady never cried' – finally wished her out to sea in a 'bottomless boat'. Margery roared her way around the Holy Places from the Church of the Holy Sepulchre to the sites of the Last

Supper and Pentecost, then on to the Jordan, the Mount of the Temptation, Bethany and Ramleh. Finally, and much against her will, she returned via Venice to Rome. Apart from a side-trip to Assisi for a visit to the Chapel of the Portiuncula, Margery stayed in Rome. She found a soul-sister in St Bridget of Sweden, whose canonisation had just been confirmed at the Council of Constance, and actually spoke with St Bridget's maid in her house in Rome. Here was a similar life, with the distinct difference that St Bridget had not begun her life of holiness until after her husband's death, but Margery found great comfort in her life and writing. Later, Margery's priest-secretary had discovered the life of another weeping saint, Mary of Oignies by Jacques de Vitry, and this tale had further reassured both of them.

While in Rome – we hear nothing of the pope – Margery participated in one of the pivotal experiences of her life. In the Church of the Holy Apostles she experienced, like other mystics before her, a marriage with God the Father. God told her that he was well pleased with her for her belief in the Manhood of his Son. Margery tells us that whenever she saw Roman women carrying boy children in their arms, 'she would cry, roar and weep as if she had seen Christ in his childhood'. (1, 35)

> And then the Father took her by the hand in her soul, before the Son and the Holy Ghost, and the mother of Jesus, and all the twelve apostles, and St Katherine and St Margaret and many other saints and holy virgins, with a great multitude of angels, saying to her soul, 'I take you, Margery, for my wedded wife, for fairer, for fouler, for richer, for poorer, provided that you are humble and meek in doing what I command you to do. For daughter, there was never a child so kind to its mother as I shall be to you … And that I pledge to you.

Margery now wore a ring with the words *Jesus est amor meus* inscribed on it. From now on, her life, despite many further troubles – all her heresy trials are ahead – seems to take on a quieter tone. She tells us that she now knows that silence is better than one thousand *Pater nosters*, and that fasting is for beginners. She heard the sweet music of the Holy Spirit in her ears for the next twenty-five years, and felt that flame of love in her heart. God now intends to live with her as a husband:

> Daughter you greatly desire to see me, and you may boldly, when you are in bed, take me to you as your wedded husband, as your dear darling, and as your sweet son, for I want to be loved as a son should be loved by a mother, and I want you to love me, daughter, as a good wife ought to love her husband.

After spending the Easter of 1415 in Rome, Margery set out again for home. John came to meet her briefly in Norwich, and before long, she was off on her travels again, this time via Bristol to the great shrine of Santiago de Compostela, from where she finally returned in early August of 1417. In late August and September of that year, she became embroiled in one of the more serious trials for heresy, initiated by the Mayor and Bishop of Leicester. She was accused of being a 'false strumpet' and a 'false Lollard'. Now friends showed up to support her, and even the gaoler took her to his own house rather than to the local gaol. During her detention, a Steward of the city tried to rape her, judging her to be indeed what she had been called, a strumpet. He began 'making filthy signs and giving her indecent looks', and when she rebuffed him, concluded that she was 'either truly good or truly wicked'. Leicester was overwhelmed by a terrible storm and the townspeople streamed to the gaol, demanding her release. Margery was brought before learned theologians, including the Abbot of Leicester, to be tested on her faith. She was accused of coming in white clothes – as a wolf – to lure away other wives, but was finally sent off to the Bishop of Lincoln to get a letter of approval for her way of life. This was duly produced, but the Archbishop of York insisted on examining her himself. He addressed her 'very roughly', inquiring about her crying and her clothing, but she replied, 'Sir, you shall wish some day that you had wept as sorely as I.' She was again tested on the articles of faith and it was found that she measured up to all ecclesiastical requirements. Then the Archbishop said:

'I am told very bad things about you. I hear it said that you are a very wicked woman'. Margery responded: 'Sir, I also hear it said that you are a wicked man. And if you are as wicked as people say, you will never get to heaven ...' She was, understandably enough, ordered out of the diocese as quickly as possible, but she refused to move until she was ready, and insisted that she would continue to speak her holy tales. This was not preaching , she said, because there was abundant precedence for this in the gospels.

The heresy accusations followed her through Bridlington, Hull and Beverley, where the Duke of Bedford took part in her hearings. Finally, with a letter wrested from the Archbishop of York, she was warned to leave the area on threat of burning should she return. Margery set out cheerfully and when admonished for laughing, since 'holy folk should not laugh', she acknowledged that the more troubles she had, the happier she was. As she crossed the Humber for home, she knew that accusations of Lollardy were much more likely as she travelled south. She persuaded her husband to accompany her to Lambeth Palace for another visit with the Archbishop of Canterbury, now Henry Chichele, who had succeeded Arundel. After several further escapades, she finally reached Lynn, where she spent the next eight years suffering a variety of illnesses, including dysentery. Her life was now centred around Lynn and while recovering from her travels, and ministering to the sick and poor, she experienced a great hunger of spirit. A priest was persuaded to read to her from the scriptures, together with many commentaries, the revelations of Bridget of Sweden, Walter Hilton's *Scale of Perfection*, Bonaventura's *Stimulus amoris*, and many others. She haunted churches to hear visiting preachers, and describes the crowds running to the church when a new preacher came to town. It was at this period that she began to struggle with the contrast she perceived between God's love and the sufferings of the damned. Her crying increased again with these worries and she was often expelled from sermons because of her disruptive weeping. Her reputation received a huge local boost on the occasion of the great Guildhall fire in Lynn in on 23 January 1421. Her prayers apparently brought an unexpected snowfall and though the Guildhall was damaged, the nearby Church of St Margaret was saved. She now achieved some kind of peace: 'So by the process of time her mind and her thoughts were so joined to God that she never fogot him, but had him in mind continually and beheld him in all creatures.' (1, 72)

Her husband, now over sixty, fell down the stairs one day and was eventually found by the neighbours, only 'half alive'. Margery was sent for and had to be persuaded at length to set her own wishes aside and care for her faithful husband in his last days. (1, 76) He turned childish and needed all the care, washing and feeding of a small child. He died around 1431, and shortly afterwards, the only child we hear about, her son, died also. This boy had led a carefree life but then, under Margery's influence, turned toward religion. He had married and lived in Germany and sometime in 1431 Margery's German daughter-in -law was living with her. This woman stayed on after her husband's death, and when she finally wished to return home to her young child, Margery, now in her sixties, decided to accompany her. This time she sailed from Ipswich and having travelled through Norway, reached the port of Danzig. On the return journey, she visited as many shrines and relics as possible, including the Four Holy Relics in Aachen. After a sojourn in the Bridgettine Syon Abbey, she reached Lynn. In 1436, the final edition of her book was begun – a previous edition was illegible. We hear little more of her and it is thought that she died sometime after 1439.

Recent interest in Margery Kempe has centred around the fact that her autobiography is the first one in English known to us, and as feminist scholarship tackles the vexed subject of writings one's own life, many have turned to the *Book of Margery Kempe* as a worthy subject for analysis.[20] Margery was faced with an enormously difficult task. She was illiterate, the wife of a well-known burger of Lynn, and ecclesiastically, a nonentity. The goal she set herself was to ensure that she would be known and remembered in a particular way, that her holiness would be recognised and acknowledged at the highest level, that the cultural suppositions that hedged around the life of a wife would be transcended, and that the privileges enjoyed by the only women with any recognition in the church would be hers, namely the virgins. At the same time, she had to ensure that such recognition would be granted her in heaven, and furthermore that that heavenly recognition would be acknowledged here on earth, by her neighbours, her confessors and whatever other clergy chose to question it. And to top it all off, in that particular place and time, she had to ensure that such endeavours would not lead to her being accused and burned as a heretic Lollard. That Margery survived at all is something of a miracle. That she maintained her sense of herself, her sense of humour and her natural spirit of defiance is remarkable. That besides, she gained some reputation for holiness in her own day and also in ours – even though ours is a great deal more begruding in bestowing that honour on her – points to something akin to genius in the art of living.

All are agreed that the autobiographical task is one of constructing one's life in a particular way. Certainly in Margery's time, and to some extent still in our time, it is a male task. The self-awareness that constructs one's life as an illustration of how one left one's unique mark on the world was not available to women. They led a prescribed life; they lived out of a male-written script. Their lives were more of an illustration of how the world left its mark on them. Many of the other women writers studied in these pages also struggled to have their voices heard, and their writings continually illustrate the necessary compromises of self-negation and other-affirmation – even if that other were divine – that made it safe for them to put pen to paper, and even more claim authority for spiritual insight. Margery speaks to us through two, or even three, secretaries. It is hard to know how much of her own voice we really hear, but the homeliness of the metaphors, and the distinctly popular turn of phrase, lends some credence to accepting the text as written as a good example of her thought and desires. She has definitely ensured that she is known and remembered in a particular way, even though both her narrative skill and her spirituality are still denigrated. When put in the context of the obstacles she had to overcome, she nevertheless deserves to accept with honour her position of the first English autobiographer known to us.

Margery's concern, however, was not with the literary critique of her work, but its spiritual message, placed alongside the other holy women of the tradition. Here, her challenge was to ensure that she would be remembered as Bride of God alongside her role as wife and mother of fourteen children. Here, her concern was not only with the external symbols of this paradoxical role, namely the white robes and the gold ring, but also with the inner certainty that she was pleasing to God in the depths of her soul. She also had to be sure that the religious hierarchy confirmed her orthodoxy of belief and practice, even as she defied every bourgeois and ecclesiastical convention of the time. Margery was a wife who did not live with her husband. She was a teacher who had no theological training. She was a prophet who had been sent directly by God. She had a message from God that superseded that power of any Archbishop, Mayor, Doctor of Divinity or spiritual director. She had a spiritual path to follow that differed from the accepted paths of anchorites, Dominicans, Benedictines, Carmelites, Franciscans, or Bridgettines. She took guidance from all of these, but she obeyed God alone. Margery did not have a profound spiritual message. It was not a systematic spiritual thesis such as that of Julian. But she was absolutely convinced of God's love and of her own unique place in the working out of God's plan of salvation. In dealing with her earthly marriage, she saw herself contracting a marriage with her 'dear worthy darling', God the Father. In dealing with the trials and tribulations of her contradictory role, she saw herself joined to the sufferings of Jesus Christ. In dealing with the gift and burden of her 'boisterous sobbings', she saw herself participating in the work of intercession for all the sinners and sufferers of the world. She saw herself in the tradition of all the holy women of Christianity, from the Virgin Mary and Magdalen, down to her own contemporaries, Bridget of Sweden, Catherine of Siena and Julian of Norwich. In all of this, her self-confidence is amazing, her lack of humility is endearing and her defiance is reassuring. Margery set out to tread the same paths as the women of the desert, the women of the great monasteries, the Beguines and the mystics, but with none of their supports or guidance. She succeeded, however, in perhaps the most difficult task of all, that of convincing her family, neighbours, townspeople and local clergy. For that alone, she deserves to be remembered.

CHAPTER TEN

Two Models:
The Virgin Mary and Mary of Magdala

Throughout the middle ages, the general and abundant ideas on the nature of 'the woman' were crystallised into two models: Mary, the Mother of Jesus, who was also, Virgin, Queen, Bride and Advocate, and Mary Magdalen, Repentant Prostitute, life-long Hermit Penitent, Apostolic Preacher in southern France, and Model of prayerful meditation. Neither image owed a great deal to their biblical forerunners, but each illustrates the multi-faceted clerical reflection on the roles, both religious and social, of medieval women. These two models are the creation of wildly imaginative clerics, but they are quite brilliantly conceived because both women correspond in very different ways to the profound aspirations of the human heart in all ages. It is not only in the abundance of art and literary works that such devotions continue to reverberate through the ages. The complex construction of spiritual devotion, both popular and scholarly, as well as the outpouring of artistic images is not easy to analyse. So much more is always going on than meets the eye. Here we shall look first at Mary the Mother of Jesus and the ways in which the majestic iconic imagery of the early Christian centuries gave way to a wonderful pastiche of homely and heavenly portraits, and then at Mary Magdalen, who received a brilliant afterlife in the vivid imaginings of medieval monks and clerics.

For the first one thousand years of Christianity, Mary was always seen in the context of Christology. The concreteness of Mary's human motherhood of Jesus was extraordinarily useful to patristic theologians in their discussions of the divine and human natures of Jesus during the early series of ecumenical

councils from Nicea in 325 to Chalcedon in 451. The naming of
Mary as *Theotokos* at Ephesus in 431 helped to hold together in
one person the growing reflection on the two natures of Christ.
It was also at Ephesus that the first signs of a widespread and
enthusiastic popular devotion to Mary emerged, partly orches-
trated by Bishop Cyril of Alexandria for his own purposes. The
fact that Ephesus was one of the centres of devotion to the mother
goddess has always been seen as the root of this popular upsurge of enthusiasm for Mary, and it is one of many examples of
the Christian penchant for 'baptising' pagan sites and shrines as
a tool of mission and evangelisation. Nevertheless, the imaging
of Mary for the first one thousand years remained eastern and
iconic – Mary is seen as the majestic *Theotokos* presiding over the
heavenly court in the same way as the Empress, the mother of
the Emperor, presides over the earthly court. In many ways,
popular devotion to Mary is confined to the monastic setting,
and her virginity is emphasised, both as a necessity for the doctrines of christology and for the ascetic and monastic propaganda
which was central to the church's sense of itself.

From the sixth century on, the major Marian festivals were
imported from the east, so that by the end of the first millennium,
the four major feasts of the Nativity of Mary, the Annunciation,
The Purification, and the Dormition/Assumption, were being
celebrated widely throughout western Christendom. Accompanying these were a host of liturgical prayers, the dedication of
hundreds of churches to the Virgin, and the insertion of prayers
invoking Mary and honouring her in every liturgical celebration. As Christianity encountered the Germanic cultures, the
need for a more palpable presence of Mary was felt and a host of
new accretions became apparent. One of the most lasting of
these in its universal influence was the Legend of Theophilus.
This is a Faustian story about Bishop Theophilus, who in his
anger at not attaining his desired episcopal posting, sells his
soul to the devil and instantly begins to prosper. Eventually he
repents, and after invoking the Virgin, is freed from the devil's
influence. The thematic structure of this tale, with its images of

Mary's response to prayer, her power over the devil, her care for the souls even of the damned, and her enormous influence with her Son, even to the extent of countermanding his judgemental orders, spread like wildfire through the middle ages. The symbolic power of her figure grew to include images of the divine not available elsewhere at that time. As the images of God the Father and Christ became ever more remote, judgemental and masculinised, female images of the divine began to accrue to Mary.[1] She claimed her place in human hearts as the one who revealed and practised a merciful love that was accessible and involved in even the smallest details of daily life.

Once this process was begun, it seemed unstoppable. The growing devotion to Mary showed up unfailingly the perceived gaps in the stance of the church towards the ordinary person. The church became more centralised and powerful under a series of powerful popes. The clergy were enabled to assume greater power both socially and religiously as the universities provided exclusive clerical theological training, and the theologies and practice of the sacraments of eucharist, penance and matrimony developed in the direction of greater clerical control over people's lives. People felt disenfranchised and orphaned and therefore less sure of their salvation. The increased sense of sin and of the demonic presence, which was one of the results of the development of the sacrament of penance, left people feeling far removed from a God who had become judgemental. Besides, the impression was widely created that such a God – and indeed, such a Christ – were best left to the clergy, who had now moved into a different sacred circle, so to speak, with their new and awesome powers to confect the eucharist and to pardon sin. Mary easily moved to fill this gap, not only in popular devotion, but also in learned speculation. One of the earliest and certainly one of the most influential commentators on Mary was the great Bernard of Clairvaux, whose writings on Mary are few in the context of his whole corpus, but whose influence far outweighed that of anyone else. He was joined in his Marian speculation by Peter Abelard, Albert the Great, Thomas Aquinas,

Bonaventure and many others, but it is Bernard who will engage us here.

In one of his most famous homilies on Mary, Bernard seemed to take up and express theologically the longings of people for a more accessible relationship with God:

> If you will not be submerged by tempests do not turn away your eyes from the splendour of the star. If the storms of temptation arise, if you crash against the rocks of tribulation, look to the star, call upon Mary. If you are tossed about on the waves of pride, of ambition, of slander, of hostility, look to the star, call upon Mary. If wrath or avarice or the enticements of the flesh upset the boat of your mind, look to Mary. If you are disturbed by the immensity of your crimes ... if you begin to be swallowed up by the abyss of depression and despair, think of Mary. In dangers, in anxiety, in doubt, think of Mary, call upon Mary ... If she holds you, you will not fall, if she protects you, you need not fear.[2]

After such preaching by Bernard, the first name to spring to the lips of any troubled Christian was the name of Mary. Mary, Star of the Sea had arrived, to be joined by whole litanies of names that have lingered on the lips of many believers ever since. Many Catholics of an older generation need but a slight nudge to be able to recite these Marian titles: House of Gold, Arc of the Covenant, Refuge of Sinners, Comforter of the Afflicted. The role of Mary as powerful intercessor for the people took deep hold of the devotional life of generations. Bernard was also to add his unique theological expression of the precise role of Mary as intercessor in what has been called his 'Aqueduct' homily. Mary is described as the aqueduct, the carrier of the graces of God to all. Through the incarnation, Mary brought the Son of Man to earth, now all the graces won by Christ will come through Mary. As Bernard says, it is the will of God to 'give everything through Mary'. This dictum became one of the basic principles of mariology, and has been repeated in thousands of homilies through the ages. Preachers turned to the biblical scene of the wedding feast of Cana, where Mary was seen to initiate the miraculous activity of her Son, and Bernard, again, added his own stamp to the teaching by calling Mary the 'neck' of the mystical body of Christ. People were invited to direct their prayers through the 'neck', and it was only through this same neck that the requested graces would return to the petitioner. Bernard is aware of the theological implications of this teaching, which have indeed haunted Roman Catholic Marian doctrine ever since. He knows that Christ is the one mediator before God, but he is also God and Judge, says Bernard, and people are rightly afraid of him in these roles. Bernard here is picking up on an earlier homily by a nameless cleric which suggested that there are two departments in heaven, that of justice and that of mercy. Christ is in charge of the justice department and is completely preoccupied with his endless work there. The department of mercy is run by Mary and she has nothing to distract her from the exercise of mercy. What we need, says Bernard is a 'mediator to the mediator' and there is none more suited to this role than Mary. Mary is forever sweet and gentle and no one need ever be afraid of her.[3] It is easy to see why Bernard was long credited with the composition of the prayer, *Salve Regina*, the 'Hail holy Queen' which so perfectly sums up this teaching. The 'poor banished children of Eve' of the middle ages turned unhesitatingly to the 'Mother of mercy', their life, sweetness and hope.

It was an extraordinary change in the devotional life of multitudes, and the nature of prayer was altered for centuries. The dangers are obvious now, and finally articulated by the Second Vatican Council, that such Marian devotion could and did overshadow the role of Christ in the Christian dispensation.[4] It is clear now also that the image of the Godhead was shrouded in a cloak of wrath, which could easily be aroused. This teaching provided the Christian God with a dark side from which 'he' has barely recovered. Mary, on the other hand, was the one heavenly figure with no dark side. She was all sweetness and light, ever attentive to her children's cries and, as mother of the judge, was all-powerful in her influence. There seemed to have been no confusion in the medieval mind with the multiple imaging of

Mary as mother, daughter, bride, queen; in fact her devotees seem to have revelled in the multiplication of images. In order to provide the people with words for their Marian devotions, some of the psalms were rewritten substituting Mary for God as the divine dispenser of grace: 'Sing to Our Lady a new song, for she hath done wonderful things. In the sight of the nations she hath revealed her mercy, her name is heard even to the ends of the earth.' She was even addressed as 'Our Mother, who art in heaven ...' and asked to continue bestowing their daily bread on the faithful. Even the ancient doxology, the *Te Deum*, was partially rewritten in her honour.

Medieval scholars, including Albert the Great, often reminded the faithful that such veneration of Mary was not on the same level as the worship of God, reminding people of the oft-quoted distinctions between *latria*, the worship due only to God, and *dulia*, the honour rendered to the saints. The veneration of Mary was deemed to fall somewhere in between and was termed *hyperdulia* but, though it is impossible to know what exactly was going on in most medieval minds, such admonitions did nothing to halt the multiplication of Marian honours and devotees. Thus generations of second millennium believing Christians looked to Mary for what Christians of the first millennium had expected only from God. As many feminists have pointed out, all this shows how easy it is to look not for a feminine dimension in God, but at God fully encapsulated in a female figure. It is not coincidental that the women mystics from the same era who are known to us through their writings, looked to the eucharistic Christ for such graces. In no sense did Mary replace Jesus in such mystical devotion for the simple reason that the qualities of mercy, forgiveness, accessibility and love still attached easily to his eucharistic presence. The women mystics felt that they had direct access to God and Christ and so had no need of a 'mediator to the mediator'. Nevertheless the same quality of human longing for love and forgiveness penetrated both forms of prayer. It was this sense of personal love given and returned which changed the nature of prayer and, of course, is not unrelated to the contemporary fashion of courtly love poetry and practice. The language of love practised in the earthly courts, where knights pined for the presence and favour of their 'Lady', easily attached itself to the Lady of the heavenly court. This is the period when qualities of beauty and adornment attach themselves to Mary in just one more superlative addition to her image. The soubriquet 'Our Lady' became henceforth one of the most frequent names for Mary, a fitting consort to 'Our Lord', making her available for an even greater number of titles, such as 'Our Lady of the Wayside'. This trend continues to this day as the names of countries, cities, towns and even space is added on to the ever convenient 'Our Lady of …'

The scholars meanwhile were as deeply involved in this veneration as the people they tried to guide. They debated the words of the Hail Mary which, from the days of St Jerome, had been so influential: 'Hail Mary, full of grace …' They wondered about the fullness of Mary's grace, and discussed in the context of scholastic theology, whether or not she might have received all the sacraments and when precisely this might have happened. Here, one of the most ancient suggestions presented itself again, namely, that Mary herself had been conceived without sin in the womb of her mother, Anne. Two of the greatest theologians of the age, Bernard and Thomas, were deeply perturbed by this suggestion, but the spirit of the age was against them. Demands for a feast day honouring Mary's Immaculate Conception continued to grow. The world took sides on this issue, Dominican against Franciscan, and the learned theologians against the mass of the Christian people. Among the supporters of the Immaculate Conception doctrine, devotion to St Anne, the mother of Mary, grew and art began to reflect this in its portrayal of a kind of secondary Trinity composed of Anne, Mary and Jesus. Pitched battles were fought between the camps to the extent that the pope forbade people even to mention this doctrine. As we know the battle was concluded in 1854 with the proclamation of the Bull *Ineffabilis Deus* by Pope Pius IX.[6]

One of the guiding theological principles of these discussions was the principle of appropriateness, whereby the theologians argued about 'appropriate' behaviour by God with regard to Mary. It was often articulated in the short-hand formula *potuit, decuit, fecit,* namely God was able to do this, it was deemed fitting that God do this, as for example, give Mary in advance all the graces of the redemption, and therefore that it can be held with certainty that God in fact did just that. Thus, the whole medieval Marian scene was subject to constant inflationary pressure both on the theological and devotional fronts. The amount of this complicated construct of ideas and images that survives to the present is amazing, but some particular devotions took pride of place. Among these were the veneration of the Christmas Crib, the Rosary and the prayer of the Angelus, not to mention the much loved prayers called generally the *Salve Regina* and the *Memorare.* Both the Franciscans and Dominicans are credited with these various devotions, but it is generally impossible to assert their origin with any degree of certainty. Of all of them, it is perhaps the Rosary which took pride of place in popular devotion.

The Rosary is composed of precisely one hundred and fifty Hail Marys, that is the most popular of all Marian prayers. The first half of the prayer is biblical, being composed of the supposed words of the Angel Gabriel at the Annunciation, 'Hail, full of grace, the Lord is with you' (Lk 1:28),[7] and the words of Elizabeth to Mary in the Visitation scene, 'Blessed are you among women, and blessed is the fruit of your womb' (Lk 1:42). These phrases had formed a Marian prayer by the tenth century and were also associated at that time with Mary's day, Saturday. As the recitation of the psalms became a standard part of clerical prayer, the practice began of recommending to the laity the recitation of one hundred and fifty Hail Marys to parallel the clerical recitation of psalms in the Office. Eventually the Hail Marys were divided into groups of ten, preceded by the *Pater Noster* and ending with the *Gloria,* and even later an appropriate biblical scene was attached to each group of ten or decade. Thus over centuries, one of the most favoured Roman Catholic prayers was created. When the petition for a happy death for 'us sinners' was added, the Rosary was complete. With the addition of the Apostles' Creed at the beginning, the Rosary was seen as the perfect form of prayer for the laity, containing as it did, everything that they needed to know. It was even sometimes called *biblia pauperum*, the Bible of the poor.[8]

While there is no denying the enormous devotional impact of this devotion to Mary in the middle ages, there is also no doubt about the negative spiritual and theological results. In this devotion we can see exactly what being a lay medieval Christian felt like. One felt 'banished' from the central core of the church, rated as unworthy to approach God directly, and always under judgement by a God who opted, according to all the brilliant teachers, for justice rather than mercy. The functioning of the inquisitional procedures against heresy, the growing power of the clergy and the increasing distance in ecclesial worth between clergy and laity, added to the growing emphasis on personal sin. The overwhelming medieval sense of the presence of the devil only added to the general feeling of abandonment. It is no wonder that Mary appeared as the only hope of the average believer. While the underlying theological distortion of all this is obvious today, it was not apparent then, even to the most scholarly monks and bishops. Both the church on earth and in heaven had become one concerted forum for rendering justice, meaning almost universally just and unavoidable punishment for what was considered sin. The appearance of Mary as the great figure of intervention on behalf of the sinner, with powers akin to and even superior to divine power, must have seemed like a miraculous gift. While there is absolutely no evidence that any medieval Christian ever spoke of her as God, nevertheless, Mary had attracted to herself many of the most beneficent powers of the biblical Jesus and did, in fact, function as the divine face of mercy and forgiveness for generations of believers. Her virginal motherhood of Christ was the foundation of the whole enterprise. Hers was the face of the ideal woman, pure, virginal, merciful, queenly, and absolutely untouched by sin. Only a woman could have fulfilled this role, and even though it has been asserted that in a church which gave such honour to one woman, all women were similarly honoured, that has not been the case. The contrary is closer to the truth. There was so much that Mary had to offer to the believer, but one thing was missing. Mary could not offer an image of repentance or penitence, and even more, she could not offer an image of a woman repenting of her supposed core sinfulness, namely sexuality. For this, a different woman was needed, and it is the same middle ages which offers us, for this purpose, the image of Mary Magdalen.

Mary Magdalen

Just as the image of the Virgin Mary had been pieced together over the centuries, so had the image of Magdalen, the sinner saint, attracted to itself a multiplicity of images. The imagery attaching to both of these women illustrates perfectly the genius of Christianity for encoding, decoding and recoding imagery as necessary, and the resulting, iconic figures – as in both of these cases – need have little to do with the originating biblical story. In this case, the originator of the Magdalen imagery is said to have been Pope Gregory I, who died in 604, having been pope since 589. His achievement was gained by conflating several of the female characters of the New Testament into one image of the repentant woman. His achievement has been termed both 'a great stroke of genius' and one of the 'greatest historical falsifications', the latter, in terms of biblical testimony, being closer to the truth. Nevertheless, the creation of Gregory was to exert an enormous influence on ecclesiastical attitudes toward women, not only in the denial of Mary Magdalen's apostolic role, but also in the creation of the sinful woman in a state of permanent repentance because of her female sexuality.

Gregory's new woman started from the assumption that the biblical healing of Mary from Magdala was for the sin of prostitution. This was achieved by identifying her with the repentant woman in Luke's gospel (Lk 7:36-39) who washed the feet of Jesus with her tears and dried them with her hair, thereby equipping Magdalen with the extraordinary cascades of hair beloved of all artists. She was also given that other piece of essential equipment, her jar of expensive ointment, which 'filled the house with its perfume', and was another sign of her occupation as a prostitute, skilled in seducing men with such bewitching tools of her trade. The money required for such expensive purchases posited a wealthy family for Magdalen, and another conflation provided this. She was identified with Mary of Bethany, sister of Lazarus and Martha, supposedly from one of the most aristocratic families in the city of Magdala. With occasional hints of the woman taken in adultery from the eighth chapter of John, and the Samaritan woman with her five husbands from the fourth, this newly created woman was complete. Indeed this Mary Magdalen has taken such a hold on the Christian imagination that all the exegesis in the world seems unable to dislodge it.[9]

The earliest representation of Mary Magdalen in art is in the little church of Dura Europos, dated to about 230 CE. Here she is one of the women at the tomb, come to anoint the body of Jesus, and already she has her ointment jar in her hand, and is dressed in the elegant style that became one of her trademarks in art. It is on the Ruthwell Cross from seventh-century England that we get the earliest image of her as the weeping woman at the feet of Jesus, and we know that her life story is already being elaborated.[10] By the eleventh century, Mary Magdalen is being venerated all over Europe, her feastday has been established on 22 July, dozens of churches are claiming to possess her relics, and her life story has become the stuff of common knowledge. The eleventh century is a boom-time for Magdalen veneration and the image of the submissive woman repenting her sexuality at the feet of Jesus suited the church's agenda excellently. It was, indeed, the flip side of the ecclesiastical attempts to make marriage and sexuality unappetising to the clergy and offered a fitting model to the hopefully repentant wives. Besides it filled out the picture of earthly womanhood in giving a clear model for all those who could not dream of attaining the purity of the Virgin Mary.

It was at Vezelay in Burgundy, situated almost in the very centre of France, that devotion to Mary Magdalen grew until this monastery became the fourth most important Christian pilgrimage site, after Jerusalem, Rome and Compostela. One cannot cease to be amazed at the power of this fictional composite image of supposed biblical and Christian virtue, when the real biblical image of Magdalen as the leader of the women disciples and the 'apostle to the apostles' had never stirred any similar enthusiasm, even among most women. The medieval love affair with Mary Magdalen grew with the contemporary development of the relic industry. It is almost comical that the standard word for the discovery of relics – invention – has lost the meaning of discovery today and indicates something closer to the notion of creative fiction which was a large part of the relic industry. Relics were needed, however, in abundance. In 1140, Gratian had decreed that every altar should have at least one relic. The eucharist could not otherwise be celebrated there. Relics were needed for the swearing of oaths, for the healing of the sick, for the protection of monarchs and they were carried into battle. Every convent, monastery, church, ruler vied with each other in the scope and significance of their relic collection. Dismemberment had long been accepted, and the bodies of most holy people were carved up and boiled to make distribution easier. This was later to be the fate of the body of Thomas Aquinas. The hair-raising story of the famous Hugh, Bishop of Lincoln, gives some indication of the seriousness of the hunt for relics. Hugh travelled to northern France where, at the monastery of Fécamp, there was reputed to be an arm of Mary Magdalen. He tried in vain to break off a piece, and then in utter frustration put it into his mouth and gnawed at it with, it was reported, 'not only his incisors but his molars'. The monks, we are told, were horrified, but Hugh got his dream relic.[11]

Several churches claimed to have locks of Magdalen's hair, some of the ointment from her ever-present jar, or even a piece of her forehead touched by Jesus in the much loved *noli me tangere* scene. It was Vezelay, however, which claimed to have 'invented' the complete corpse of Mary Magdalen, and this soon was seen to eliminate all other claims, as well as all other versions of her biography. Earlier versions of her life had placed her tomb at Ephesus with a later translation to Constantinople to be placed beside the body of Lazarus. It was France, however, which won out in the claim to have the definitive body and life-story of this remarkable composite saint. After the resurrection, Mary Magdalen, Martha and Lazarus preached throughout the Holy Land, this story goes, until they aroused the anger of the Jews. All three were shoved out to sea in a rudderless boat, which eventually deposited them at Marseille. Here, their apostolic lives of preaching continued, and some artistic representations would indicate that Martha and Lazarus became bishops. Magdalen, however, was said to have retired, either as a penitent sinner or as a profoundly meditative hermit, to the sacred and very aptly named cave of La Baume, high in the hills.

The monks at Vezelay were never too forthcoming about the reasons why her body should have arrived there, but from the eleventh century, the word was out that this one abbey possessed this great treasure.[12] Vezelay had grown to be one of the largest abbeys of Christendom, and it was from here, as we have seen, that Pope Eugenius III had sent the united forces of the Christian world, including the followers of Eleanor of Aquitaine, off to the second crusade.[13] From 1026 when the Benedictines from Cluny took over the direction of the abbey, its fortunes increased miraculously under the patronage of Mary Magdalen. By mid-century, Vezelay was confirmed by the Bull of Pope Leo IX as one of the main owners of the relics of the saint and she became the sole patron of the abbey. Pilgrims flocked to Vezelay, and vast wealth accrued to both abbey and town. So many freed prisoners came to donate their chains that the abbot was able to erect a huge iron railing around the high altar. Sinners flocked for forgiveness and peace descended even on the warlike Burgundians. Even though no one had ever seen the relics, their existence at Vezelay was confirmed by three popes in succession as well as by the French monarchy. Vezelay became one of the

most important meeting places for pilgrims en route to
Compostela.

By the thirteenth century, the fortunes of the abbey were de-
clining, and it was then that the burial place and indeed the
body were discovered – invented – in the most dramatic fashion.
Questions had always persisted – in the face of the rival claims
of Marseille and La Baume – about the hows and whys of
Magdalen's presence at Vezelay. Even reports of an angry
Magdalen appearing to one of the monks, claiming 'It is really
me', did not squelch the questions. One of the abbots was said to
have attempted to open the tomb, only to be surrounded by
thick darkness and a strong warning about doubting her presence. The pilgrims continued to dwindle, however, and drastic
action was seen to be necessary. The monks published the ancient story of the journey from Palestine to Provence and then
explained the saint's presence at Vezelay through the execution
of a *sacra furta*, or holy theft. Such thefts were widely seen as
praiseworthy, and in this case, a new vision of Magdalen confirmed it. The saint now is confirmed as a penitent hermit, naked
and clad only with her hair. She is said to have been discovered
half-dead by a priest, who eventually buried her. Several versions of her story were in circulation, but all end with the relics
being centred at Vezelay. Apart from the honour brought to
Vezelay, France how had on its own soil a direct link with
Christ. Lazarus, now seen as the first Bishop of Marseille, was
buried there. Martha, it was said, had retired to Tarascon which
was being plagued then by a death-dealing dragon. In a truly
early feminist re-writing of the story of George and the dragon,
Martha is said to have tamed the dragon and to have led it back
repentant to the village.[14]

After a gruelling few decades at the opening of the thirteenth
century, when abbots were deposed and monks were in revolt,
finally in 1265, during the night of 4-5 October at matins, the
bones of a saint were discovered wrapped in silk under the high
altar in the crypt, accompanied, it was reported with awe, by 'an
extraordinary amount of female hair'. This could be none other

than Magdalen. The monks had the relics officially confirmed and then bones, hair and document of confirmation were quickly re-sealed with the body to prevent theft. The most Christian king, Louis IX, was invited to the Mass of celebration on 24 April 1267, when the relics were displayed in a new silver reliquary. The king had demanded and received a large part of the bones and he won instant acclaim by distributing bits to the crowds. For the crowds were back. The king sent gorgeous reliquaries and relics to the monastery over the next few years, including the apron from the washing of the feet and some thorns from the crown. It was only fitting, he said, that these should rest near Magdalen in death, since she was so near to them in life.

For about a decade Vezelay enjoyed a revival, but to their horror, it was reported in 1279 that practically a complete body, definitely that of Mary Magdalen, had been found in Provence, near her famous cave of repentance. The following year, the bones were solemnly exhumed and a document was found with them saying: 'Here lies the body of Mary Magdalen.' New gold and silver reliquaries were created, including a gold head-shaped reliquary for her head, topped with a gold crown. In 1295, Pope Boniface VIII confirmed this new relic and Vezelay fell into decline. Her festival is still celebrated among the Provencals in the week of 21-28 July.

Mary Magdalen was the favourite saint of the middle ages, even though her devotion was initiated by nothing more than monastic rivalries. She filled a gap and had the widest appeal of any saint because of her quasi erotic and penitential represent-ation. As the image of a redeemed prostitute, she offered both an image of repentance, but also sufficient titillation in her naked hair-covered body to add a frisson of sexual interest to her cult. Despite her fictional nature, this composite Mary Magdalen was listed first among all the saints, and it was ruled that the Creed should be recited at her festal liturgy, just as it was for feasts of Jesus, Mary, and the apostles. The church even instituted penal-ties for those who failed to celebrate her feastday appropriately, and these earthy penalties were often confirmed by a display of heavenly displeasure. Many trades adopted her as their patron, including gardeners, apothecaries, perfume-makers, hair-dressers and wool-weavers. Hospitals, prisons, brothels and churches were dedicated to her, and eventually the colleges at Oxford and Cambridge.

Mary Magdalen offered so much to the believer. She was a favourite of Jesus, a model of conversion and repentance and, above all, a redeemed whore. Since she had become identified with Mary of Bethany, and portrayed in the gospels as one of the closest friends of Jesus, the story of her eventual fall into prostitution had to be explained. The story that was developed described her as the future betrothed of John the Evangelist and beloved disciple of Jesus, whose wedding was being celebrated at Cana. The presence of Jesus and the great wine-making miracle so impressed John that he did not go through with the nuptials and abandoned Mary to follow Jesus. The rage of Mary led her into a life of absolute profligacy. Her conversion took place at the feet of Jesus in the house of Simon the Pharisee. It may have been the paradoxical nature of Mary's life that was found to be so attractive. She was lovingly described as 'most chaste prostitute' and 'most blessed sinner'. As we have seen above, her story helped to make the lives of real prostitutes a little more bearable throughout the middle ages. The hope of conversion was always present.

The ecclesiastical ideals of the middle ages found in her a perfect female model. Though Magdalen had not achieved marriage, she was seen as a wonderful model for all married women, still labouring under sin as daughters of Eve. The confusion of marriage with prostitution was not uncommon throughout the medieval period, especially for women. It had originated in the push to destroy clerical marriage and continued in the ever-present ecclesiastical disquiet with female sexuality. Mary Magdalen could represent both the necessarily ongoing presence of female sexuality, and at the same time, provide a model for its defeat and redemption. Magdalen also offered a more delectable female model than the Virgin Mary. Her once sinful body was always at hand in art. She is forever draped in voluptuous reds and purples. As the image of grief, her body is bent and contorted in the most revelatory ways. As a penitent, her naked body is presented, gaunt and emaciated, but nevertheless covered only in hair and always suggestive of the female temptress she once was. Devotion to Mary Magdalen must have been a veritable voyeur's paradise for the medieval monk, in a way that could never be offered by the imagery of the Virgin Mary. Even though the Virgin Mary was seen theologically as the new Eve, she could never portray the reality of that ancient fornication as Magdalen could. In fact, Mary of Magdala was Everywoman, especially every married woman.

As the list of women's failings poured endlessly from the pens of medieval clerics, it must have been some small consolation for them to look on Magdalen. Albert the Great warned all to look on a woman only as a 'venomous serpent and horned devil'. Woman is further described as 'the confusion of man, an insatiable beast, a continuous worry, an incessant warfare, daily ruin, a house of tempests, a hindrance to devotion ...' and one who ensnares men and robs them of all their strength.[15] The discovery of Aristotle's description of a woman as an accidental male, and his description of marriage as the union of two unequal beings, only added certainty to the monkish and clerical imaginings. It was at this period that women and men were separated in churches, and the image of Mary Magdalen sitting silently at the feet of Jesus returns to rebuke the reported restlessness and 'jangling' of women in church. The supposed aristocratic and wealthy background of Magdalen gives preachers wonderful opportunities to preach on her inevitable worldliness, and her use of cosmetics and jewellery to deceive the hearts of men. The extent of the use of Magdalen's image is extraordinary. There are hundreds of semons and stories, all directed at women. At no time was the repentance of Peter or Thomas used to such effect. These twin devotions to two male-constructed female models provide a perfect example of how religious traditions can be endlessly creative in proposing theological, spiritual, and liturgical models as a vehicle for the male, and in this case, clerical control of women.

Conclusion

The medieval world has long been associated with towering cathedrals, papal power and grandeur, the brilliant achievements of scholastic theology, the institution of the great universities, the foundation of new religious orders with their still popular saints and founders, and the extraordinary advances in law, philosophy and what might be called natural science. In a word, the medieval world and Christendom are co-terminous. It is not, however, in these still recognisable institutions that we seek traces of women's presence. Certainly the women were there, but their lives and spiritual presence were not considered necessary, either for the founding or maintenance of these institutions. Indeed, women were deliberately forbidden to attend university and to take any public part in the life of the church. Nevertheless, even though the conventional historical memory of the Christian women of the middle ages has come down to us only in prohibitions and negative definitions, many women left their mark on this extraordinary age. We meet these women in convents, in houses of prostitution, in the courts of the Inquisition, along the pilgrim paths of Europe and the Holy Land, in hospitals, prisons, leprosaria, and market squares, and occasionally in papal and episcopal courts.

What is even more important for us, at this distance from the medieval world, is that we can still hear the voices of these women as they describe their momentous encounters with the God who created and recreated them. The medieval period presents us with one of the greatest outpourings of the voices of women in Christian history. These brilliant, eccentric and passionate women were visionaries, mystics, teachers, preachers, abbesses, recluses, pilgrims and profoundly creative theologians. They exercised these ministries in a world that felt no need of such ministry from women, and often resented and tried to prevent it. The world of women was severely prescribed as to its parameters. They were defined as passive matter in relation to male potency and rationality, but passivity is not a word one would ever use to describe this group of women. They constantly transcended the set boundaries not only of familial life, but of the centuries-old patterns of religious and social life.

Reform was the watchword of the church as the second millennium dawned; in this case, reform of the clergy and the removal of lay influence from the heart of ecclesiastical life. Clerical reform always indicated a lessening of lay involvement, but in this case, with the new emphasis on the imposition of clerical celibacy and the obliteration of clerical marriage, it was women especially whose activities had to be curtailed. Perhaps it was in response to this reform movement, perhaps it was the expanding horizons of the time and the development of town life, or perhaps, eventually it was the influence of the returning crusaders with their stories of the Holy places – whatever combination of reasons we would like to assign the phenomenon, there is no doubt that women moved in precisely the opposite direction to the one indicated by a reform-minded church.

The spiritual lives of women flourished in spite of the fulminations of council after council and the exaction of law after law. From the abundance of writing left by these women, we know that they were haunted by the knowledge of their creation in the image of God and their recreation by the grace of Christ. In writing after writing, we find the women longing to return to the place 'where they were before they were'. They set out, often with little to guide them except their own fidelity, to find the paths that led to God. They explored with creativity and tenacity the landscape of their own souls, and shared their discoveries with anyone who cared to listen. Those within a monastic setting were blessed in this regard with a supportive and critical audience, but even there, it was the common belief of these women that the path to God was open to all.

When medieval women wrote, it was mostly in the vernacular, a new language for a completely new phenomenon. They designed the language as they went along, making their own path as they walked it. They were convinced that God was choosing the weak to confound the strong, and that 'many a learned master was a fool in God's sight'. They spoke of God with the familiarity of a most intimate relationship, and with the utter conviction of those who have seen the face of God, especially in their relationship with Christ. The celebration of the eucharist and the yearly round of liturgical life was often the focus of this intimate relationship but, again without exception, the women learned that they could not just remain there. They set out with burning energy to share their message of the compassion of God with all, and to invite all to tread the same path.

In the process, the medieval women mystics brought a whole new accent to the spiritual life of the age. Among so many themes that are characteristic of these writings, there are two in particular that must be mentioned. First is the unanimous emphasis on the compassionate love of God. This insight is common to all. When they had negotiated the difficult road to the vision of God, they found there a God of the utmost compassion. Julian of Norwich struggles for language to describe this compassion and insists that God is truly a mother in this regard. Mechtild of Magdeburg uses the language of courtly love to describe this attribute of God and joins with Julian in writing at length on the exquisite courtesy of God in our regard. Marguerite Porete addresses God as Lady Love and deliberately sets up two contrasting worlds and churches where those who accept God's love grow in intimacy, while those who depend on reason ultimately fall away and die. None of these women found an aloof, distant or angry God at the end of their God-seeking. From the conviction born of this experience of love arises the gift of prophecy in so many of the mystics. They experience the need to pass on this love to the church and to challenge both the hypocrisy of a church which preaches but does not practise love, as well as the individual lives of clerics and others, including popes and emperors, who do not practise this love in their own lives.

Because of the universal experience of God's love, the medieval women mystics demonstrate a real difficulty with the concepts of sin and damnation. Though present in all the female mystical writing, this is perhaps most evident in the writing of Julian of Norwich. Julian cannot assign fault to the sinner, but judges sin to be a sense of worthlessness and futility, maybe even a failure of nerve in the individual. The recluse in her cell at Norwich looked out on the world with a compassionate eye. She cannot accept that God will abandon any sinner. The assumption of human nature by Christ and the recreation of this nature makes the thought of hell and divine judgement almost impossible for her. Julian continually acknowledges the teaching of the church in this regard, but returns to the subject again and again, challenging God to explain the divine attitude toward the sinner.

The cumulative effect of reading the writings of these women is profound. One feels that a new voice is being heard, that the core of divinity and humanity have been touched, that the heart of the Christian message is being approached. It is surely a tragedy and an almost irreparable loss to the Christian tradition that such wisdom was at no time allowed to modify the mainstream development of Christian teaching. Perhaps now is the time to attend to the voices of medieval women, so that what Hildegard described as the 'small voice of the trumpet' may become a clarion call to hear again the many forgotten dimensions of the Christian story.

Select Bibliography

Achtenberg, Jeanne, *Woman as Healer*, Shambala, 1990.

Allen, Prudence, RSM, 'Six Canadian Women: Their Call, their Witness, their Legacy', *The Canadian Catholic Review*, Vol. 5/7, July-August, 1987, pp. 246-258.

Allen, Prudence RSM, *The Concept of Woman: The Aristotelian Revolution, 750BC-AD 1250*, Eden Press, 1985.

Atkinson, Clarissa W., *Mystic and Pilgrim: The Book and World of Margery Kempe*, Cornell University Press, 1983.

Atkinson, Clarissa, W., et al., *Immaculate and Powerful: The Female in Sacred Image and Social Reality*, Women's Studies in Religion, Harvard University Press, 1985.

Atkinson, Clarissa, W., *The Oldest Vocation: Christian Motherhood in the Middle Ages*, Cornell University Press, 1991.

Babinsky, Ellen A., Editor and Translator, *Marguerite Porete: The Mirror of Simple Souls*, Classics of Western Spirituality, Paulist Press, 1993.

Baker, Derek, Editor, *Medieval Women*, Basil Blackwell, 1978.

Barber, Malcolm, *The Trial of the Templars*, Cambridge University Press, 1978.

Barratt, Alexandra, Translator, *The Herald of God's Loving-Kindness, Books One and Two*, Cistercian Publications, 1991

Barstow, Anne Llewellyn, *Married Priests and the Reforming Papacy: the Eleventh Century Debates*, The Edwin Mellen Press, 1982.

Barstow, Anne Llewellyn, *Witchcraze: A New History of the European Witch-Hunts*, Pandora, 1994.

Beers, William, *Women and Sacrifice: Male Narcissism and the Psychology of Religion*, Wayne State University Press, 1992.

Bell, Catherine, *Ritual Theory: Ritual Practice*, Oxford University Press, 1992.

Bell, Rudolf, *Holy Anorexia*, The University of Chicago Press, 1985.

Bennett, Judith, et al., Editors, *Sisters and Workers in the Middle Ages*, Oxford University Press, 1989.

Benstock, Shari, Editor, *The Private Self: Theory and Practice of Women's Autobiographical Writings*, The University of North Carolina Press, 1988.

Bordo, Susan, *Unbearable Weight: Feminism, Western Culture and the Body*, University of California Press, 1993.

Borresen, Kari Elisabeth, Editor, *The Image of God: Gender Models in Judaeo-Christian Tradition*, Fortress Press, 1995.

Bowie, Fiona, *Beguine Spirituality*, Spiritual Classics, Crossroad, 1990.

Bradford, Clare M., 'Julian of Norwich and Margery Kempe', in *Theology Today*, 35 (1978)153-158.

Brady Ignatius, OFM, Editor and Translator, *The Legend and Writings of St Clare of Assisi*, St Bonaventure, 1953.

Bridenthal, Renate and Koonz, Claudia, *Becoming Visible: Women in European History*, Houghton Mifflin Company, 1977.

Briggs, Robin, *Witches and Neighbours*, Fontana Press, 1996.

Bullough, Vern L. and Brundage, James, Editors, *Sexual Practices and the Medieval Church*, Promotheus Books, 1982.

Bunnik, R. 'The Question of Married Priests', *Cross Currents*, 15 (1965), pp. 407-431 and 16 (1966), pp. 683-705.

Cantor, Norman F., Church, *Kingship and Lay Investiture in England 1089-1135*, Princeton, 1958.

Carroll, Bernice, *Liberating Women's History: Theoretical and Critical Essays*, University of Illinois, 1976.

Cohn, Norman, *The Pursuit of the Millennium*, Pimlico Edition, 1993.

Colledge, Edmund and Walsh, James, Editors, *A Book of Showings to the Anchoress Julian of Norwich*, Pontifical Institute of Medieval Studies, Toronto, 1978.

Cooey, Paula M., et al, *Embodied Love: Sensuality and Relationship as Feminist Values*, Harper and Row, 1987.

Cooey, Paula M., *Religious Imagination and the Body*, Oxford University Press, 1994.

Curtayne, Alice, *Saint Catherine of Siena*, Sheed and Ward, 1929, and Tan Books, 1980.

Dalarun, Jacques, 'The Clerical Gaze' in *A History of Women, Vol. II, The Silences of the Middle Ages*, edited by Christiane Klapisch-Zuber, Harvard University Press, 1992, pp. 15-42.

Dronke, Peter, *Women Writers of the Middle Ages: A Critical Study of Texts from Perpetua (d. 203) to Marguerite Porete (d. 1310)*, Cambridge University Press, 1984.

Duby, Georges and Perrot, Michelle, General Editors, *A History of Women*, 5 Vols., Harvard University Press, 1992 – 1994.

Eigo, Francis A., Editor, *All Generations Shall Call Me Blessed*, The Villanova University Press, 1994.

Erler, Mary et al, *Women and Power in the Middle Ages*, University of Georgia Press, 1988.

Fatula, Mary Ann, OP, Editor, *The Way of the Christian Mystics: Catherine of Siena's Way*, Michael Glazier, Inc., 1987.

Finnegan, Mary Jeremy, *The Women of Helfta: Scholars and Mystics*, The University of Georgia Press, 1991.

Fletcher, Richard, *The Conversion of Europe: From Paganism to Christianity, 371-1386 AD*, Fontana Press, 1997.

Fox, Matthew, Editor, *Historical Roots: Ecumenical Routes*, Fides/Claretian, 1979.

Fox, Matthew, Editor, *Hildegard of Bingen: Book of Divine Works with Letters and Songs*, Bear & Company, 1987.

Fox, Matthew, *Illuminations of Hildegard of Bingen*, Bear & Company, 1985.

Fraser, Antonia, *The Warrior Queens*, Viking, 1988.

Fuchs, Eric, 'Sex and Power in the Church', in *Power in the Church, Concilium*, Vol. 197, pp. 23-28, T. and T. Clark, 1988.

Fulkerson, Mary McClintock, *Changing the Subject: Women's Discourses and Feminist Theology*, Fortress Press, 1994.

Gies, Frances and Joseph, *Life in a Medieval Village*, Harper Perennial, 1991.

Gies, Frances and Joseph, *Women in the Middle Ages*, Harper, 1978.

Ginzburg, Carlo, *Ecstasies: Deciphering the Witches' Sabbath*, Penguin Books, 1992.

Glascoe, Marion, Editor, *The Medieval Mystical Tradition in England*, Boydell and Brewer, 1984.

Graef, Hilda, *Mary: A History of Doctrine and Devotion*, 2 Vols., Christian Classics, Westminster MD, 1985.

Grundmann, H., *Religious Movements in the Middle Ages*, University of Notre Dame Press, 1995.

Haddad, Yvonne Yazbeck and Findly, Ellison Banks, Editors, *Women, Religion and Social Change*, State University of New York Press, 1985.

Halligan, Theresa A, Translator, *Book of Special Graces*, Pontifical Institute of Medieval Studies, Toronto, 1979.

Hart, Mother Columba and Bishop, Jane, Editors and Translators, *Hildegard of Bingen: Scivias, Classics of Western Spirituality*, Paulist Press, 1990.

Haskins, Susan, *Mary Magdalen: Myth and Metaphor*, HarperCollins, 1993.

Hastings, Adrian, Editor, *A World History of Christianity*, Cassell, 1999.

Herlihy, David, *Medieval Households*, Harvard University Press, 1985.

Jantzen, Grace M., *Julian of Norwich: Mystic and Theologian*. Paulist Press, 1987.

Jedin, Hubert and Dolan, John, *History of the Church, Vol. III, The Church in the Age of Feudalism*, Burns & Oates, 1980.

Jedin, Hubert, Editor, *History of the Church, Vol. IV, From the High Middle Ages to the Eve of the Reformation*, Burns & Oates, 1980.

Johnson, Elizabeth A., 'Mary and the Female Face of God', in *Theological Studies*, 50 (1989).

Johnson, Elizabeth A., *Friends of God and Prophets: A Feminist Theological Reading of the Communion of Saints*, Continuum, 1998.

Johnson, Elizabeth A., *SHE WHO IS: The Mystery of God in Feminist Theological Discourse*, Crossroad, 1992.

Johnson, Penelope, *Equal in Monastic Profession: Religious Women in Medieval France*, The University of Chicago Press, 1991.

Kadel, Andrew, *Matrology: A Bibliography of Writings by Christian Women from the First to the Fifteenth Centuries*, Continuum, 1995.

Kearns, Conleth, OP, Editor and Translator, *The Life of Catherine of Siena by Raymond of Capua*, Michael Glazier, Inc., 1980.

Kelly, Joan, *Women, History and Theory*, Chicago, 1984.

Kirshner, Julius and Wemple, Suzanne F., *Women of the Medieval World*, Basil Blackwell, 1985.

Klapisch-Zuber, Christiane, Editor, *A History of Women, Vol. II, The Silences of the Middle Ages*, Harvard University Press, 1992.

Kleinberg, Aviad M., *Prophets in Their Own Country: Living Saints and the Making of Sainthood in the Later Middle Ages*, The University of Chicago Press, 1992.

Kleinberg, S. Jay, *Retrieving Women's History: Changing Perceptions of the Role of Women in Politics and Society*, Oxford University Press, 1988.

Küng, Hans, *The Religious Situation of Our Time*, SCM Press Ltd., 1995.

Labarge, Margaret, W., *Women in Medieval Life*, London, 1984.

Lachman, Barbara, *The Journal of Hildedgard of Bingen*, Bell Tower, 1993.

Le Goff, Jacques, Editor, *The Medieval World*, Collins and Brown, 1990.

Lea, Henry D. *History of Sacerdotal Celibacy in the Western Church*, London, 1932.

Lerner, Gerda, *The Creation of Feminist Consciousness: From the Middle Ages to 1870*, Oxford University Press, 1993.

Lerner, Gerda, *The Creation of Patriarchy*, Oxford University Press, 1986.

Levack, Brian P. *The Witch-Hunt in Early Modern Europe*, Longman, 1995.

Lopez McAlister, Linda, Editor, *Hypatia's Daughters: Fifteen Hundred Years of Women Philosophers*, Indiana University Press, 1996.

Malone, Mary T. *Who Is My Mother? Rediscovering the Mother of Jesus*, Dubuque, Iowa, 1984.

Malone, Mary T., 'The Unfinished Agenda of the Church: A Critical Look at the History of Celibacy', in *Celibacy, The Way Supplement*, Vol. 77, 1993, pp. 66-75.

McDonnell, Ernest, *The Beguines and Beghards in Medieval Culture: With Special Emphasis on the Beguine Scene*, Rutgers University Press, 1954.

McGinn, Bernard, Editor, *Meister Eckhart and the Beguine Mystics*, Continuum, 1994.

McLaughlin, Eleanor, 'Women, Power and the Pursuit of Holiness in Medieval Christianity', pp. 101-129 in *Women of Spirit: Female Leadership in the Jewish and Christian Tradition*, Edited by Rosemary Ruether and Eleanor McLaughlin, Simon and Schuster, 1979.

McManners, John, Editor, *The Oxford Illustrated History of Christianity*, Oxford University Press, 1992.

McNamara, Jo Ann Kay, *Sisters in Arms*, Harvard University Press, 1996.

Meale, Carol M. Editor, *Women and Literature in Britain 1150-1500*, Cambridge University Press, 1993.

Menzies, Lucy, Translator, *The Revelations of Mechtild of Magdeburg*, Longman, Green & Co., 1953.

Merton, Thomas, *Conjectures of a Guilty Bystander*, Doubleday/Image, 1968.

Miles, Margaret, *Carnal Knowing: Female Nakedness and Religious Meaning in the Christian West*, Beacon Press, 1989.

Monson, Craig A., Editor, *The Crannied Wall: Women, Religion and the Arts in Early Modern Europe*, University of Michigan Press, 1992.

Murk-Jansen, Saskia, *Brides in the Desert*, Traditions of Christian Spirituality Series, Darton, Longman and Todd, 1998.

Newman, Barbara, *Sister of Wisdom: St Hildegard's Theology of the Feminine*, University of California Press, 1987.

Nichols, John A., and Shank, Lillian Thomas, Editors, *Peace Weavers: Medieval Religious Women*, Vol. 2, Cistercian Publications, Inc., 1987.

Noffke, Susan, *The Letters of St Catherine of Siena*, Medieval and Renaissance Texts and Studies, Binghampton, New York, 1988.

Noffke, Susan, *The Texts and Concordances of the Works of Caterina da Siena*, Madison, Wisconsin, 1987.

O'Carroll, Michael, CSSp., *Theotokos: A Theological Encyclopedia of the Blessed Virgin Mary*, Michael Glazier, Inc., 1983.

O'Dwyer, Peter, *Mary: A History of Devotion in Ireland*, Four Courts Press, 1988.

Osborne, Martha Lee, *Woman in Western Thought*, Random House, 1979.

Pelikan, Jaroslav, Flusser, David, Lang, Justin, *Mary: Images of the Mother of Jesus in Jewish and Christian Perspective*, Fortress Press, 1986.

Pernoud, Regine, *Joan of Arc*, A Scarborough Book, 1982.

Perrot, Michelle, *Writing Women's History*, Basil Blackwell, 1984.

Personal Narratives Group, *Interpreting Women's Lives: Feminist Theory and Personal Narratives*, Indiana University Press, 1989.

Petroff, Elizabeth Avilda, *Body and Soul: Essays on Medieval Women and Mysticism*, Oxford University Press, 1994.

Petroff, Elizabeth Avilda, Editor, *Medieval Women's Visionary Literature*, Oxford University Press, 1986.

Radford Ruether, Rosemary, *Women and Redemption: A Theological History*, Fortress Press, 1998.

Radice, Betty, Editor, *The Letters of Héloïse and Abelard*, Penguin, 1974.

Raitt, Jill, Editor, *Christian Spirituality: High Middle Ages and Reformation*, Crossroad, 1987.

Rosaldo, Michelle Zimbalist and Lamphere, Louise, *Women, Culture and Society*, Stanford University Press, 1974.

Rose, Mary Beth, Editor, *Women in the Middle Ages and the Renaissance*, Syracuse University Press, 1986.

Ross, Ellen M., 'Spiritual Experience and Women's Autobiography: The Rhetoric of Selfhood in The Book of Margery Kempe', *Journal of the American Academy of Religion*, LIX/3, 1991, pp. 527-546.

Ruether, Rosemary Radford, Editor, *Religion and Sexism: Images of Women in the Jewish and Christian Tradition*, New York, 1979.

Savage, Anne and Watson, Nicholas, Editors, *Anchoritic Spirituality: Ancrene Wisse and Associated Works*, Classics of Western Spirituality, Paulist Press, 1991.

Schillebeeckx, E., *Ministry: Leadership in the Community of Jesus Christ*, Crossroad, 1981.

Schine Gold, Penny, 'Male/Female Cooperation: The Example of Fontevrault', in *Distant Echoes: Medieval Religious Women*, Vol. I, Cistercian Publications Inc., 1984, pp. 151-168.

Schmitt, Miriam and Kulzer, Linda, Editors, *Medieval Women Monastics: Wisdom's Wellsprings*, The Liturgical Press, 1996.

Sells, Michael, A., *Mystical Languages of Unsaying*, The University of Chicago Press, 1994.

Shahar, Shulamith, *Childhood in the Middle Ages*, Routledge, 1992.

Shahar, Shulamith, *The Fourth Estate: A History of Women in the Middle Ages*, Methuen Press, 1983.

Sheldrake, Philip, *Spirituality and History: Questions of Interpretation and Method*, Crossroad, 1992.

Smith, Sidonie, *A Poetics of Women's Autobiography: Marginality and the Fictions of Self-Representation*, Indiana University Press, 1987.

Southern, R. W., *Western Society and the Church in the Middle Ages*, Penguin Books, 1970.

Strehlow, Dr Wighard and Hertzka, Gottfried, *Hildegard of Bingen's Medicine*, Bear & Company, 1988.

Talbot, C. H., Editor and Translator, *The Life of Christina of Markyate, A Twelfth Century Recluse*, Oxford, 1959.

Tobin, Frank, *Mechtild von Magdeburg: A Medieval Mystic in Modern Eyes*, Camdedn House, 1995.

Tuchman, Barbara W., *A Distant Mirror: The Calamitous 14th Century*, Alfred A. Knopf, 1978.

Ulrich, Ingeborg, *Hildegard of Bingen: Mystic, Healer, Companion of the Angels*, The Liturgical Press, 1990.

Walker Bynum, Caroline et al, *Gender and Religion: On the Complexity of Symbols*, Beacon Press, 1986.

Walker Bynum, Caroline, *Fragmentation and Redemption: Essays on Gender and the Human Body in Medieval Religion*, Zone Books, 1992.

Walker Bynum, Caroline, *Holy Feast, Holy Fast: The Religious Significance of Food to Medieval Women*, University of California Press, 1987.

Walker Bynum, Caroline, *Jesus as Mother: Studies in the Spirituality of the High Middle Ages*, The University of California Press, 1982.

Walker Bynum, Caroline, *The Resurrection of the Body*, Columbia University Press, 1995.

Walters, Clifton, Translator, *Julian of Norwich: Revelations of Divine Love*, Penguin Books, 1966.

Warner, Marina, *Joan of Arc: The Image of Female Heroism*, Knopf, 1981.

Warner, Marina, *Monuments and Maidens: The Allegory of the Female Form*, Picador, 1985.

Wiethaus, Ulrike, Editor, *Maps of Flesh and Light: The Religious Experience of Medieval Women Mystics*, Syracuse University Press, 1993.

Williams, Marty Newman and Echols, Anne, *Between Pit and Pedestal: Women in the Middle Ages*, Markus Wiener Publishers, 1994.

Wilson, Katharina, *Medieval Women Writers*, University of Georgia Press, 1984.

Windeatt, B.A., Translator, *The Book of Margery Kempe*, Penguin Classics, 1985.

Winkworth, Margaret, Editor, *Gertrude of Helfta: The Herald of Divine Love*, Paulist Press, 1993.

Zum Brunn, Emile & Epiney-Burgard, Georgette, *Women Mystics in Medieval Europe*, Paragon House, 1989.

Notes

CHAPTER ONE

1. Jacques Dalarun, 'The Clerical Gaze' in *A History of Women*, Vol. II, *The Silences of the Middle Ages*, edited by Christiane Klapisch-Zuber, Harvard University Press, 1992, pp. 15-42.

2. Quoted in *The Oxford Illustrated History of Christianity*, edited by John McManners, Oxford University Press, 1992, Chapter Six, 'Christian Civilization', (1050-1400), by Colin Morris, pp. 196-232.

3. Jacques Le Goff, Editor, *The Medieval World*, Introduction, Collins and Brown, 1990.

4. Jacques Le Goff, *op. cit.*, Introduction, pp. 20ff.

5. Quoted in *How to Read Church History*, Vol. 1, edited by Jean Comby, SCM Press, 1986, p. 133.

6. The joint declaration of Paul VI and Patriarch Athenagoras of 7 December, 1965, traces the rewrites the offensive language of the original document. They acknowledge that this gesture of reconciliation 'is not enough to put an end to the differences, older or more recent', which continue to exist between the churches, but express the hope of arriving at a 'common understanding and expression of the apostolic faith...'

7. Peter Damian, *De celibatu sacerdotum*, quoted in Anne Llewellyn Barstow, *Married Priests and the Reforming Papacy: The Eleventh Century Debates*, The Edwin Mellen Press, 1982, p. 119.

8. See Chapter 13, 'Never Better Ruled by any Man: Women as Consorts, Regents and Rulers', in *Between Pit and Pedestal: Women in the Middle Ages*, Marty Newman Williams and Anne Echols, Markus Wiener Publishers, 1994, p. 188.

9. A similar list is published in Hans Küng, *Christianity: The Religious Situation of Our Time*, SCM Press Ltd, 1995, pp. 383-384.

10. See the chapter, 'Matilda, Daughter of Peter', in *The Warrior Queens*, by Antonia Fraser, Viking, 1988, pp. 131ff.

11. *Op. cit.* p. 142. My account depends principally on Antonia Fraser's excellent chapter.

12. This manuscript can be seen in the Pierpont Morgan Library in New York, *op. cit.* p. 148

13. See Jo Ann Kay McNamara, *Sisters in Arms*, Harvard University Press, 1996, pp. 214ff.

14. *Ibid.* p. 217

15. Susan Haskins, *Mary Magdalen*, Harper Collins, 1993, pp. 98ff.

16. Norman Cohn, *The Pursuit of the Millennium*, Pimlico Edition, 1993.

CHAPTER TWO

1. Surprisingly, there are few full-length treatments of the history of celibacy and none that has replaced Henry D. Lea's *History of Sacerdotal Celibacy in the Western Church*, London, 1932. This is now dated and I have used it sparingly. Instead, I have relied on the following: Anne Llewellyn Barstow, *Married Priests and the Reforming Papacy: The Eleventh Century Debates*, The Edwin Mellen Press, 1982; R. Bunnik, 'The Question of Married Priests', *Cross Currents*, 15 (1965), pp. 407-431 and 16 (1966), pp. 683-705; Eric Fuchs, 'Sex and Power in the Church', in *Power in the Church, Concilium*, Vol. 197, pp. 23-28, T. and T. Clark, 1988; E. Schillebeeckx, *Ministry: Leadership in the Community of Jesus Christ*, Crossroad, 1981. It is Norman F. Cantor who comments on the world revolutionary nature of these events in *Church, Kingship and Lay Investiture in England 1089-1135*, Princeton, 1958.

I have also referred to the relevant sections of Hans Küng, *Christianity: The Religious Situation of our Time*, SCM Press Ltd., 1995 and Hubert Jedin and John Dolan, *History of the Church*, Vol. III, *The Church in the Age of Feudalism*, Burns and Oates, 1980. The last mentioned has abundant reference to the appropriate documentary evidence. See also Mary T. Malone, 'The Unfinished Agenda of the Church: A Critical Look at the History of Celibacy', in *Celibacy, The Way Supplement*, Vol. 77, 1993, pp. 66-75.

2. See Chapter One, p. 34.

3. Quoted in Barstow, *op. cit.*, p. 60.

4. See her Chapter Three, pp. 105-156. The next section relies substantially on this work.

5. Abbot Conrad of Marchtal, quoted in R. W. Southern, *Western Society and the Church in the Middle Ages*, Penguin Books, 1970, p. 314.

6 *A History of Women*, Vol. II, edited by Christiane Klapisch-Zuber, Harvard University Press, 1992.

7. For Grace's story, see Paulette L'Hermite-Leclercq, 'The Feudal Order', in *Silences of the Middle Ages*, pp. 202ff.

8. Carla Casagrande in 'The Protected Woman', *Silences of the Middle Ages*, p. 70ff.

9. A host of writers took up their pens to address the position of women at this time. They include Alan of Lille, James of Vitry, Vincent of Beauvais, William Peraldo, Gilbert of Tournai and John of Wales. The quotation is from Peraldo. See Casagrande, *op. cit.* p. 85.

10. Penelope D. Johnson, *Equal in Monastic Profession: Religious Women in Medieval France*, The University of Chicago Press, 1991, p. 257.

11. *Ibid*.

12. *Sisters in Arms: Catholic Nuns Through Two Millennia*, Harvard University Press, 1996, p. 211ff.

13. Silvana Vecchio, 'The Good Wife', in *A History of Women*, Vol. II, p. 105ff.

14. *Ibid*.

15. *Ibid*., p. 120ff.

CHAPTER THREE

1. I have used the work of Amy Kelly extensively in this chapter: *Eleanor of Aquitaine and the Four Kings*, Harvard University Press, 1978.

2. Christine Klapisch-Zuber, *Silences of the Middle Ages*, p. 14.

3. *Historia Calamitatum* or *The Story of My Misfortunes*, St Paul, 1922.

4. Quoted in *Hypatia's Daughters*, Edited by Linda Lopez McAlister, p. 26, Indiana University Press, 1996.

5. *Ibid*.

6. See the translation of *The Letters of Héloïse and Abelard* by Betty Radice, Penguin, 1974. See also Andrea Nye, 'A Woman's Thought or a Man's Discipline: The Letters of Abelard and Heloise', in *Hypatia's Daughters*, pp. 25-47. It is the quotations from Nye that I have used here.

7. See the section on Heloise's convent in Jo Ann Kay McNamara, *Sisters in Arms*, p. 290ff.

8. Quoted in Kelly, *op. cit.*, p. 20-21.

9. *Ibid*., p. 30f.

10. See Kelly's account of Rosamund in Chapter 14, *op. cit.*

11. *Ibid*., p. 311-312.

12. See *Between Pit and Pedestal:Women in the Middle Ages*, pp. 194-195, Markus Wiener Publishers, 1994, by Marty Williams and Anne Echols.

13. Quoted in R. W. Southern, *Western Society and the Church in the Middle Ages*, Penguin, 1970, p. 312.

14. See the fine account in 'Male/Female Cooperation: The Example of Fontevrault' by Penny Schine Gold in *Distant Echoes: Medieval Religious Women*, Vol. I, Cistercian Publications, Inc., 1984, pp. 151-168.

15. *Ibid*. p. 154.

16. *Ibid*., p. 162.

CHAPTER FOUR

1. Hubert Jedin, Editor, *History of the Church*, Vol. IV, *From the High Middle Ages to the Eve of the Reformation*, Burns & Oates, 1980, p. 39ff.

2. Hans Küng, *Christianity: The Religious Situation of our Time*, SCM Press, 1995, p. 390ff.

3. Other groups such as the followers of Peter Waldo, the 'poor man of Lyons', whose teachings were similar to the Albigensians, somehow managed to survive. The Waldensians eventually became part of the re-form movements of the sizxteenth century.

4. See Caroline Walker Bynum, *Jesus as Mother: Studies in the Spirituality of the High Middle Ages*, University of California Press, 1982, especially Part III, 'Did the Twelfth Century Discover the Individual?', pp. 82-109.

5. The literature on the spirituality of women in the middle ages is abundant and increasing daily. I mention here only two of these contributors: Caroline Walker Bynum and Elizabeth Avilda Petroff. Apart from Bynum's work metioned above, there is also the very helpful *The Resurrection of the Body*, Columbia University Press, 1995. Petroff's *Medieval Women's Visionary Literature*, Oxford Univeersity Press, 1986 has been enormously helpful in all my teaching and writing as well as her *Body and Soul: Essays on Medieval Women and Mysticism*, Oxford University Press, 1994.

6. For one of the best introductions to women's spirituality, see Petroff's Introduction to *Medieval Women's Visionary Literature*, pp. 3-59

7. *The Life of Christina of Markyate, a Twelfth Century Recluse*, was translated and edited by C. H. Talbot (Oxford, 1959). A large extract from this translation is published in Petroff, *Medieval Women's Visionary Literature*, 144-150.

8. Petroff, p. 144.

9. Eleanor McLaughlin, 'Women, Power and the Pursuit of Holiness in Medieval Christianity', pp. 101-129, in *Women of Spirit: Female Leadership in the Jewish and Christian Tradition*, Edited by Rosemary Ruether and Eleanor McLaughlin, Simon and Schuster, 1979.

10. We will see more of recluses when we explore the life of Julian of Norwich in Chapter Nine.

11. See Christopher J. Holdsworth, 'Christina of Markyate', pp. 185-204, in Derek Baker, Editor, *Medieval Women*, Basil Blackwell, 1978.

12. Scholarship on Hildegard has been booming for the past few years. I list here just a few of the more accessible works and commentaries which have been used in this text: *Hildegard of Bingen: Scivias*, Translated by Mother Columba Hart, Jane Bishop, Classics of Western Spirituality, Paulist Press, 1990; *Hildegard of Bingen: Book of Divine Works, with Letters and Songs*, Edited by Matthew Fox, Bear & Company, 1987; Barbara Newman, *Sister of Wisdom: St Hildegard's Theology of the Feminine*, University of California Press, 1987; Ingeborg Ulrich, *Hildegard of Bingen: Mystic, Healer, Companion of the Angels*, The Liturgical Press, 1990; and the relevant sections in Elizabeth Avilda Petroff, *Medieval Women's Visionary Literature*, pp. 136ff.; Miriam Schmitt, Linda Kulzer, Editors, *Medieval Women Monastics: Wisdom's Wellsprings*, The Liturgical Press, 1996, pp. 149ff.; Emilie Zum Brunn & Georgette Epiney-Burgard, Editors, *Women Mystcis in Medieval Europe*, Paragon House, 1989, pp. 3ff.; Prudence Allen, RSM, *The Concept of Woman: The Aristotelian Revolution, 750 BC-AD 1250*, Eden Press, 1985, pp. 292-316 and 409-412; Barbara Newman, 'Divine Power Made Perfect in Weakness: St Hildegard on the Frail Sex', pp. 103-122, in *Peace Weavers: Medieval Religious Women*, Volume Two, Edited by John A. Nichols and

Lillian Thomas Shank, Cistercian Publications, Inc., 1987; Helen J. John SND, 'Hildegard of Bingen: A New Twelfth-Century Woman Philosopher', pp. 16-24, in *Hypatia's Daughters: Fifteen Hundred Years of Women Philosophers*, Edited by Linda Lopez McAllister, Indiana University Press, 1996. See also *Illuminations of Hildegard of Bingen*, Commentary by Matthew Fox, Bear & Company, 1985; *The Journal of Hildegard of Bingen*, Barbara Lachman, Bell Tower, 1993; and Dr. Wighard Strehlow & Gottfried Hertzka, *Hildegard of Bingen's Medicine*, Bear & company, 1988.

13. Quoted from Petroff, *op. cit.*, p. 151.

14. See Barbara Newman, *Sister of Wisdom*, for general details in this biographical outline, and Emilie Zum Brunn, *op. cit.* for the quoted extracts from the letters.

15. See the discography on p. 273 of Barbara Newman, *Sister of Wisdom*.

16. For this following section, I am indebted to Prudence Allen, *The Concept of Woman*, pp. 292ff.

17. Quoted in *Peace Weavers*, p. 118-119.

18. Quoted in Lena Eckenstein, *Women Under Monasticism: Chapters on Saint- Lore and Convent Life, Between AD 500 and AD 1500*, Russell and Russell, 1963, p. 257. Not a great deal of attention has been paid to the writings of Elizabeth of Schönau until recently. The most accessible account is in Anne L. Clark, *Elizabeth of Schönau: A Twelfth-Century Visionary*, University of Pennsylvania Press, 1992. Her writings are collected in Vol. 195 of *Patrologia Latina*, cols. 119-194, but there is no critical English edition of her work. Petroff, *Medieval Women's Visionary Literature*, has Book Two of the *Visions*, edited and translated by Thalia A. Pandiri. See also, M. Colman O'Dell, 'Elizabeth of Schönau and Hildegard of Bingen: Prophets of the Lord', in *Peace Weavers: Medieval Religious Women*, Vol. 2, pp. 85-102; and Anne Beard, OSB, 'The Visionary Life of Elizabeth of Schönau: A Different Way of Knowing', in *Medieval Women Monastics*, pp. 167-182.

19. Petroff, p. 142.

20. *Visions*, Book Two, p. 159 in Petroff.

CHAPTER FIVE

1. Philip Sheldrake, *Spirituality and History: Questions of Interpretation and Method*, Crossroad, 1992. See Part One, p. 9ff.

2. The literature on the Beguines is now proliferating. Sheldrake's work *supra* has a very interesting case study on the Beguines, Chapter 6, pp. 133ff. The standard work used by all is Ernest McDonnell, *The Beguines and Beghards in Medieval Culture: With Special Emphasis on the Beguine Scene*, Rutgers University Press, 1954, together with the recently translated work of H. Grundmann, *Religious Movements in the Middle Ages*, University of Notre Dame Press, 1995, translated by Steven Rowan. The new Traditions of Christian Spirituality Series presents an excellent short work by Saskia Murk-Jansen, *Brides in the Desert*, Darton,

Longman and Todd, 1998, and Spiritual Classics from Crossroad had previously published *Beguine Spirituality* Edited by Fiona Bowie in 1990. Other works include Emilie Zum Brunn & Georgette Epiney-Burgard, *Women Mystics in Medieval Europe*, Paragon House, 1989 and *Meister Eckhart and the Beguine Mystics*, Edited by Bernard McGinn, Continuum, 1994. See also the appropriate and very helpful sections in *Medieval Women's Visionary Literature*, Edited by Elizabeth Avilda Petroff, Oxford University Press, 1986; *Sisters and Workers in the Middle Ages*, Edited by Judith M. Bennett et al, University of Chicago Press, 1989; and *Medieval Women*, Edited by Derek Baker, Basil Blackwell, 1978. There is a host of other studies, some of which will be mentioned at the appropriate place.

3. Zum Brunn, p. xiii-xiv.

4. See the *Life of Mary of Oignies*, translated by Margot King, reproduced in Petroff, pp. 179-183.

5. *Western Society and the Church in the Middle Ages*, Vol. 2, The Pelican History of the Church, Penguin Books, 1970, p. 319.

6. *Ibid*.

7. Southern, p. 329.

8. Southern, p. 330.

9. See Murk-Jansen, p. 34ff.

10. Petroff, Introduction to *Medieval Women's Visionary Literature*, pp. 3-59.

11. Jacques de Vitry's friend, Thomas de Cantimpre wrote this extraordinary life, perhaps as a case of one-up-manship. It is translated by Margot King and published in *Vox Benedictina*. Some sections are to be found in Petroff. See also 'The Sacramental Witness of Christina Mirabilis: The Mystic Growth of a Fool for Christ's Sake' in *Peace Weavers*, Volume Two of *Medieval Religious Women*, Edited by John A. Nichols and Lillian Thomas Shank, Cistercian Publications, 1987, pp. 145-164.

12. Petroff, pp. 9-10.

13. Quoted in Petroff, p. 179, translation by Margot King.

14. Quoted in Caroline Walker Bynum, *Fragmentation and Redemption: Essays on Gender and the Human Body in Medieval Religion*, p. 119, Zone Books, 1992.

15. Bynum, p. 122.

16. Bynum, p. 123.

17. As well as the discussion in the above article, see also Caroline Walker Bynum, *Holy Feast, Holy Fast: The Religious Significance of Food to Medieval Women*, University of California Press, 1987, and Rudolf M. Bell, *Holy Anorexia*, University of Chicago Press, 1985.

18. Bynum, p. 147.

19. *Holy Feast, Holy Fast*, p. 52ff.

20. See Emilie Zum Brunn for a good introduction to and analysis of Hadewijch's work.

21. Quoted from Petroff, *Medieval Women's Visionary Literature*, p. 190, translation by Mother Columba Hart

22. *Ibid*. p. 177.

23. Bowie, p. 96.

24. Murk-Jansen, Letter 6, p. 71.

25. Zum Brunn, p. 100.

26. *Ibid*. p. 105.

27. Letter XX, quoted in Zum Brunn, p. 108.

28. Letter XXVIII, quoted in Zum Brunn, p. 109.

CHAPTER SIX

1. See the chapter on The Medieval West in *A World History of Christianity*, Edited by Adrian Hastings, Cassell, 1999, pp. 110-146 for a very good summary of the century's developments.

2. There is no complete individual study on Helfta in English, though much has been written on its individually famous nuns and on the characteristics of the spirituality that was practised there. See expecially the lengthy study in Chapter V of Caroline Walker Bynum's *Jesus as Mother*, University of California Press, 1982. The chapter is entitled, 'Women Mystics in the Thirteenth Century: The Case of the Nuns at Helfta', pp. 170-262. This remains the standard study, but it has been supplemented by other general works on thirteenth century women's mysticism, especiall by studies of the writings of the three famous Helfta mystics, Mechtild of Hackborn, Gertrude of Helfta and Mechtild of Magdeburg. These will be referenced throughout.

3. This has been translated by Theresa A. Halligan from a fifteenth century English edition and published by the Pontifical Institute of Medieval Studies, 1979. See also the work of Mary Jeremy Finnegan, *The Women of Helfta: Scholars and Mystics*, The University of Georgia Press, 1991, and the same author's article in *Medieval Women Monastics*, pp. 231-242. See also Bynum, p. 209ff.

4. There are two recent translations of this work: *The Herald of God's Loving-Kindness, Books One and Two*, translated by Alexandra Barratt, Cistercian Publications, 1991; and *Gertrude of Helfta: The Herald of Divine Love*, translated and edited by Margaret Winkworth, Paulist Press, 1993. See also the selections in Petroff, *Medieval Women's Visionary Literature*, pp. 222-230; and the chapter in *Medieval Women Monastics*, by Jane Klimisch OSB, pp. 245-259. The section on Gertrude in Bynum's work starts on p. 186.

5. Quoted from Bynum, p. 202.

6. *Ibid*. p. 206.

7. *Herald* 2.3. Quoted in 'The God of My Life: St Gertrude, A Monastic Woman', pp. 239-273 by Lillian Thomas Shank in *Peace Weavers: Medieval Religious Women*, Cistersian Publications, 1987.

8. The English translation of Mechtild of Magdeburg's *Flowing Light of the Godhead* is by Lucy Menzies, *The Revelations of Mechtild of Magdeburg*,

Longman, Green & Co., 1953. See also the appropriate sections in the books mentioned above. See especially, Frank Tobin, *Mechtild von Magdeburg: A Medieval Mystic in Modern Eyes*, Camden House, 1995, and *Meister Eckhart and the Beguine Mystics*, Edited by Bernard McGinn, Continuum, 1994.

9. *Flowing Light of the Godhead*, 3.10. Quoted in Rosemary Radford Ruether, *Women and Redemption: A Theological History*, Fortress Press, 1998, p. 102.

10. *Flowing Light*, 5.8. Quoted in Edith Scholl, 'To Be a Full-Grown Bride: Mechtild of Magdeburg', p. 229 in *Peace Weavers*, pp. 223-237.

11. *Flowing Light*, 3.21-22. See Bynum's discussion of Mechtild of Magdeburg in *Jesus as Mother*, pp. 228ff.

12. *Flowing Light*, 6.36 in Bynum, *op. cit.*

13. *Flowing Light*, 4.16.

14. *Ibid.* 5.32 , quoted in Edith Scholl, as above, p. 232.

15. *Ibid.* 6.28, 7.1.

16. Elizabeth Avilda Petroff publishes the *Testament* of Clare in *Medieval Women's Visionary Literature*, pp. 242-245. This quote is from the introduction to the document, p. 232. There is an abundance of material on Clare, much of it focusing on her supposed emotional relationship with Francis. For more recent treatment, see the three excellent articles in *Peace Weavers*, pp. 165-210, 'St Clare' by Rosalind B. Brooke and Christopher N. L. Brooke, in *Medieval Women*, edited by Derek Baker, pp. 275-288. Her writings are edited and translated by Ignatius Brady OFM in *The Legend and Writings of Saint Clare of Assisi*, St Bonaventure, 1953. See also the article by Elizabeth Avilda Petroff in *Body and Soul: Essays on Medieval Women and Mysticism*, Oxford University Press, 1994, pp. 66-82.

17. Petroff, *Medieval Women's Visionary Literature*, p. 232.

18. Baker, p. 286-287.

CHAPTER SEVEN

1. Barbara W. Tuchman, *A Distant Mirror: The Calamitous 14th Century*, Alfred A. Knopf, 1978.

2. The most recent edition is in The Classics of Western Spirituality series, newly translated and edited by Ellen L. Babinsky, Paulist Press, 1993. Several recent studies of Marguerite's mysticism have been published, as well as excerpts from her book. See especially, *Meister Eckhart and the Beguine Mystics*, Edited by Bernard McGinn, Continuum, 1994; Emilie Zum Brunn & Georgette Epiney-Burgard, *Women Mystics in Medieval Europe*, Paragon House, 1989; Elizabeth Alvilda Petroff, Editor, *Medieval Women's Visionary Literature*, Oxford University Press, 1986; Michael A. Sells, *Mystical Languages of Unsaying*, The University of Chicago Press, 1994; Saskia Murk-Jansen, *Brides in the Desert: The Spirituality of the Beguines*, Darton, Longman & Todd, 1998; and the article, 'Living Without a Why', in *Doctrine and Life*, September, 1999, by Mary T. Malone.

3. For the historical details and citations from the work, I follow, for the most part, the edition of Ellen L. Babinsky.

4. See Malcolm Barber, *The Trial of the Templars*, Cambridge University Press, 1978.

5. See McGinn, p. 4ff.

6. The word 'station' is from Michael Sells, in 'The Pseudo-Woman and the Meister: 'Unsaying' and Essentialism', in McGinn, *op. cit.*, pp. 114ff.

7. In general, I am following the text and analysis of Babinski.

8. *Mirror*, chapter III.

9. Chapter 86.

10. Chapter 56.

11. Chapter 70.

12. Chapter 82.

13. Michael Sells, *Mystical Languages of Unsaying*, passim.

14. *Mirror*, Chapter 87.

15. Chapter 130.

16. Chapter 135.

17. Chapter 68, 115.

18. Chapter 67.

19. Chapter 85.

20. Chapter 135.

21. See the discussion by Amy Hollywood in 'Suffering Transformed: Marguerite Porete, Meister Eckhart, and the Problem of Women's Spirituality', in McGinn, *Meister Eckhart and the Beguine Mystics*, pp. 87-113.

22. See McGinn for the mosr recent editions and commentaries on Eckhart's work. See also 'An Eckhart Bibliography' in *The Thomist*, Vol. 42, pp. 313-337, 1978 for a fairly exhaustive bibliography to that date.

23. See 'Marguerite Porete and Meister Eckhart: The Mirror of Simple Souls Mirrored', in McGinn, pp. 65-86.

24. For the complete writings, see Suzanne Noffke, *The Texts and Concordances of the Works of Caterina da Siena*, Madison, Wisconsin, 1987; also by the same author, *The Letters of St Catherine of Siena*, Medieval and Renaissance Texts and Studies, Binghampton, New York, 1988. Mary Ann Fatula, OP, has edited Vol. 4 of *The Way of the Christian Mystics: Catherine of Siena's Way*, Michael Glazier Inc., 1987. The life by Alice Curtayne is still extremely useful: *Saint Catherine of Siena*, first published by Sheed and Ward, 1929 and republished by Tan Books in 1980. All research on Catherine goes back to *The Life of Catherine of Siena*, written by her Dominican director and closest friend, Raymond of Capua. This is published by Michael Glazier Inc., in a translation by Conleth Kearns, OP, 1980. Elizabeth Petroff has translated and published a selection from the letters in *Medieval Women's Visionary Literature*, pp. 263ff. For a commentary on Catherine's mystical teaching, see 'Foundations of Christian Formation in the Dialogue of St Catherine of Siena', in *Peace Weavers*, pp. 274-288; and for a commentary on the

Letters, see Carola Parks, OP, 'Social and Political Consciousness in the Letters of Catherine of Siena', in *Western Spirituality: Historical Roots, Ecumenical Routes*, Edited by Matthew Fox, Fides/Claretian, 1979.

25. Quoted in Paul Johnson, *A History of Christianity*, Penguin books, 1978, p. 221.

26. See Barbara W. Tuchman for a good brief account of the plague, *A Distant Mirror: The Calamitous Fourteenth Century*, Chapter 5, Alfred A. Knopf, 1978.

27. Jo Ann Kay McNamara, *Sisters in Arms*, p. 319, Harvard University Press, 1996.

28. Quoted in Curtayne, p. 91.

29. *Holy Anorexia*, The University of Chicago Press, 1985. See also Carolyn Walker Bynum, *Holy Feast, Holy Fast: The Religious Significance of Food to Medieval Women*, University of California Press, 1987.

CHAPTER EIGHT

1. See Stephen Wessley, 'The Thirteenth Century Guglielmites: Salvation Through Women', pp. 289-304 in Derek Baker (Ed.), *Medieval Women*, Basil Blackwell, 1978. See also 'If Ignorance Were a Woman's Passport to Paradise: Women in Heretical Sects', Chapter Nine in *Between Pit and Pedestal: Women in the Middle Ages*, by Marty Williams and Anne Echols, Markus Wiener Publishers, 1994, pp. 133-142.

2. See Petroff, *Medieval Women's Visionary Literature*, p. 284 for the Confession of Na Prous Boneta.

3. Petroff, p. 284.

4. Regine Pernoud, *Joan of Arc*, A Scarborough Book, 1982, translated from the French by Edward Hyams.

5. Pernoud, p, 209.

6. Pernoud, p. 218.

7. Peroud, p, 233.

8. Pernoud, p. 269.

9. *Ibid*.

10. See Robin Briggs, *Witches and Neighbours*, Fontana Press, 1996, for an excellent discussion of the witch-craze from this perspective. A complete bibliography will be given in the next volume when the sixteenth and seventeenth century witch-craze will be covered, but see also, Anne Llewllyn Barstow, *Witchcraze: A New History of the European Witch-Hunts*, Pandora, 1994; Carlo Ginzburg, *Ecstasies: Deciphering the Witches' Sabbath*, Penguin Books, 1992; Brian P. Levack, *The Witch-Hunt in Early Modern Europe*, Longman, 1995. See also the article, 'Abracadabra: Superstitions and 'Witchcraft', in Williams and Echols, *Between Pit and Pedestal*, pp. 143-155.

11. See especially *Sexual Practices and the Medieval Church*, edited by Vern L. Bullough & James Brundage, Prometheus Books, 1982, especially Chapters 4, 14, 16.

CHAPTER NINE

1. For a good introduction, see *Anchoritic Spirituality: Ancrene Wisse and Associated Works*, The Classics of Western Spirituality, translated and introduced by Anne Savage and Nicholas Watson, Paulist Press, 1991. Referred to as *AS* from now on. See also Jean Leclercq, 'Solitude and Solidarity: Medieval Women Recluses', pp. 67-84 in *Peace Weavers: Medieval Religious Women*, Cistercian Publications, 1987; and *ibid.*, Patricia J. F. Rosof, 'The Anchoress in the Twelfth and Thirteenth Centuries', pp. 123-144.

2. See *AS*, pp. 41-207.

3. See *AS*, pp. 223-243.

4. 'Six Canadian Women: Their Call, Their witness, Their Legacy', by Prudence Allen, RSM, in *The Canadian Catholic Review*, Vol. 5, 7, July/August 1987, pp. 246-258.

5. For Julian see Edmund Colledge and James Walsh Eds., *A Book of Showings to the Anchoress Julian of Norwich*, Pontifical Institute of Medieval Studies, Toronto, 1978. See also *Julian of Norwich: Revelations of Divine Love*, translated by Clifton Walters, Penguin Books, 1966. This is the edition that I mostly use. For an overview and excellent analysis of Julian's teaching, see Grace M. Jantzen, *Julian of Norwich: Mystic and Theologian*, Paulist Press, 1987.

6. Quoted in Jantzen, p. 15, from the Short Text, 6.

7. *Conjectures of a Guilty Bystander*, Doubleday/Image, 1968.

8. See the discussion of Julian in Rosemary Radford Ruether, *Women and Redemption: A Theological History*, Fortress Press, 1998, p. 104-111.

9. Long Text, 7.

10. Long Text, Ch. 86.

11. Long Text, Ch. 27.

12. Long Text, Ch. 50-Ch. 51.

13. Long Text, Ch. 55.

14. Quoted in Carolyn Walker Bynum, *Jesus as Mother*, University of California Press, 1982, p. 135-136.

15. Long Text, Ch. 58.

16. Long Text, 60.

17. Long Text, Ch. 5.

18. Long Text, Ch. 9.

19. *The Book of Margery Kempe*, translated by B.A. Windeatt, Penguin Classics, 1985. There is a great deal of interest in Margery Kempe in recent times. See the following: Clarissa W. Atkinson, *Mystic and Pilgrim: The Book and World of Margery Kempe*, Cornell University Press, 1983; Ellen M. Ross, 'Spiritual Experience and Women's Autobiography: The Rhetoric of Selfhood in the Book of Margery Kempe', *Journal of the American Academy of Religion*, LIX/3, 1991, pp. 527-546; Janel M. Mueller, 'Autobiography of a New 'Creature': Female Spirituality, Selfhood, and Authorship in the *Book of Margery Kempe*', in Mary Beth Rose, Editor, *Women in the Middle Ages and the Renaissance*, Syracuse University Press,

1986; Clare M. Bradford, 'Julian of Norwich and Margery Kempe', in *Theology Today*, 35 (1978) 153-158; A. E. Goodman, 'The Piety of John Brunham's Daughter, of Lynn', in Derek Baker, Editor, *Medieval Women*, Basil Blackwell, 1978, pp. 347-358; Chapter 4, 'The Book of Margery Kempe: This Creature's Unsealed Life', pp. 64-83 in *A Poetics of Women's Autobiography: Marginality and the Fictions of Self-Representation*, by Sidonie Smith, Indiana University Press, 1987.

20. See Sidonie Smith, *op. cit.* above; also Shari Benstock, Editor, *The Private Self: Theory and Practice of Women's Autobiographical Writings*, The University of North Carolina Press, 1988; and The Personal Narratives Group, *Interpreting Women's Lives: Feminist Theory and Personal Narratives*, Indiana University Press, 1989.

CHAPTER TEN

1. The writing on medieval images of Mary is voluminous. See especially, Hilda Graef, *Mary: A History of Doctrine and Devotion*, 2 Vols., Westminster, MD, Christian Classics, 1985; Peter O'Dwyer, *Mary: A History of Devotion in Ireland*, Four Courts Press, 1988. Especially helpful were several articles by Elizabeth Johnson, especially, 'Marian Devotion in the Western Church', in *Christian Spirituality: High Middle Ages and Reformation*, edited by Jill Raitt, Crossroad 1987, pp. 392-414; and 'Toward a Theology of Mary: Past, Present and Future', in *All Generations Shall Call Me Blessed*, Edited by Francis A. Eigo, OSA, The Villanova University Press, 1994. See also Mary T. Malone, *Who is My Mother?: Rediscovering the Mother of Jesus*, Dubuque, Iowa, 1984. For Marian specifics of doctrines, dates, authors and devotions, one cannot be without *Theotokos: A Theological Encyclopedia of the Blessed Virgin Mary*, by Michael O'Carroll, C.S.Sp., Michael Glazier, Inc., 1983.

2. Homily, 'In Praise of the Virgin Mother', 2.17. Quoted in Malone, p. 48.

3. Malone, p. 49.

4. See Chapter Eight of *Lumen Gentium*, the Dogmatic Constitution on the Church, as well as the brilliant document of Paul VI, written over a decade later, *Marialis Cultus*.

5. Quoted in Elizabeth A. Johnson, CSJ, 'Mary and the Female Face of God', in *Theological Studies* 50 (1989), p. 508.

6. For a brief discussion of the development of this dogma, as well as that of the Assumption of Mary, see Malone, Chap. 9.

7. The Greek words translate to something like 'Hail, highly favoured one' , a phrase which in itself does not in any way support the theological freight attached to the words 'full of grace'. It would take a very brave liturgist to attempt the alteration of this prayer today!

8. See Malone, p. 57ff.

9. See especially Susan Haskins, *Mary Magdalen: Myth and Metaphor*, HarperCollins, 1993. This is perhaps the most complete treatment of the religious and social implications of the image of Magdalen. See also

Ingrid Maisch, *Mary Magdalen: The Image of a Woman Through the Centuries*, The Liturgical Press, 1998, Carla Ricci, *Mary Magdalen and Many Others*, Burns & Oates/Search Press Limited, 1994, and Jane Dillenberger, 'The Magdalen: Reflections on the Image of the Saint and Sinner in Christian Art', p. 115-146 in *Women, Religion and Social Change*, edited by Yvonne Yazbeck Haddad and Ellison Banks Findly, State University of New York Press, 1985.

10. See Dillenberger, p. 117ff for an excellent overview of the artistic representation of Mary Magdalen.

11. For most of what follows in this section, see Haskins, p. 100ff.

12. Haskins, p. 113ff.

13. See above, Chapter Three, p. 80.

14. For a summary of these tales, see Elizabeth Moltmann-Wendel, *The Women Around Jesus*, SCM Press, 1982.

15. See quotations in Haskins, p. 150ff.

Index of People and Places

Also by Mary Malone

Women & Christianity
Volume 1
The First Thousand Years

Paper ISBN 1-57075-366-0

Cloth ISBN 1-57075-365-2

"A warm and lively account of the broader role of the
half-visible female population in the history of
Christianity...."
— *The Expository Times*

"This excellent book is the first volume in what
promises to be an invaluable series on the history of
women in the Christian tradition. It is a welcome
addition to the literature, well-grounded, accessible,
and able to inform even as it
raises consciousness."
— *Mary Jo Weaver, Indiana University*

"Brings to light both the persistent courage and innovative quality of women's lives. This outstanding work
of
scholarship is well-grounded and accessible; an infor-
mative synthesis that also raises consciousness."
— *The Other Side*

"An unqualified and urgent recommendation."
— *Consensus*

Please support your local bookstore,
or call 1-800-258-5838.

For a free catalogue, please write us at

Orbis Books, Box 308

Maryknoll NY 10545-0308

Or visit our website at www.orbisbooks.com

Thank you for reading *Women & Christianity*.

We hope you enjoyed it.

DATE DUE

The Library Store   #47-0103